born on the
BORDER

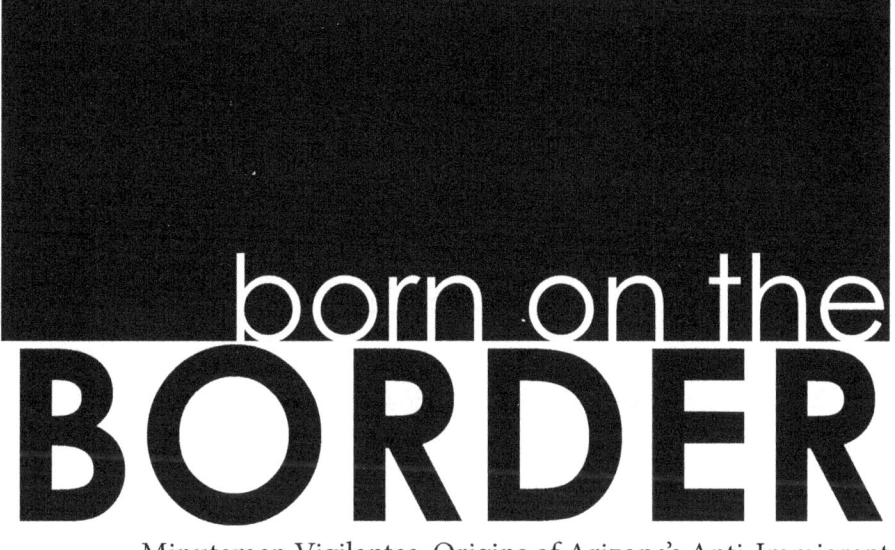

born on the
BORDER

Minutemen Vigilantes, Origins of Arizona's Anti-Immigrant Movement, and a Call for Increased Civil Disobedience

Ray Ybarra Maldonado, Esq.

First Edition | 2013
Published by the Hispanic Institute of Social Issues
Phoenix, Arizona

FIRST EDITION

Published by the Hispanic Institute of Social Issues
Book cover and interior designed by Yolie Hernandez
Cover photograph by Eduardo Barraza
Copyright © 2013 by Ray Ybarra Maldonado, Esq.

All rights reserved.

No part of this book may be used or reproduced in any manner whatsoever without the written permission of the publisher and author.

Hispanic Institute of Social Issues
PO Box 50553
Mesa, AZ 85208-0028
www.hisi.org
books@hisi.org

Ybarra Maldonado, Ray

Born on the Border, Minutemen Vigilantes, Origins of Arizona's Anti-Immigrant Movement, and a Call for Increased Civil Disobedience/
Ray Ybarra Maldonado —1st ed.
pp. 260

ISBN 13: 978-1489516367

Printed in the United States of America.

Acknowledgments

More people played a part in making this book a reality than there are words in the following pages. I must of course begin with my parents, whose unconditional love I have benefited from since the day I was born. I will always remember the sacrifices you made to ensure that Alex, Bobby, Amber, and I had a better life. It was your daily examples of struggling and reaching forward that has guided me on the path I find myself today.

My beautiful wife, my partner, my co-conspirator, and the one I truly feel blessed to wake up with every morning. Without your encouraging me to complete this process this story would have remained experienced, but never read. What a joy it is to experience this life and start a family with such an intelligent and passionate human being.

Every person who put on a legal observer t-shirt will always have a special place in my heart. It was an honor to stand with you out in the desert behind a bunch of armed crazies to protect the rights of someone we never met. I am especially thankful for those who stood up when others walked away, people like Dr. Michelle Landis Dauber who organized behind the scenes to make sure the legal observer project would go forward.

I must also acknowledge the plaintiffs and many great lawyers in the *Vicente v. Barnett* case. I have many fond memories of driving through Michoacan and the process involved in starting a lawsuit. A big thank you as well to all of the volunteers at *Centro de Atencion a Migrante Exodus* (CAME) in Agua Prieta, Sonora.

I also want to thank all of the people who read first drafts and helped me edit this book. I hesitate to put down names because I did such a horrible job of keeping track of everyone who provided the feedback, but here it goes: Alvaro Soria, Yara Lomeli-Loibl, Diane Chin, Mario Moya, Amber Ybarra, Xavier Zaragoza, Olivia Para, Ramon Villalpando, Oscar Casares, Cecilia Balli, Juan Carlos Cancino, Gloria Borges, Dr. Miguel Unzueta, and Dr. Joseph Nevins.

To my publishers, thank you so much for believing in this book and for the invaluable work you do on a daily basis. After our first meeting I knew this was where my book belonged, thank you for your valuable insights into the world of publishing and commitment to this project.

For those who strap on a backpack and hit the desert in pursuit of your dreams, may the sun be gentle, the water plentiful, the Border Patrol and vigilantes blind to your presence, and may the future erase the need to risk your life to pursue work or be reunited with family. I have made a living, and a book, based mainly on your stories and on governments' attempts to make your lives miserable. I hope my line of work will someday be ancient history.

I am so grateful to have had the opportunity to work alongside or have encounters with many great people who have dedicated their lives to fighting for human rights. People like Tom Saenz, Danny Ortega, Padre Cayetano Cabrera, Rev. John Fife, Isabel Garcia, Margo Cowan, and Sarah Roberts. A double shot out goes to Danny for introducing me to my wife (at a protest against Sheriff Joe Arpaio nonetheless) and to Padre Cayetano for his presence at our wedding.

For my son, Ray Emerson, the day I held you in my arms I finally understood why people are willing to risk so much, may you enjoy many, many years of resistance, happiness, and love. I hope you are inspired to follow your dreams and passions, to recognize that your time on earth is so precious and limited, that you dedicate yourself to being completely present in every encounter you have and strive to simply exist. Do not ask yourself where you can do the greatest amount of good, but ask yourself where you will be truly happy. Above all else, please remember that your mother and I love you unconditionally.

Contents

9	Playing the Game
23	Back in Douglas
45	*Rancho Escondido* (The Hidden Ranch)
107	Choosing Death
119	Legal Observing Part I
149	Out of the Desert and into the Interior
165	Return to the Desert
181	The Beginning of Mass Mobilizations
195	Back to Arizona
237	Walking through the Desert

Chapter One

Playing the Game

It used to be a game. We would play it while visiting my grandparents in Douglas, Arizona—a border town across from Agua Prieta, Sonora. My brothers would take turns running through one of the many holes in the chain-link fence that stood as the only barrier between the United States and Mexico. The fence was the same size as the chain-link fence that stood around the perimeter of the elementary school where I would soon be attending kindergarten.

The only difference was that the fence my brothers were running through had many more openings and looked ignored. It was a simple game, similar to games made up by children in their own backyards throughout the world. Standing on the U.S. side of the fence, the kids would take turns to see who could duck through one of the holes, run into Mexico, and touch a building. Each kid would take turns trying to touch a further spot then the one before him.

I was always too afraid to play. My two big brothers were certainly not. I remember looking on nervously but not wanting to have to go back to my grandparent's house where they were certain to be talking amongst themselves in a language that I could not then understand.

So I simply watched as my brothers and their friends played with the international divide the same way other kids played with a jump rope. We were less than half a mile from the official port of entry, but we could be out there for hours before a Border Patrol truck would come by. According to the United States Border Patrol, in 1984 the agency recorded

1,138,566 apprehensions along the entire U.S.-Mexico boundary, and we witnessed more than a few while out playing baseball on the empty dirt lots of Douglas.

But this scorching summer day in August of 1984, there were not enough people to get a decent game of baseball going. Sure enough, after a few hours of taking turns jumping through the fence, a Border Patrol truck finally came by.

There were two agents in the truck, one male, one female and both white. "What are you kids doing out here?" asked the agent.

My oldest brother, Alex, responded without any hint of nervousness or intimidation, "Just playing." Though Alex was only 14 years old, he was already an expert at standing his ground against authority figures. As a matter of fact, he was the one who talked back to the theatre owners that had kicked us out of a movie a few days before. I knew the Border Patrol agents would be in for the same tongue lashing if they tried to get smart with us.

"Are you kids from around here?"

"No, we live in Scottsdale, we are here visiting our grandparents who live right there," said Alex as he pointed in the direction of the house that was less than 100 yards away.

"Well, this is not Scottsdale, this is a very dangerous area, with lots of dangerous people coming through," said the Border Patrol agent.

"Yeah right," said Alex, "don't we look pretty dangerous to you?" The Border Patrol agent obviously did not want any more lip and he simply drove off after again cautioning us to be careful. The laughing and joking that began as soon as the Border Patrol agents drove away signaled to me that the game of jumping through the fence was about to continue as soon as the agent's truck was out of sight.

The encounter with the agent caused the queasiness in my stomach to increase even further, and I was ready to run home to mom. I told my brothers I was going to walk home and my brother Bobby instructed his friend Mike to walk me back.

Mike walked me the one block from the boundary fence to First Street. He asked if I wanted him to time me as I ran from the corner, past Mary's house, to the gate in front of my grandparents' house. This was the kind of challenge that I was certainly not too afraid of, so I agreed.

Mike began to count and I took off, pushing my short, chubby legs as fast as I could. I was probably somewhere around the count of six or seven when the Pro-Wings shoes on my feet collided with a bump in the sidewalk and I went head first into the concrete, landing on my left-arm.

I wailed so loud that everyone inside the house came out and I quickly found myself being picked up by my grandfather and carried into his truck for a trip to the hospital.

A few weeks later, I would show up to my first day of kindergarten. I was one of the few brown kids and certainly the only kid with a cast on his broken left arm.

Early lessons on standing up for justice

About a year before I started school, my parents migrated from the small border town of Douglas to the metropolitan Phoenix area in order to provide their children with more opportunities. We began our adventure by having our entire family—my mother, father, two older brothers and myself—living in one room of my uncle's house.

I remember my father holding down two full-time jobs, one of them being as a security guard at the apartment complex we eventually moved into. My mom got a job through a relative at the local Dairy Queen and I soon found myself at my own private pre-school in the backroom next to the syrup boxes of soda, mops, and brooms. It was also the spot of my first job. When the store was empty my mom would give me a dollar to wipe off the tables—just enough money for me to buy a Dilly Bar.

School was in South Scottsdale —a city adjacent to Phoenix on the east side— but for every holiday, family reunion, and summer vacation it was a four-hour trip that began by going east and then south down Interstate 10. Sitting in the back of the car meant staring out the window as cactus after cactus went by. The monotony of the desert changes after getting onto Interstate 80 and venturing through southeastern Arizona. Small rolling hills dot the terrain as the gigantic blue sky grows even larger. Gone were the large trailer trucks as the two-way highway took us through Benson, Tombstone, St. David, and the quaint former mining town and now small artist colony of Bisbee. From Bisbee, I-80 heads directly south and curves east just a few miles north of the border at the point where the Paul Lime Plant —a supplier of limestone for copper melting— still stands ten miles west of Douglas.

"There's where *Tata* works," someone in the car would always point out in reference to my grandfather. It would only be a few minutes before we would be at the house where one of us kids would fight to get to see who would get the honor of taking Tata's work boots off as he leaned back in his recliner. Three more miles down the road sits my sister's and my alma mater, Cochise College, —founded in 1964— perhaps the only school in the country that literally sits in the middle of the desert, situated between two small mining communities. Continuing about two more miles down Interstate 80 would take us past the Hanigan Ranch. I remember driving by the ranch and listening to my father tell stories of the ranchers who brutally tortured three Mexican migrants, a local incident that drew international attention.

On August 18, 1976, George Hanigan and his two sons abducted and tortured three undocumented migrants crossing their property. The migrants were searching for water and one of the Hanigans claimed to have recognized one of them as someone who had stolen from the ranch previously, and decided to become judge, jury, torturer, and almost executioner. The migrants were ordered at gunpoint to strip naked and were forced to give the small amount of change in their pockets to the Hanigans. The

Hanigans dragged the hog-tied migrants to a bonfire and carved chunks of hair off of their heads while using a metal rod to burn the soles of their feet. They tied a rope around one of the migrant's neck and strung him up on a tree, but fortunately his feet touched the ground.

One of the brothers, Thomas, took the red hot metal rod from the fire and passed the rod over the face and genitals of the migrants while brother George ran the blade of his knife over and around the genitals of the migrants and threatened to castrate them. The Hanigans then forced the migrants to walk back naked across the border while they were firing shotguns at them. Later, doctors found 47 shotgun bird pellets in the back of Bernabe Herrera Mata and 125 shotgun pellets in the back of Manuel García Loya, two of the tortured migrants.

The first legal case brought against the Hanigans resulted in an all-white jury acquitting them. Immigrant activists quickly swung into action and began a campaign to get the federal government to prosecute. The person given the most credit for organizing against the Hanigans was a young law student born and raised in Douglas, Antonio (Tony) D. Bustamante. My father would tell stories of Tony yelling into a bullhorn as people in the streets passed by, encouraging the residents of Douglas to get involved. My father was younger than Tony, but knew him well since Tony's younger brother was my father's best friend in high school, Ray Bustamante. Unfortunately, Ray passed away in high school, which is why the name on my birth certificate reads "Ray."

After marches and protests in front of the U.S. Attorney's Office and mass organizing, the U.S. Attorney's Office charged the Hanigans with violating the Hobbs Act, a federal statute enacted in 1946 that prohibits certain interferences of interstate commerce. Unfortunately for the people of Douglas and those crossing the border, vigilantes like the Hanigans would eventually return years later.

Though my mother was living in Douglas at the time, she does not remember much about this incident that garnered national and international attention. Instead we would hear stories about her mother, Maria Jesus Enriquez Luzania, organizing a union within the *maquiladora* —an assembly plant— in which she was employed as a seamstress. Though the plant would eventually shut down before recognizing the union, my mom would still have my *nana* recount parts of the story. "Tell the kids about the time you spoke to Cesar Chavez on the phone," my mom would instruct her in Spanish as we sat around the kitchen table inspecting each bean to see if it was worthy enough to be boiled and then cooked in my *nana's* small, narrow kitchen.

I've heard the story often, and it wasn't until I was much older that I would be able to ask more specific questions. My nana was a strong woman with a keen sense of right and wrong. It was no surprise to me that even though she only had a few years of education in Mexico that she was the one leading the organizing drive amongst the workers. Her house was a revolving door of family and friends enjoying her hospitality and listening to her sing, play the guitar, and out-curse anyone. Her home, kitchen, and her heart were always open to family and strangers alike. Despite the closure of the plant, the organizers managed to have Cesar Chavez —the legendary labor leader and cofounder of the United Farm Workers Union— call my *nana* to congratulate her on her courageous stand for justice.

Many years later, while attending Cochise College on a baseball scholarship, I would ask my *nana* to retell the story. My Spanish was still quite poor but every time she told it I would stop her and ask the definition of different words, for example, *"Qué significa huelga?"*

My grandmother would then use simpler words to describe what a strike meant and then would ask, *"[e]ntiendes?"* I would nod and say either yes or no and she would attempt to explain the meaning of the word or go on with her story. She would explain at the time of the organizing that my *tata* was the president of his local chapter of the United Steelworkers and that she had encouraged him to take the position because all of the other workers were too afraid.

"*Por qué voy a tener miedo* (Why am I going to be afraid)?," grumbling the only words he was likely to say during my nana's storytelling. She would always conclude with talking about the phone call that probably only lasted a few short minutes and would remind me that even though they lost their jobs, they were victorious because they stood up for their rights.

As I walked out of their house, I would raise my hand to slap the back of the small wooden sign that hung from the bottom of the porch. As children, my brothers and I would take turns jumping up to try to hit the 7, 2, or 1 numbers of the street address, and now it was easily within reach.

Leaving the Game

The drive to Cochise College, where I was a student, never took longer than fifteen minutes and, regardless of where I was at in town, it never took longer than five minutes to find myself on Interstate 80 surrounded by the desert. But it was not the mountains or brush that I remember seeing; rather it was the people who were standing on the side of the road waiting for help. I had no idea who they were, but knew exactly what they wanted. They had just crossed the U.S.-Mexico border and were hoping for a ride, or maybe simply wanted some food or water. I did not want to be late to baseball practice so I continued to drive past the Hanigan Ranch and toward the school. After all, their suffering was not my problem. What I really needed was someone to hit me fly balls as I had recently been moved from catcher to the outfield where I had never before played.

Playing in a small town in the southeastern corner of Arizona meant a lot of long bus rides up north. Our return trips from playing other community colleges in Tucson, Phoenix, and northern Arizona often resulted in our arriving back in Douglas at 2 or 3 a.m. It was on more than one occasion when I remember seeing groups of 100 to 150 people in our school parking lot being detained by a single Border Patrol agent. Groggy-eyed and freshly woken-up, everyone in the bus would look but nobody would say a thing. It was just another return trip back home.

The year was 1999, and Arizona was quickly becoming the border's number one crossing point for migrants from Mexico and other countries of Latin America. This new trend happened due to a shift from the traditional crossing points of San Diego, California, and El Paso, Texas, which occurred in the early 1990's, under the Clinton Administration. In 1993, the head of the El Paso Sector of the Border Patrol, Silvestre Reyes, implemented a border control plan he referred to as Operation Blockade. The idea was to place Border Patrol agents right on the international line, within view of one another, to create a line of defense that would deter anyone from even thinking about crossing. More resources were placed in the city area, additional fencing was built and the border that separates Ciudad Juarez, Chihuahua and El Paso, Texas became almost impenetrable. Apprehensions by Border Patrol agents skyrocketed and then quickly plummeted; to Reyes this meant that the plan had worked. No longer were migrants running through the streets of El Paso, and after putting a more politically correct title of Operation Hold-the-Line on his strategy, Reyes was elected a Congressman for the El Paso area in 1996.

Piggybacking on Reyes, Doris Meissner, the Commissioner of the Immigration and Naturalization Services under President Clinton, and Janet Reno, the U.S. Attorney General, decided to conduct Operation Gatekeeper in San Diego beginning in 1994. Despite a dearth of evidence to support its claims, the Clinton Administration precipitously proclaimed the new strategy a "dramatic success." Meissner testified before Congress that migration in the El Paso area had been cut by approximately 75 percent in the first months of Operation Hold the Line, and by approximately 60 percent in the San Diego area following the implementation of Operation Gatekeeper.

While the numbers may have been accurate, a question worth asking is what happened to those immigrants who were no longer crossing in the

El Paso or San Diego area. While the Clinton Administration may have wanted the public to believe those individuals made a cost-benefit analysis and chose to go back home, the fact is that they simply changed their traditional points of entry, headed to Arizona and began crossing in the most remote and deadly areas of the U.S.-Mexico border.

Instead of running through the freeways south of San Diego, migrants were now hiding in the trees or behind the dugout at Cochise College before our practices started. With terrified looks on their faces, they would quickly resume their trip north through the treacherous desert once someone showed up. I still remember those faces. I found it odd that they would have such a look of terror. This was my school, and more importantly, this was my field. I couldn't think of any other place on Earth where I felt more comfortable than on a baseball field. No matter what was going on at home or whether or not I was having difficulties with girlfriends, school, work, or buying the latest "necessities," the bases were still 90 feet apart, and it was 60 feet, six inches from the rubber line on the pitcher's mound to home plate. I thought that nobody should be that scared so close to a baseball field. After all, the birds that flew over our head in perfect formation smoothly crossed the border and continued on toward their destination without looking at all uncomfortable. I remember how calming it was to watch them glide through the sky in unison.

Not that every day on the baseball field was necessarily calming. I do not remember exactly what day it was. I remember it being toward the end of the season and not on a game day. I had just had a bad round of batting practice, and my 30 ounce bat was so heavy it felt like I had forgotten to take the three-pound donut off of it before stepping up to the plate to take my swings. I was not having as great of a season as I had hoped and in fact was finding myself in the starting line up less and less. Angry, frustrated, and confused I longed for the days when I was behind the plate instead of in the outfield and when the fastballs were slower and the breaking balls hung higher. I took my position in the outfield and for whatever reason finally began thinking about the faces of the people I had seen driving to school for practice or coming back from a game. Though I loved the game, it was just that, a game. Why was I so angry and upset when these people who crossed the border were risking their lives to make things a little bit better for themselves and the ones they loved? Many years before, my grandfather had crossed the border as an undocumented immigrant and it was quite possible that one of the people I saw on the side of the road was a relative. It was at that point that I thought I should return to Arizona State University to finish my degree and see if I could do something to help out the people who were crossing. Who knows, I thought, maybe I could even go to law school.

While baseball was becoming more difficult, I found my studies becoming more intriguing. I was not quite ready to give up baseball, so I enrolled full-time at both Arizona State and Mesa Community College (MCC). My brother had played at MCC and I knew the coaches there would give me a fair shot because of the work ethic and quality character of my older brother. I made the team, but toward the end of fall practices began feeling a sharp pain that shot from my right elbow down to the tips of my fingers occasionally when I would throw. I was thankfully back behind home plate, but found the shooting pain occurring with greater frequency until it reached the point where I felt it just about every time I threw. I went in for an MRI test and learned that I had a bone spur in my right elbow that would require surgery. This would mean I would miss the regular season. I went to talk to assistant coach Zeke Zimmerman about the possibility of getting a medical redshirt so that I could return next year for my last year of eligibility at the community college level. He was raking the pitching mound in the bullpen and when I asked about the possibility of getting a medical redshirt, he stopped smoothing the dirt, placed the rake in his right hand and took a deep breath. Zeke looked me straight in the eye and asked, "Son, what do you want to do with your life?"

"I guess go to law school," I replied.

I told him I was close to graduating and when I told him what my grade point average was he said, "Jesus Christ!" He explained that the other two catchers on the roster were both freshman and this meant that next year I would be competing with two individuals who already had a season under their belt. In the direct, yet respectful, manner in which Zeke speaks, he suggested that I forget about the game and concentrate on my studies. I cannot accurately describe the emotional pain, but it hurt more than anything I had experienced in my life. Change is painful. My entire identity was wrapped up in being a baseball player. My way of life would never be the same, but I had to come to grips with the changing reality of my world.

Arizona: How we got here?

As I said goodbye to baseball and began focusing more on issues pertaining to Arizona and the U.S.-Mexico border, my new goals and aspirations provided me with a total new set of experiences, but the lens through which I analyzed these experiences were very much influenced by my first lessons on social justice I experienced growing up along the border. The events of my early years eventually put me on a path that led to the work I now have the privilege to undertake on a daily basis. Along this journey I have met some of the key players of the border enforcement debate, and received an up close look at the most recent events that continue to put Arizona in the limelight of the nation, principally the "Minuteman Project."

Perhaps due to my "world crushing" experience of living life without baseball as mentioned above, I also have empathy for people like the Minutemen. The Minutemen —the citizens' vigilante group— see their communities changing. No longer is America the same America they experienced growing up. Latinos are moving into areas they have never been before, standing on *their* street corners, taking over *their* radio stations, and looking at *their* women. One common complaint I hear from Minutemen is that everything is now in Spanish and that they have to wait when calling any phone number to push a button to hear someone talk in English. This is the United States of America and we speak English! Change is indeed painful. So just as I dealt with my emotional pain of leaving baseball by reading books and eating food —in fact I gained a good 80 pounds in less than three years— other people deal with their pain by taking guns and going to the border, like the Minutemen.

However, I've never met a Minuteman that I hate. I am probably the one person outside of the vigilante/border watchers movement that has had the most conversations with Minutemen: I spent a total of three months in the Arizona desert tracking the Minutemen and splinter border vigilante groups. During those 90 days, I spent approximately 16 hours a day following the Minutemen through the desert areas in Arizona, New Mexico, and Texas.

From 2004 to 2006, I documented vigilante activity on the U.S.-Mexico border thanks to an Ira Glasser Racial Justice Fellowship awarded by the American Civil Liberties Union, where I spent time on the 2,000 mile border from San Diego, California to Brownsville, Texas. As part of this work, I stood on the beach in Tijuana and looked at the corroding fence that runs into the sea, rode with Grupo Beta on the Mexican side of the border from Tijuana to Tecate, felt the heat of the 120 plus degree desert in Arizona, encountered Marines in the middle of the night in New Mexico, and drove along the levees east of El Paso looking for the Minutemen.

Throughout this period, I've also been very fortunate in having the opportunity to learn from many great people. I've greatly benefited from conversations with the pre-eminent academics who study the border, immigrants' rights activists, elected officials, Mexican Consulates, college students, law students, filmmakers, and reporters. My best understanding of the issue has not come from any of the previous conversations, any of my classes in law school, nor from any of the books or studies I have read, but from the people on the ground, including border activists on the left or right of the issue, border residents, migrants, and government officials. These interactions took place in small villages in central Mexico, at migrant shelters on the Mexican side of the border, in the open desert on the U.S. side of the border, and in communities deep within the United States.

As I ponder about this reality and reflect on this past and current work, I realize that migration and the border are issues I cannot escape from. From a personal perspective, I was born in the border town of Douglas, Arizona and the house where I used to live sits one block from the international divide. My mother was born less than a few miles from the hospital where I was born, but because she was born on the Mexican side of the line, in Agua Prieta, Sonora, she was born a Mexican citizen and I a U.S. citizen. My family members who attended a graduation party held for my sister, our three cousins and myself shed light on how migration and the border are not simply concepts I have read about, but instead are ones that I have been forced to live. At the family party there were mothers whose children were jailed and accused of being *coyotes*, or people smugglers, relatives who jumped the fence and were held in the Border Patrol's detention centers, uncles and aunts who could not bring their children across the line because they had been deported from the United States, relatives who help migrants out of the kindness of their heart, those who do it for a little money on the side, an uncle who is a paramedic and saves migrants lives when they are near death or transports the dead bodies of migrants out of the desert, someone who takes care of the Border Patrol's horses, citizens, permanent residents, drug smugglers, non-immigrants who possess border crossing cards, and yes, even undocumented migrants.

Over the past decade I have seen my home state turn into the laughing stock of the nation. From allowing private citizens to carry guns and hunt for immigrants to passing the most draconian anti-immigrant legislation, Arizona has been a breeding ground for the anti-immigrant sentiment that has spread throughout the country. The U.S. Government has poured more resources into guarding the border than ever in the history of our nation yet the incompetent, fear-mongering elected officials in Arizona continue to claim the federal government is not doing enough. With a wag of her finger, Governor Jan Brewer further embarrassed Arizona during President Obama's 2012 visit, and vigilantes have murdered children and even toddlers in cold blood. Local school districts have banned books meant to educate Latina/o youth, and the steps government officials will take to punish immigrants and the Latina/o community seems endless.

In the following pages, I will provide background information that will help the reader understand how Arizona came to be the epicenter of the immigration debate and how these fringe vigilante groups helped encourage mainstream hate. I'll conclude with calling for a more radical approach from those on the left, one that follows the path of the migrants I describe meeting in the following pages. As you can tell by now, I am not a reporter who came down to the border for a short period of time, interviewed people on both sides of the issue, then wrote a book. Arizona is my home. It's where I was born, where I met my wife, where my baby was born, and hopefully where I will die. I love this state, but am sick and tired of the insanity surrounding the immigration issue, from local, state, or federal governments and private citizens. I am most certainly biased and do not even pretend to be neutral. My eyes and ears have seen and heard suffering that I never thought imaginable, and I will share with you these stories. I will take you into the middle of the desert and tell you about encounters with vigilantes in the middle of the night and migrants who have been walking for days. I will speak about my experiences living along the U.S.-Mexico border and searching for victims of vigilante abuse in small villages in Central Mexico. I promise to not hold back and will even share with you stories of engaging in illegal activity.

And just as my *grandfather* grumbled those defiant, confident words during my grandmother's storytelling, I can also say, *por qué voy a tener miedo?*

Chapter Two

Back in Douglas

With each quick movement in the bushes, I imagine a snake slithering out to bite me or a rat crawling up my pant leg. "No lights," barks Chris Simcox in a low-voice so that if there was a real person in the bushes, instead of a snake or a rat, they would not hear him. I turn off the flashlight and wrap my arms around my legs as my knees near my face and my bottom sits on the desert floor. With black tape covering the red light on my camera, the only lights tonight are coming from the stars in the open sky.

A quick question pops into my mind. What the hell am I doing in the middle of the desert with the founder of Civil Homeland Defense, his "legal" immigrant girlfriend and their vigilante goon friends? It was a Friday night, and I was tagging along on this romantic date of hunting for migrants in the middle of the Arizona desert to help protect the motherland. We were lying in wait to capture human beings-the ultimate safari.

Simcox ordered us to remain quiet, we spoke only in whispers. With the video camera running and my cousin holding the microphone inches from Simcox's face, he told of his reason for starting a civilian border watch organization, which he had previously called a citizen's Border Patrol militia on the front cover of his small-town newspaper. He abruptly stops mid-sentence and he puts his finger to his mouth to signal for everyone else to be silent. My heart takes off and it becomes increasingly difficult to breathe; the look on Simcox's face is that of a soldier listening for the approaching enemy who is about to jump out of the darkness and begin unloading rounds of ammunition. I felt like I was watching a war movie, but instead I was living it. "It's nothing," Simcox whispers as he places his unlit cigar back in his mouth. "We'll know when they are coming. It's like a stampede; you can feel the ground shaking. That might have been one of the scouts they send ahead of the group, let's see if they decide to head this way."

It was the fall of 2004 and the idea of the Minuteman Project had yet to even enter anyone's mind, but Simcox was already leading small patrols into the desert on a regular basis. There were a few other groups in Cochise County, Arizona that engaged in similar activities: American Border Patrol, Ranch Rescue, and Roger Barnett and his family. I had spoken with each group over the phone or met with them in person, but this was the first patrol I was on with one of the vigilante groups. I had only been working a few months but was eager to head to the desert to see what the mythic characters really did in the darkness of the night. I had met with Simcox the summer before and he was willing to take me out on one of his patrols so that he could show me that he was not racist and that he treated people with respect. His friends became irate when they learned I worked for the American Civil Liberties Union (ACLU) and one even refused to talk to me. On the actual patrols, everyone was friendly but I was sure the situation would change if they actually tried to detain a group of migrants, especially if I informed the migrants that they were legally free to keep walking.

I waited for the stampede. The whispers were occasionally accompanied with the sound of hands slapping at ones skin because the mosquitoes were having quite a feast. Carmen –Simcox's girlfriend– and I volunteered to head back to Simcox's truck to get more bug spray while everyone else stayed behind. I was leery of leaving my cousin alone with the vigilantes, but I figured that since we had only hiked in about ten minutes, I would be back shortly. Little did I know that it would take us over an hour to find our way back. We could not see more than a few feet in front of our face and Carmen would not think of disobeying Simcox and turning on the flashlight. A branch snapped back from Carmen and scratched my left arm as we attempted to navigate our way through the bushes that all looked the same. Carmen finally radioed back to Simcox that we were lost and though you could hear that he was annoyed, he quickly turned his flashlight on and pointed it straight up to the sky to give us his position. The bright light would have to spring out of the darkness and into the night sky two more times before we finally made it back. If we got lost going on a short hike, I wondered how difficult it would be to navigate the route from the U.S.-Mexico border to the city of Phoenix, that was about 230 miles away, as many migrants have to do.

Migration from the Mexican side of the border, experiences from a migrant shelter

When not following vigilantes, I was volunteering at a migrant center in Agua Prieta, Sonora, Mexico every evening. The center is run by the Catholic Church and offers migrants a free place to sleep, receive food, clothing, and a safe environment. CAME is one of dozens of migrant shelters run by churches on the Mexican side of the U.S.-Mexico border and south down the migrant route into Central America.

At around 5:50 every evening, I would get in my car and make the five-minute drive to the migrant center. The short drive took me down First Street in Douglas, passing the domestic violence shelter that once housed an underground drug tunnel connecting to a house on the other side of the border. After taking a left to head through the port of entry, I would turn right, just past the Mexican customs agents. I would then take the first left down the streets that were obviously less well kept than the streets in Douglas. Only a few minutes from my house, I was already in a different world. The economic disparity was obvious not only from the poorly kept streets, but also the size and structure of the houses. Six blocks down, I made a right-hand turn and parked in front of the white church. Situated in one of the poorer neighborhoods in the sprawling city of over 100,000 residents, the migrant center quickly became my second home.

It was much more difficult to be accepted by the folks at the migrant center than it was by Chris Simcox. I believe I was viewed as a nosy, useless foreigner given the less than warm reception I received. All of the volunteers were local parishioners, with the vast majority being poor people who live walking distance from the church. There was no paid staff and each night two different volunteers would be in charge of screening migrants, doing intake interviews, providing migrants with clothing and bedding, preparing dinner, and sending everyone in to the dormitory. The priest who started and ran the migrant center, Padre Cayetano Cabrera, is a pudgy man with a black goatee and a gigantic smile. Well versed in the field of liberation theology and therefore obviously familiar with the writings of Bishop Oscar Romero from El Salvador and other liberation theologians, Padre Cayetano had created a system where the poorest people in one of the poorest border communities were assisting the migrants, while at the same time meeting weekly to study migration and biblical teachings related to migration.

My grandfather, who met Padre Cayetano through church retreats, introduced me to him knowing we both had an interest in migration. He invited me to come to one of their weekly meetings and after that I went the next three months without missing a single day at the center. At first I was absolutely useless. Everyone had their routines and roles and I often felt like I was simply getting in the way. I tried to help out wherever I could: washing dishes, cleaning floors, hanging laundry out to dry, or making beds.

Eventually I worked my way-up to doing the screening and intake interviews and facilitating discussions amongst the migrants, but it took me only a few days to learn about the tragedies that occur on a daily basis. I was sweeping the floor when Doña Esther brought over a young man she thought I might be able to help. He stood just over five feet tall and his skin was the dark color of an indigenous person who had just spent days in the sun. He spoke in an almost whisper-like monotone, eyes fixed on the ground as he told his story.

About 20 days earlier, he was walking with a group that crossed the border near Sasabe, Arizona. Late in the middle of the second night of the journey, his brother, Salvador, disappeared after everyone scattered when they thought they saw Border Patrol agents. He returned to the area about an hour later, but all he found was his brother's backpack. The coyote told him they had to keep going forward, but he could return later and search for his brother in the Sierrita Mountains, northeast of Sasabe.

He made it all the way to Phoenix, then decided to head back to the border, hoping his brother had been picked up by the Border Patrol and deported to Nogales, Sonora. His search in the border town west of Agua Prieta yielded no results, which brought him to Agua Prieta in hopes his brother had made it to a city he had never been in before.

It was extremely unlikely that his brother would show up in Agua Prieta, but I decided to make a few calls to see if I could locate where he was. I called the Border Patrol and they had no record of detaining Salvador, and neither the Mexican consulate in Nogales nor in Douglas had any information. In fact, calls to their offices were quickly directed to a person in the office whose cold, disinterested handling of the case gave me the impression that they had received hundreds of calls from people looking for lost relatives.

There was no trace of Salvador in Nogales or Altar, Sonora, another town on the migrant trail route where he might have ended up. In a last ditch effort, his brother searched in Agua Prieta, but no one had seen him.

He and I met up the next day at CAME, and our grim faces told us both that neither had learned anything. As the other migrants ate their first meal of the day at 6:30 p.m., his bloodshot eyes stared at a map. He showed me where he thought his brother was lost, but after walking for two days, he wasn't sure which direction they were heading.

Salvador was left without money, phone numbers, food, or water. His brother was carrying the contact information for relatives because Salvador does not speak Spanish, only a native dialect called Mixteco. The brothers had traveled from the Mexican state of Guerrero, never dreaming they would be separated.

Salvador had come to the United States because two incomes were reduced to one when his wife, Graciela, died a year before, and he no longer could support his eight children by working in the fields outside Chimaltepec.

Those who are at all familiar with the U.S.-Mexico border, have assumed by now the fate of this five-foot-two, 130-pound 44 year-old.

But one cannot look into his brother's eyes and tell him that Salvador has become another victim of a failed U.S. policy that forces people to risk death in order to meet labor demands. I couldn't bear to look into his eyes and tell him that he was probably amongst one of the over 4,000 people that have died in less than twenty years.

One can only wonder what pain is being endured by Maria, 2; Luis, 4; Virginia, 6; Felicardo, 8; Mario, 11; Marcelino, 13; Martino, 15; and Palemon, 18. They may have lost both parents within one year, and they know their father made the trip to support them. This is not another story of a man led to death by an evil *coyote*, the name given to a paid guide for the migrants. Activists on the left and right like to blame *coyotes*, but they are usually poor people of color reacting to a failed policy created and implemented by the U.S. Government. Salvador's tragic story is a result of one of the most inhumane U.S. polices ever implemented.

When I began going to the center I was oblivious as to how many stories like these I would hear about. I had read many articles and books about migration and the border, but was unprepared for what became my nightly lesson on the reality of migration. I already knew that before 1917 anyone could cross the border with relative ease, and the Border Patrol was not even created until 1924 and that was more to keep out the Chinese and not the Mexicans. From reading Professor Douglas Massey, I knew that between 1986 and 2002 the number of Border Patrol officers *tripled* and the number of hours they spent patrolling the border grew by a factor of around eight, thereby forcing migrants to cross in even more isolated areas. But my instructors here on the border did not have PhD's, nor were they well paid to write reports. Instead, my professors were those individuals who had just been sent back to Mexico after having walked through the desert for four, five, or six days. Many had been near death and retold their stories about filling their water jugs from animal troughs or small green-watered ponds. From those who had spent thirty days on the train coming from Central America, I heard horror stories of being robbed and witnessing murders by gangs who controlled the trains, mainly the *Mara Salvatrucha*.

The stories told by the Central Americans were by far the worst. The second they stepped onto Mexican soil they were the targets of robberies and extortion from gang members and Mexican government officials. Because they were "illegally" in Mexico they were forced to forego the traditional routes of boarding an airplane or taking a bus to a Mexican border town and instead were forced to clandestinely cross by jumping on freight trains or hiding in trucks heading north.

Abuse was so common that when asked the question, "have you been the victim of an abuse," the question was most always answered in the negative. However if the next series of questions were, "have you been robbed, assaulted, or threatened," the question was very often answered in the affirmative. Being threatened at gunpoint, extorted by a government official or witnessing physical violence are so common that they are simply considered part of the expected experience. The most horrific stories would come out after the migrants had stayed at the center for a few days and were comfortable enough to share the worst of their experiences. Too many times people shared that someone in the group had been raped, or talked about witnessing gang members stab someone and throw them off the train.

With each passing day, I realized how little I knew of the migrants' reality. The standard form to interview everyone asked a series of questions in addition to whether or not they were abused. Where are you from, how much education, what is your profession, why are you coming to the United States, etc. They came from just about every state in Mexico, including, Chiapas, Oaxaca, Michoacán, and Jalisco. The most common profession listed was *albañil*. I had no idea what the word meant and for fear of seeming ignorant I did not ask. I assumed it meant general worker or day laborer, and I finally got-up the courage one day to ask Padre Cayetano what it meant.

"*Albañil*," he repeated after I asked him the question. "*Es como de construcción o carpintería*. Car-penter o Construc-shin," he stated in his best attempt at English. "*Como Jesús*." The same field as Jesus.

Each day someone new arrived at our little manger in the desert. "*Quién sigue*," I call out the door to ask who is next after stepping out from behind the desk. Somebody new arrives each day and after the second month there was no longer anything that shocked me. I was afraid of becoming coldhearted and distant. I consistently had to remind myself that each person who walked through the door deserved the respect and attention that every human being merits.

There were of course occasions that disrupted the daily routine. I arrived one evening to find three men who had stayed the night before sitting in the dining hall of the migrant center. When I opened the door all three of their heads shot straight up in my direction. The look on their faces was one of fear, as if an assassin was about to walk in. I smiled and walked to the plastic table and pulled out a chair to sit across from the men who were sitting shoulder to shoulder. They appeared to be staring beyond me and looking through the window to see if anyone was approaching. Knowing they had seen me walk through the courtyard, I was surprised that I was met with such startling looks, even when they knew it was I who was about to walk in the door. "So, what's up," I asked.

The man with speckles of dry blood on his shirt began to speak, "They tried to rob us."

"Who tried to rob you?" I asked.

"The coyotes, well they said they were coyotes," replied José Angel.

"We were sitting in the plaza and this man came up to us, offering a much lower price than what we thought we were going to have to pay. He said that for six hundred dollars each he would get us to Phoenix."

The average price to get someone to Phoenix was about twelve hundred dollars and this discount offer turned out simply to be a rouse to try to corner the migrants and rob them. The men were led to a house not far from the city center and when the door was closed they were ordered at gunpoint to take off their shoes. José Angel and Luis complied, but the third man they were with refused to obey the order. He was smacked in the face with the butt of the rifle and blood exploded from his nose. He stood up to show me the blood that was also on his pants.

The men were ordered to take everything out of their pockets and were then threatened with death if they could not produce more money. With only a few dollars in their pockets it is safe to assume that the "coyotes" were planning on holding the migrants hostage until relatives or friends could wire them money. I have heard similar stories of this happening in city areas in the United States. Someone pays twelve hundred dollars to get to Phoenix; but is then held in a house along with other migrants until family members can come up with an additional twelve hundred dollars.

In this instance, the robbers would not see the profits as the three men made a daring escape when the front door was left unguarded. They ran through the streets of Agua Prieta, not looking for the police station, but trying to make it back to the church. José Angel and Luis ran without shoes and were still only in their socks as we were speaking. I soon learned the men were so afraid because when they were forced to empty their pockets, they left their migrant center passes which had their name, and the address of the migrant center. The men were terrified that at any moment the robbers would be the next ones to come through the door. So was I.

What to do? We brainstormed options, and the first one that was dismissed was returning home. José Angel insisted that he could not return home with his arms empty; his family was relying on him. Like many migrants, the entire family pooled together what little money they had to pay for the journey. They hoped that in the long term the money that José Angel made in the United States would cover the up-front costs of migrating and then the money sent back from the United States would subsidize the low wages of the family members who stayed behind. This way the entire family could survive.

Since the North America Free Trade Agreement (NAFTA) and Mexico's neo-liberal economic policies did away with heavy tariffs that protected traditional economies such as farming, people have been forced to use migration of at least one family member, as a self-help remedy. For José Angel, migration was no longer an option; but something that had to be done—regardless of the fact that he was barefoot, out of money, and probably being sought by armed kidnappers. While the Mexican government did a good job protecting Mexican families with high tariffs that protected the market from U.S. agribusiness prior to the implementation of neo-liberal economic policies, they are unable to protect the migrants, despite the fact that migra-dollars are reportedly the second highest source of revenue for the nation behind oil.

We decided that the best option would be to find a way to another border town where they could cross. I stepped outside to try to figure out how to get the three men to another border city and also how to get shoes for José Angel and Luis. I stood outside of the dining hall with my arms crossed staring at the ground. Then, I heard footsteps approaching. During our brainstorming session, I forgot that the kidnappers might show-up at any moment. Padre Cayetano and the migrant center had already received threats and warnings not to meddle from those who profit from migration. Apparently, the center's attempts to help and the Border Patrol was sending them back over the line was the smugglers' profits, and they had no problem vocalizing their anger to the center. Frightened and anticipating a rifle-carrying smuggler, I looked up. To my surprise and relief, it was a man whose skin color told me he had been walking in the desert for days.

"*Buenas tardes*," stated the man.

"*Buenas tardes*," I responded.

"Excuse me, but is this where you give lodging to migrants?" asked the man in Spanish.

I responded that he had found the right place. The man was from Veracruz. He began to tell me that he had just been dropped off by the Border Patrol at the port of entry after spending five days walking in the desert, the last four of which he had no food. The Border Patrol had given him a small juice and some crackers before dropping him off, and it was obvious that the man was still desperately in need of water and food. He told me he had two kids back in Veracruz, one was four years old and the other six. He could no longer support them with the earning of his job since they were at the age when they were entering school.

After getting the man from Veracruz and the other migrants settled in, and cautiously dropping off the others at the bus station, I returned home that evening. With simply showing my driver's license, I was allowed back into my country. I was thoroughly looking forward to my daily walk with my two dogs AJ and Chow-chow. It was about 8:45 p.m. when I grabbed the leashes and they ran around the living room announcing to the neighborhood that they were about to enjoy their favorite 20 minutes of the day. We walked outside and began heading east down First Street. A block down the street, Chow-chow was only stopped from sprinting to freedom by the firm grip of the leash by my left hand, while AJ planted himself into the concrete because he had to investigate the markings left by the previous K-9. I thought I was simply in for another night of trying to balance the desire to move forward with the passion of enjoying the current moment, but things soon changed.

As we were crossing the second street that runs north-south from our house, my attention was drawn to my right as I heard a car quickly coming to a stop. On the Mexican side of the large wrought-iron fence, I saw three people jump out of a car. One man frantically began hollering out instructions, "*¡Súbele, súbele!*" I pulled back with my left hand to try to bring Chow-chow to a slower pace. I watched the people try to get a grip on the rectangular bars so they could climb to the top and somehow throw themselves over the 14 foot barricade. I could tell by the speed of their movement and the sense of urgency in the man's voice that they didn't need someone with two large dogs watching them as they tried to cross the border. I decided not to stop and watch as if jumping the fence were an Olympic sport.

As we continued to walk down the street, I kept looking backwards to see if the people would run by. Sure enough, I saw a man and a women turn right on First Street, heading in my direction, but on the opposite side of the street. The overweight man was leading the female by the hand as they moved faster then they probably ever had. Just then, I saw a Border Patrol truck roaring by my house and heading toward us. I assumed the people were about to get caught, but the agent turned left and headed north up the street where the couple would have been running down if they had not turned onto First Street. I am positive the Border Patrol saw the couple on camera as they jumped the fence, but as the two jumped out of the ditch, the view was probably obstructed by the houses that begin on International Avenue.

AJ and Chow-chow looked up to see the couple run by. As soon as they passed us, the dogs returned to investigating the sidewalk. "*Andale, ándale,*" the man said as he cut through someone's yard and began pounding on the white-steel screen door. "*Buenas noches.*" I was surprised at how calm he sounded given that his heart was probably beating as if he were a soldier in the middle of a war zone. *"Yo y mi mujer…"*

Before he could finish his statement and before the old man could open the door, a woman who was standing on her porch told the couple, *"Ven acá, ven acá."* The couple followed the women's motion to get into her backyard as an older man and women opened the screen door and stepped onto their porch. I knew in less than a minute another Border Patrol agent would show-up in hopes of apprehending the couple. They have more than 500 agents patrolling less than 53 miles of border in the Douglas sector, and the city-area is virtually impenetrable.

Even if they filled the canal with alligators and placed archers on roof tops, the same amount of people would probably get across—very few. This does not mean that people will not eventually get across. When migrants are apprehended, Border Patrol takes them to their station for processing, which includes getting fingerprinted and photographed. The prior policy was that if the person did not have a criminal history or if they were not from a country other than Mexico, they would quickly be dropped off at the port of entry to attempt to cross again. However, in recent years the Border Patrol has changed their policies to include criminally prosecuting migrants who have never even stepped foot in this country; or deporting them through different states so they cannot reunite with their guide.

While the majority of those caught crossing do not have criminal backgrounds, it is also worth noting that those who are listed as having a prior criminal record generally include those whose only "crime" was previously being deported or some other crime related to living in the United States without status, such as document fraud. Those who are sent back to the port of entry now know how difficult it is to cross in the heavily fortified areas of the city. They will instead choose to cross in the middle of the desert, walk for days, and risk losing their lives before coming upon a city area.

The couple was already safely in one of my neighbor's backyards when I heard the rumbling of another Border Patrol truck heading our way. As we reached the next street that runs north-south, the Border Patrol agent pulled-up from behind me and politely asked me, "Excuse me sir, you didn't happen to see anyone running north, did you?"

I didn't think there was any reason to lie, so I told him that I had not. We continued walking east as I tried to make sense of the evening's events. The risks human beings endure in order to seek a better life for themselves and their families is almost unbelievable: a young couple jumping over a large fence and seeking refuge by knocking on a stranger's door; men running through the streets while blood pours from their face, or their feet grind into the pavement; a man going for days without food while walking in the barren desert, instead of choosing to turn around. Most move forward. As morbid as it sounds, it's a beautiful thing to see people willing to endure so much for the sake of another human being. If I could wipe away the needless suffering and deaths with a magic wand I certainly would in a second.

I hope that my romanticizing of suffering is not taken as even the least bit of approval of the disgusting events that take place on a daily basis on the border. These stories, and hundreds more, make me question how the human beings can be so cold and heartless. How can we as a society continue with murderous policies; knowing with certainty that the effects will lead to continuous death and suffering?

The actions of people such as the woman who instructed the couple to get in her backyard show signs of hope. Knowingly hiding someone from the Border Patrol is a federal crime. I imagine the woman who let the couple hide out in her backyard knows that. Everyone on the border knows that it is unlawful to deceive federal agents. Thankfully, many people do not see this as at all being immoral, especially in border towns such as Douglas; where the people on both sides of the line remain connected through bloodlines and marriages irrespective of the disgusting fence.

If these laws were enforced on every individual who violated them, there would be no border communities and a large section of the Latino community would be behind bars. I am proud to admit that many of my family members have in some way violated these laws. Knowing the work that I do, every family gathering includes relatives sharing how they helped someone in one way or another. Of course, there are family members who do it for profit as well, but the vast majority simply see an individual in need, and so they help them.

I hope I am not being too stereotypical in saying that a large section of the Latino community would be behind bars as well, but I cannot count the times I have had people tell me that they picked up a family member somewhere along the border and drove them to safety. I remember when I was younger and driving with my grandfather, and he stopped to give someone a ride who was walking on the side of the highway. I asked him why he did that, and he gave me a response that accurately reflects my purpose for this book. You see, my grandfather is what many would regard as a simple man. His formal education lasted until third grade in Mexico and the notes he leaves me in Spanish generally have every other word spelled wrong. He originally crossed without the proper permission slip and went on to adjust his status to become a permanent resident. His response when I asked him why we picked up this person was, "because we could."

That seems to be the general sentiment I get from those who have knowingly violated the law to help out a fellow human being. They had the ability or privilege to help someone in need and did this without expectations of monetary compensation. They were acting in accordance with the Golden Rule. In fact, Irish philosopher Edmund Burke aptly described their actions when he said, "[i]t is not what a lawyer tells me I *may* do; but what humanity, reason, and justice tell me I ought to do."

Now, on the other hand, there are no doubt residents who live along the border who call the Border Patrol when they spot people who they believe are undocumented immigrants. In fact, these are the people who are often portrayed by politicians as being "under attack and "afraid to live in their own homes." While these people make great quotes for newspaper articles and documentaries, the majority of border residents are hands-down in favor of human beings attempting to better their lives.

No place like home

Within these stories of pain and struggle are also stories of resistance, persistence, and hope. It is easy to look at these stories and see victims: migrants being forced to leave home because of poor economic policies planned and implemented by elites; border residents being suspected of being criminals because of the color of their skin; and citizens' humanitarian actions construed as criminal. However, looking beneath the surface one can find so much more.

It was facilitating the human rights discussions amongst migrants at the migrant shelter in Agua Prieta that really opened my eyes not only to the victimization of migrants, but to their analysis of the world and their rights. After dinner at the migrant center, we would transform the dining area into a small classroom. I brought in the easel pad from my car and placed it in front of the tables that had just been wiped clean. On one side of an easel pad I wrote "Civil Rights," and beneath that there would be a long list of the rights guaranteed by local, state, and federal governments. I went over amendments in the Bill of Rights, labor laws in the United States, and the right to speak to consular representatives. On the right-hand side of the chart were the words "Human Rights." I explained that civil rights are recognized by governments and given the power of the state to be enforced through government intervention. I talked about how a government could imprison someone or a court could award damages to someone if an individual's civil rights were violated. I went on to explain that human rights are rights that one possesses regardless of whether there is any government to protect and enforce those rights. Then I would ask people what they believe their human rights are. One of the first answers was always the right to cross borders to find work. I had not encountered this right in any of my textbooks in law school or in any other book I had read, but it was consistently repeated. Nobody cited an international treaty or the work of any great philosopher; instead they were using their life experience to analyze the world around them.

While these discussions were often stimulating, some evenings made me feel like people just wanted to shower and go to bed. But these discussions gave me the impression that migrants should not simply be seen as victims of a policy, but thoughtful human beings who are actively reshaping the world and challenging the sanctity of the concept of sovereignty of nation-states. What happens when the human right to mobility collides with the right of a nation-state to choose whom they want to admit and whom they want to exclude? Here we were in a small room, in an isolated little border town, and I was receiving a much better education than I did at the prestigious law school that cost thousands of dollars. I wondered why I had ever taken out all those school loans when I could have just come here every night for free.

Plus, I was at home. Please do not misunderstand; living in a bordertown is not paradise, especially if your skin is as dark as mine. The first day I was back in Douglas I went for a run and was pulled over by the Border Patrol and asked what my citizenship was. I thought that my shoes that cost over one-hundred dollars and my short running shorts would have given me away as a U.S. citizen, but the Border Patrol agent did not think so. I have been pulled over taking my grandmother to dialysis treatment in Sierra Vista, Arizona, taking my grandfather to meet with an eye doctor in Tucson, and on many, many other occasions. Regardless of how many college degrees I have, when a Border Patrol agent sees me, all they see is another illegal or a terrorist. Does it matter if my family's presence in this area pre-dates the acquisition of the land by the U.S. Government? Not a bit, nor does it matter if they were here before the land was "owned" by any nation-state.

When I go for a run, I know that I am being monitored by a National Guardsmen sitting in a room filled with television screens at what has been called the world's largest Border Patrol station. I've looked out of my bathroom window to see Border Patrol agents staring at footprints in my backyard, and just about every time I walk into a restaurant there will be someone there with a badge and a gun. Normally, it is someone from out of state who has no desire to be in our small, sleepy border town and is instead waiting to be transferred to Florida, San Diego, or to some other branch of the U.S. Government.

I also have to be careful when going grocery shopping. In September of 2004, the FBI arrested vigilante Casey Nethercott in Douglas, stemming from a guns-drawn showdown he had with Border Patrol agents who attempted to pull his vehicle over. Nethercott is one of those old-fashioned militia types who not only hates people of color, but also hates the federal government. Apparently, the thought of being pulled over by a federal agent was too much for him, so he decided to let the Border Patrol agent follow him all the way to his compound where Nethercott's militia members were waiting with high-powered assault rifles. Imagine what would happen to me if the next time I am being pulled over by the Border Patrol I drive all the way to my house and my grandfather and cousins are waiting in the front yard with high-powered assault rifles.

Fearing a showdown at the compound that is filled with bunkers, watch-towers, hand grenades, and high-powered assault rifles, the FBI chose to arrest Nethercott in the parking lot of our local Safeway store while he was going for groceries. As the FBI agents identified themselves, Nethercott's companion Kalen Riddle pulled out his gun and was shot by the FBI agents. Just a few weeks earlier Riddle had been outed by the Anti-Defamation League as a known Neo-Nazi who was leading the recruiting effort for Nethercott's splinter group and actively recruiting other White Supremacists to come to the compound in Douglas. A September 10, 2004 press release from the Anti-Defamation League states:

> The recruiting effort [of Ranch Rescue] is being led by Kalen Riddle, a self proclaimed Nazi and white supremacist. On his website, Riddle, pictured toting a rifle and dressed in a Nazi uniform complete with swastika armbands, claims that two of his favorite things are "ethnic cleansing and weapon making." Riddle's occupation is listed as "National Socialist." In addition Riddle requests that "any WN [White Nationalist] volunteer is asked to keep WP [White Power] or Third Reich imagry (sic) to a minimum and not to talk to any press.

The most militant-looking group, Ranch Rescue members outfit themselves in full battle dress uniforms including face paint and perform patrol units along the U.S.-Mexico Border. Well, at least they used to. Even before migrating to Arizona, Ranch Rescue members were drawing headlines. In March of 2003, members assaulted and unlawfully detained a pair of migrants from El Salvador. The incident occurred in Jim Hogg County, Texas and would result in a fatal blow to the Ranch Rescue organization.

Based on the incident in Jim Hogg County, Nethercott was indicted on charges of aggravated assault and unlawful restraint after one of the migrants claimed he was pistol-whipped by Nethercott. I'll never forget running into Nethercott in the bathroom of a local Douglas fast-food restaurant and having him slap me on the back and pledge to me that he was innocent. The criminal court eventually agreed with him, but this would not be Nethercott's last day in court. While all the excitement was happening in Douglas, local attorneys in Texas along with the Southern Poverty Law Center and the Mexican American Legal Defense and Education Fund filed a civil lawsuit against Nethercott. A judgment was eventually entered against Nethercott, and the legal owners of the former Ranch Rescue compound are now Fatima Del Socorro Leiva Medina and Edwin Alfredo Mancia Gonzales, the migrants who Nethercott claimed he never touched.

Only in Douglas can I run into vigilantes while using the restroom at a fast-food restaurant, catch Border Patrol agents looking for footprints in my backyard, come home to find migrants hiding in my backyard, have helicopters fly over my house, and know I am being monitored when I go out for a run. I have often thought of counting the number of federal agents I see in a day, but since many now drive unmarked cars and do not wear uniforms, it would be impossible.

By this time, you might be wondering just how much this border "thing" costs. Customs and Border Protection's (CBP) fiscal year 2007 budget was $7.7 billion, with $2.4 billion going to enforcement between the ports of entries, the latter *doubling* the amount of money given to the Border Patrol as recently as 2001. The CBP's fiscal year 2008 Budget was increased to $9.2 billion. The spending did not stop once President Obama took office; rather the 2009 budget for CBP was $11.2 billion, followed by an increase in 2010 to $11.4 billion. President Obama also sent 1,200 National Guard troops to the border in 2010 and signed a bill that funded an additional 1,500 Border Patrol agents. The 2012 budget supports 21,370 Border Patrol agents and 21,186 Customs and Border Protection officers, the largest deployment of such officers in the agency's history. The 2012 budget included $242 million for technology alone along the border with Mexico. What exactly do we get for all this money, besides being able to see me in my short shorts when I go for a run? The money has gone to purchase items that make the U.S.-Mexico border look like a war zone. The Border Patrol has received an infusion of unmanned aerial vehicles, humvees, sensors, cameras, Black Hawk helicopters, roving watch towers, all terrain vehicles, and fencing. The recent spike in funding for border enforcement has led private corporations to head for the trough. The Boeing Company was awarded a contract to erect a "virtual fence." Boeing's idea was to construct 1,800 towers equipped with cameras, use of the same drones used by the Israeli army, and installing underground seismic sensors and heat detectors utilized by U.S. forces in the Middle East.

The project was eventually scrapped in 2010, because it was ineffective and too costly, but only after $1 billion was already spent. Meanwhile, the hospital in Douglas was so strapped for cash that they no longer deliver babies, resulting in women about to give birth having to drive 40 minutes to get to a hospital in Sierra Vista. There really is nothing like home.

CHAPTER THREE

Rancho Escondido (The Hidden Ranch)

In the late 1990s, a rancher east of Douglas began making national headlines. Roger Barnett boasted of having over $30,000 worth of sensors installed on his land that could notify him when migrants were crossing. His brother, Donald, has a night-vision scope mounted on the top of his pick-up truck. The family's weekend adventure consists of tracking human beings.

The vast majority of Roger Barnett's land, over 19,000 acres, is leased from the State of Arizona for the sole purpose of grazing cattle. Activist pro-immigrant groups have attempted to pressure the State Land Department to revoke Barnett's lease, but efforts have fallen on deaf ears. Barnett's actions drew headlines in *USA Today* —a daily newspaper— and other mainstream media outlets. In addition to his safari trips to Africa, he proudly boasts of catching thousands of migrants in Arizona. While often identified as a rancher in the media, Barnett's income actually comes from a propane and towing company in southeastern Arizona. Ironically, he profits heavily from the towing of vehicles seized by the Border Patrol in this area of the U.S.-Mexico border. Even before he saved enough money to buy a ranch, he earned a reputation of being a mean, quick-tempered man, especially toward Latinos.

Eleanor Eisenberg, the Director of the ACLU of Arizona, thought it would be a good idea if I attended her next scheduled luncheon with Paul

Charlton, the United States Attorney for the District of Arizona. Seeing that Charlton was appointed by President Bush, I doubted that the meeting would be worth my time, but Eleanor insisted that I attend their next monthly sit-down. However, the fact that a Republican appointee made the point of having a monthly lunch with the Director of the ACLU of Arizona provided me with a small amount of hope that something might actually get done.

I wanted to show Mr. Charlton that Barnett and the other vigilantes could be prosecuted under federal law. I decided to prepare a memo for the meeting that was going to take place in less than two weeks. After quickly learning that there were no legal treaties at the Douglas Public Library, I drove down the highway to Cochise College. The books were outdated, and looked and sounded as if I were the first person to open them. I spent days combing through the federal criminal code and searching through its annotations to find cases that could help my cause. The case that ended up being most helpful was the Hanigan decision from the Ninth Circuit Court of Appeals. I mentioned the Hanigan Ranch incident in Chapter One. I was excited to begin reading about the case that my parents had told me about when I was younger. As I sat on one of the tables trying to ignore the students who were more interested in chatting amongst themselves than studying, I was amazed at what this decision stated. The court held that the movement of undocumented laborers across an international boundary constituted commerce, and that by robbing the undocumented migrants, the Hanigans were guilty of violating the Hobbs Act. The Hobbs Act makes it a federal crime to interfere with interstate commerce by robbery, threats, or physical violence. Reading through subsequent cases that interpreted the Hobbs Act, I could not see any reason why the Statute would not apply to the vigilantes. However, because the books only covered up until the late 1990s, I had to drive to Tucson and figure out how to sneak into the library at the University of Arizona.

Still not owning a vehicle, I borrowed my grandfather's truck for a few days and took the two-hour drive to Tucson. I was delighted to learn that those guarding the gates of the library were not as strict as the Border Patrol or as those who guard the sacred gates of the Robert Crown Library at Stanford Law School. Being that the University of Arizona is a public school, I guess that means that all are welcome. Not that I asked before walking in with my head looking down at the ground and carrying one of my old law books from the previous year. I found the latest edition and read through each case, hoping that I would not see anything overruling the Hanigan decision. Case after case discussed the Hobbs Act, but none contradicted what was stated in Hanigan. After a few days of research, I was ready to write the memo that I was to deliver to Mr. Charlton on July 26, 2004. My grandfather was becoming upset that I had essentially appropriated his truck, so I decided it best to figure out a different mode of transportation to get to the meeting in Phoenix. When I learned that no friends or relatives would be heading to Phoenix around the time I needed to be there, I knew this meant that I would have to ride "El Shuttle." The large greyhound buses I rode on as a child no longer made their way to Douglas, and now there were only two different van services to choose from. Both cost the same and pack people and luggage in like the buses in Cuba or the subway in Mexico City. To say there is a choice between the two is misleading. The shuttles leave from just outside the port of entry, so I packed my bags and walked a few blocks down First Street.

Though Douglas is always a few degrees cooler than Phoenix, I was already drenched in sweat by the time I boarded the 15 passenger van to join the other 16 people inside. I waited patiently for the driver to turn on the van so that the air conditioning could get going. It was much more frustrating than being on an airplane and twisting the knob next to the button with the light bulb and hoping the air will come gushing out at you. I was squeezed in between two large, older women, and there was no arm rest separating us from each other. Even worse, it did not look like the vents were pointed in my direction. We eventually left and after about

20 minutes the van was cool enough to where I stopped sweating, at least temporarily. As the driver flirted with an attractive woman in the passenger seat, we listened to Mexican music on our journey north. I took out the recently finished legal memo to try to keep it fresh in my mind. As I read about the Hobbs Act I heard the air conditioning turn off. I did not think much of this and continued to read. After a few minutes the 100 plus degree weather outside was heating up the inside of the van. Those squished in the back called out to the driver to get the air turned back on. It took a couple of yells before he was finally distracted from his conversation with the young lady, and he began playing with the air conditioning controls. After turning the air conditioning on and off a few times he announced that the system was now broken. He returned to his conversation without an apology.

A few miles down the road we passed a Border Patrol truck that was off to the side of the road peering into each vehicle that drove-by. A man a row in front of me saw the truck ahead and nudged the person sitting next to him with his elbow. As we drew closer to the truck, their eyes fixed on the green and white vehicle, and their jaws dropped. Despite the perspiration undoubtedly now beginning to seep out of their pours, they appeared frozen. Our shuttle passed the Border Patrol truck, and the person in the middle tapped the person sitting next to him as his head jerked around to see if the Border Patrol truck was pulling out to follow us. A couple of us turned around as well, and we were happy to see that the road was empty. The Border Patrol agent remained off the side of the highway. Smiles, and the same look that I remember my friends and I giving to each other when the cop that was following us turned down a different street ensued. Of course, the consequences I faced as a youth paled in comparison to what would happen to the three men, and perhaps others in the van, if the shuttle was pulled over.

We passed another Border Patrol vehicle about a half-hour later and the same process was repeated. A tap on the shoulders that eventually led to smiles. One of the older women sitting next to me said to the men in Spanish, "Hopefully you'll have luck today and there will not be a checkpoint." The men seemed somewhat surprised to hear her comment; perhaps they had thought that no one else in the van knew that they did not have the proper documents to be in the U.S.A. However their shyness was quickly dissolved when the woman began a conversation with the men.

"Where are you from?" she asked.

"We are from Veracruz," responded the man. "So there might be a checkpoint coming up?"

"Yes, sometimes they have the checkpoint just outside of Tombstone, but hopefully they will not have it today," responded the woman as she fanned herself with a piece of paper.

"I hope not too," joked the man as he and his fellow travelers nervously laughed. They continued to chit-chat amongst each other while I cursed myself for not bringing my video camera along on the trip. Here was the perfect example of an everyday occurrence on the U.S.-Mexico border that is never reported in the media. The cat and mouse game is primarily played between migrants and Border Patrol agents, but border residents more often than not intervene on behalf of the migrants. It's an us-against-them attitude, and despite what the Minutemen want everyone to think, border residents tend to come out on the side of the migrants. We all know someone who has slipped past the Border Patrol at night or used a fake document to get across the port of entry. Many times the person is a relative. If your uncle lived in South Carolina and North Carolina fortified their borders, would you help smuggle your uncle across the border? The border does not just demarcate a political boundary; it separates communities and families while impeding our daily lives.

About half-an-hour later, we were nearing the city of Tombstone. Everyone in the van looked around nervously since the woman had mentioned that if there was a checkpoint it would be coming up shortly. We slowly drove through the town made famous by Wyatt Earp, hoping that the law was not in wait around the corner. I was so nervous I forgot about the heat. In the distance I could see the barricades used to slow down traffic and was afraid that we were about to lose a few of our companions. Further down the highway I could see a Border Patrol van where there were normally four or five Border Patrol vehicles. As we drove closer, I noticed that the speed limit signs that gradually slow you from 55 miles per hour down to five miles per hour and finally to a stop to be inspected by the Border Patrol agents, were not on the side of the road. While the port-a-potties used by the Border Patrol were still out, it appeared that the checkpoint was closed for the day. "We got lucky," said the woman, patting the man in front of her on his shoulder. The tension in the air disappeared as everyone in the back looked at each other, smiled and relaxed a little bit more. Meanwhile, the driver appeared oblivious to our concerns as he continued to flirt with the woman in the passenger seat.

"After Tucson we are set," the woman told the three men. With over an hour left of driving, there was still a chance of being pulled over on Interstate 10 by the Border Patrol before reaching Tucson. However, luck was on our side this day, except for the fact that the air conditioning never came back on. The drive was horrendous, but I am sure it was nothing compared to walking through the desert in the same weather. In an effort to minimize the sweltering heat, I rolled my sleeves over my shoulders and folded the bottom half of my pants over my knees. I swore to myself that before I took another trip to Phoenix I would buy my own vehicle. I looked at the cars that passed us by with great envy. I desired the freedom to turn on the air-conditioning as high as I could, listen to my own music, and drive as fast as I wanted. I wanted my privilege back. I was not walking in the desert and nobody had the right to deport me, but I was still not happy.

We finally made it to Phoenix. Though I was soaking wet, I felt a small victory. "We" had beaten the biggest, baddest government in the world. Despite its agents, fences, cameras, sensors, K-9s, unmanned aerial vehicles, annoying check points, and vehicles, we still got by. Sure, most folks in the shuttle had cell phones on them, but nobody was about to call the Border Patrol to snitch on the migrants in the shuttle. While that might have given us more room and made the journey a little more comfortable, we were all willing to sacrifice our comfort for the sake of our fellow human beings. Everyone in the shuttle had the same skin color, and we all spoke the same language. The fact that we may or may not have had the proper permission slip in our wallet was irrelevant. The laws have yet to erase the compassion from the hearts of those who live on the border. It was off to shower and prepare for my meeting with the U.S. Attorney the next day.

I arrived at the ACLU office the next morning hoping to have a strategy session before our lunch meeting, but the executive director and legal director were booked until lunch. On the drive over to meet with Mr. Charlton, Eleanor Eisenberg asked about my trip to Phoenix. I told her it went fine and asked what to expect from Mr. Charlton. She described him as a Bush appointee but explained that he was a reasonable person who hadn't done too much evil. Much to my disappointment, we ended up meeting at a steakhouse downtown. When we entered, we were escorted to the back corner where Mr. Charlton was occupying his usual booth. He got up to hug Eleanor and greeted me with a warm smile and a handshake.

I had just made the switch from vegetarian to vegan, and when I looked at the menu I realized there was nothing on it that I could eat. Not wanting to come off as too much of a bleeding heart liberal, I ordered the Caesar salad and decided I would just not say anything. My nerves resulted in me continuing to sweat despite the fact that we were in a very well air-conditioned restaurant. Mr. Charlton and Eleanor chit-chatted, and Eleanor told the same joke that I had heard her tell at least five times before. 'You know, Paul, it is getting so bad here that I am proposing to every Canadian I meet." He laughed hysterically, and I tried my best to laugh again. Eleanor continued to bash Bush to the point where I was getting uncomfortable as I was hoping to persuade Bush's appointee to take action against the vigilantes. Finally, Eleanor stopped and told Mr. Charlton about the work

I was doing on the border. I pulled out the memo and began the pitch that I had rehearsed over and over in front of the mirror. I am sure my voice was shaking from my nerves as I tried my best to talk about Barnett and the legal claims from the Hanigan Case.

"Oh, yes, Mr. Barnett," said Charlton. "Do you know he takes safari trips to Africa to hunt big game?" I had never heard of his adventures hunting big game. It was obvious that I was dealing with someone who knew more about Barnett's activities than I did. "He is not a poor man, he does this for sport; it is just ridiculous." I was extremely pleased to be hearing these words, and I quickly asked Mr. Charlton if he had ever heard of the Hanigan Case. He said he had not, and I went through the facts and talked about the holding of the case. Before I could finish my pitch Mr. Charlton interrupted me and said, "Do you have any documented cases?" I had to respond in the negative. "So you do not have any victims that could step forward?" I again had to respond in the negative. I had spent so much time developing the legal memo and using my skills learned in law school that I had completely forgot that you need real people for a lawsuit. "You know Barnett has come close to being prosecuted, but the problem is that we cannot get the victims to want to stick around." I was so embarrassed for not having come prepared to talk about this. I had heard and read stories, but had no actual proof of migrant abuses. In fact, I had never even spoken to any migrants who were abused by any of the vigilantes. Mr. Charlton kindly stated he would read the memo, and then Eleanor went back to Bush bashing as I tried to maneuver my fork around the parmesan cheese on my salad while internally cursing myself for being so stupid.

As soon as we got back to the office, I found a vacant computer and began typing an open records request to the Cochise County Sheriff's Office and to the Cochise County Attorney's Office. I also wrote a Freedom of Information Act (FOIA) request to the Border Patrol asking for any documents they had relating to private citizens detaining or abusing border crossers. An open records request can be sent to local and state agencies much like a FOIA request can be used against federal agencies to attain information. As long as the documents are not deemed matters of national security and their disclosure would not reveal private information about individuals, the government agencies cannot deny a request. Such laws emanate from the idea that the government works for the people, and anything it produces should be reviewable to interested taxpayers who are willing to bear the expense of production. I was determined to mail them before the post office closed, even though I would not hear anything for a couple of weeks.

A few weeks later, I received a letter from the Cochise County Sheriff's Office saying the documents were ready to be picked up, so I drove to Bisbee. I paid for the documents and took them with me to a restaurant. My stomach was queasy, and I grew more disgusted as I continued to turn each page. The documents revealed repeated cases of migrants being shot at, punched, kicked, bitten by dogs, and beaten with flashlights. Not surprisingly, there was not a shred of evidence pointing to a single arrest of any of the vigilantes. I was also not surprised to learn that most of the cases involved the friends of the Cochise County Sheriff's Department, the Barnett Klan.

One incident occurred in March of 2003. A group of individuals were crossing through Mr. Barnett's ranch when they heard the sound of a dog barking. The dog soon arrived and began barking viciously while circling the group as if herding sheep. The dog returned with the vigilante rancher about ten minutes later. Barnett jumped off of his ATV and pointed his 9mm pistol at the group while yelling and cursing.

Barnett yelled at one of the woman in the group, saying in Spanish, "*levántate perra*" (get up, bitch). The woman did not stand up because she was afraid of the dog that continued to bark menacingly. Barnett then roughly kicked her in the leg as she lay on the ground. Barnett attempted to kick the woman again, but she blocked the kick by placing her bag in front of her leg. The kick destroyed a statute of the Baby Jesus she was carrying with her, and she began crying in pain and fear. One woman pleaded from her knees with her hands held upright in front of her chest for Barnett to let them go. Barnett screamed back at the woman that his dog was hungry, and if they left she would get bitten in the ass.

Barnett mocked and belittled the group until Border Patrol arrived. Along with his dogs that are trained to hunt the scent of human beings, he escorted the group toward the highway. I contacted Mr. Barnett in hopes of being able to sit down and chat. As I expected, he was extremely rude and dismissive, insisting that if he wanted to talk he would call me back and then hung up the phone.

Since Barnett was not up for conversation, I thought the migrants who were unlawfully imprisoned, harassed, and assaulted might be interested in organizing to stop the vigilante rancher. The only thought that jumped into my mind was going to Mexico and looking for the individuals who were mentioned in the reports. Unfortunately, for the longest time I was the only one who thought this might work. I met with the Mexican Consulate in Douglas, Miguel Escobar Valdez, to tell him about my intentions. I waited in the small building for a few minutes and looked at the poster board on the wall filled with missing people who had probably died in the desert. Their families call the consulate's office, probably having last heard from their family members from a public phone on one of the corners in Agua Prieta. Chances are the people in the photos met a tragic death in the desert in such a remote area that their bodies will never be discovered. Their family members would forever wonder what actually happened to them.

I was summoned into the Consulate's office and presented him with a copy of some of the documents. I then told him about my plans and asked if he could help obtain the addresses of the people in Mexico. "No, we do not have those, but I remember talking to these people," he responded. "Let me tell you this, you are just wasting your time. They did not want to do anything, just like all of the other migrants. They are not concerned about justice. For them, their concern is getting sent back to the border so they can cross again. You see they have family, entire communities waiting for them back home to send money, and they cannot sit in a jail cell waiting. No, they just want to get sent back so they can cross again."

The conversation quickly turned into a monologue, and Consul Escobar took it all the way back to the days of the Spanish Conquistadors burning their ships so that their soldiers would have no other choice than to go forward. The noted author made poetic references to migrants throughout his over an hour-and-a-half monologue, which ended up with the same conclusion. It was a waste of time because the migrants were not concerned about justice. I am sure Consul Escobar was careful in choosing his words and probably just could have dismissed me as a young Chicano with visions of coming and saving the migrants. He kindly took it upon himself to place me back into reality, but all he did was encourage me to seek another path.

Then I got really lucky. I got a call from a very nice man named Vince Festa at the Cochise County Attorney's Office. Mr. Festa led the criminal division of the Cochise County Attorney's Office and would have been the person overseeing any criminal prosecution of vigilantes. He invited me to come to his office to inspect the documents I requested, and I quickly drove back to Bisbee. Mr. Festa greeted me in the reception area and guided me into a small conference room. He told me about a case he had just declined to prosecute. Apparently, an undocumented man was heading back to Mexico and attempted to cash a refund from the IRS in someone else's name. The man was working under a false social security number, but since he was heading back to Mexico he figured he would try to see if he could cash it. The bank notified the police, who arrested the man and referred the case to Mr. Festa to see if he wished to prosecute. Instead of being angry that the man had broken the law, Mr. Festa asked if there was anything I could do to get the man his money. After all, it was money he earned while working and was rightfully his. I was a little thrown off by the request and was not sure how to respond. I ended up telling Mr. Festa that I would look more into it, but doubted there was anything I could do.

"That's fine, just thought maybe you would know," responded Festa. "Here are the files, anything you want just mark it and we'll make a photocopy for you." Festa left the room, and I was left alone with piles of folders related to the specific cases I read briefly about from the documents obtained from the Cochise County Sheriff's Office. Each folder contained a copy of the Sheriff's Reports that I already had, but they also contained additional correspondence that the Sheriff's Office did not turn over. I was shocked to see a draft of a complaint that was written by the Cochise County Attorney's Office that charged the Barnetts with disorderly conduct, reckless endangerment, threatening and intimidating, and unlawful imprisonment. The complaint arose from an incident when the Barnetts shot at a group of migrants on March 18, 2001. I read as fast as I could to try to find out why the Barnetts were never formally charged. The thick folder contained letters from Escobar encouraging prosecution, Border Patrol reports, and correspondence between the U.S. Attorney's Office and the Cochise County Attorney's Office. After looking over 20 pages, I discovered that the main witness, a *coyote* or people smuggler, was becoming increasingly more difficult to locate. Unfortunately, the prosecution was deemed too risky because none of the victims could be counted on to be present throughout the process. I tagged page after page until I ran out of tabs and had to ask for more from the front desk. Here was a wealth of evidence, and nobody could ever again allege that the vigilantes were not engaging in violent activity toward migrants.

I started reading over the file from the Barnett incident where the young woman was kicked. Although I was alone in the room, I blurted out, "no way," when I saw that the addresses of all of the victims were contained on several different pages. While many of the addresses merely listed the name of a ranch and a city, there were some that contained actual street addresses in Mexico. Virtually all of the migrants were from the central state of Michoacán. After tagging essentially every page in the files, I told the receptionist I was done, and Mr. Festa quickly came out. He noticed that nearly every page was tabbed and said, "Well, I guess we'll just photocopy it all for you." I waited in the lobby until I had each of those documents in my hand. Of course, I could have left earlier since I had written the names and addresses on a separate sheet of paper.

I sent an email to Eleanor telling her about the addresses and that I was hoping to go to Mexico. It took me weeks to get a response, and it was not the one I was hoping for. I told Eleanor about what the consulate had said. She agreed and told me she could not provide funding for a trip to look for the victims. I met with a non-profit in Tucson that had been working on stopping the vigilantes. The executive director of the organization thought it was a good idea to look for the migrants but thought that it would be best for someone else to look for them, namely a Mexican national. I came to the conclusion that this meant that she wanted her organization to get credit for a lawsuit. I was beginning to feel like the boy in the classic movie the Christmas Story with everyone telling Ralphie that he'll shoot his eye out with the B.B. gun he so desperately wants Santa to bring him. I just couldn't find anyone to agree with me that it was a good idea to find these people. Even worse, I could not find anyone willing to pay for my flight.

Journey to Michoacán

It was already late September, and over a month had passed since I discovered the addresses, but there was still no prospect of me going down to Central Mexico. Things at the migrant center in Agua Prieta were going well, and I was invited to attend the annual conference of migrant centers that was going to be taking place in Ciudad Juarez, Chihuahua. I had finally gotten around to buying a car and offered to drive Padre Cayetano, Panchita, Doña Esther, and Katia—the center's volunteer staff—to the conference. We all piled into my little Honda Civic and Padre Cayetano asked if everyone had gotten their visa to travel past the short perimeter allowed with a border crossing visa. Everyone said yes, and we drove on the U.S. side of the border through New Mexico and into El Paso, Texas before driving into Ciudad Juarez. The three-day conference concerned how to better provide services to the migrants, document abuses, and work at the policy level. There were also sessions devoted to teaching about U.S. law, and there were always plenty of coffee and cookies around. The rooms were filled with Catholic priests and volunteers who ran migrant shelters in Guatemala, on the Guatemala-Mexico border, and at other points throughout the migrant journey through Mexico and all along the U.S.-Mexico border. One of the men who stuck out in the crowd was an Anglo priest who spoke good Spanish but would ask long questions at just about every session. From his sermons—I mean, questions—I learned that Padre Klotz was in charge of pastoral service for migrants in the state of Michoacán. Before the conference was over, I approached him and told him of my situation. He informed me that the cities I planned to visit were on the other side of the state of Michoacán, but he told me that he would be willing to drive me around if I were able to make it. We exchanged email addresses and I followed up with him about a month later. I was still hopeful that someone would fund my trip, but I eventually became too impatient. I finally decided to buy my own ticket. I was tired of other people theorizing about the migrants' motivations and desires, and I wanted to hear directly from those abused by Barnett.

I flew into Guadalajara on November 13, 2004, and was met by the smiling Padre Klotz, fully adorned in his priestly garb. He told me it was his birthday, and I apologized for my flight being so delayed that he had to spend his birthday in the airport. He said it was alright because he was doing God's work and that we were going to seek justice for migrants. We had a long drive ahead of us to the beautiful tourist town of Pátzcuaro, Michoacán, where Padre Klotz lived for half of the week. It was past midnight when we arrived at the church where we were staying, and the narrow, brick-paved streets were completely empty. Padre Klotz not so politely advised me that I should attend at least one mass in the morning, and when he woke me up at 6:30 a.m., I decided it best to go to the 7:00 a.m. mass in order to get it over with. Padre Klotz stood at the front of the church as he gave his lecture. He discussed in detail how he picked me up and how we were on a quest for justice. While I initially felt bad for inconveniencing him so much, I quickly realized that he was going to get plenty of mileage out of the journey.

After mass, I walked less than half a block to the center of town and enjoyed a great breakfast of chilaquiles con frijoles, fresh bread, and orange juice at *El Surtidor* Restaurant. I took in the beauty of the plaza that was beginning to wake up on this early Sunday morning as I sipped my coffee. The plaza was lined with trees that towered over the two-story colonial buildings, the lower portions of which were painted in an identical crimson red. The tops of the buildings were covered in fresh white paint, and the stores on the side streets had their names written atop their doors. There were no flashy Time Square signs competing for attention. I wondered why someone would ever want to leave a place as beautiful as this. A few hours later, the plaza filled with families and couples enjoying corn-on-the-cob smothered with mayonnaise, chile, and parmesan cheese. Young people, dressed in all white and wearing masks that resembled old-people, performed the traditional *viejito* dance. Seeing that the people I were looking for were hours away, I spent the day being a tourist and paid 30 pesos for a boat ride to the tourist island of Janitzio. I walked to the top of the mountain passing the endless vendors selling fried sardines and tourist trinkets and climbed to the top of the monument for General Jose Maria Morelos y Pavón. On the entrance ticket is one of his quotes, "Death is nothing when it is for the country that you die." The nationalist quote irked me, but since it was the government that probably paid for the statue, I should not have been surprised. I could just imagine some wealthy politician in Mexico City quoting General Morelos when discussing the tragic deaths of migrants in the desert.

Even the next day was spent sightseeing and I was starting to get frustrated. I came to look for people, and instead I was seeing every church in the area. Additionally, Padre Klotz kept introducing me as being from New Mexico with parents who were originally from Sinaloa. He was wrong on both accounts. No matter how many times I corrected him he made the same mistake. He was also trying to marry me to every woman with two legs who would stop and talk to him. I got an eerie sense that he was trying to live vicariously. His rhetoric about Mexicans was bordering on racists, and frankly he epitomized everything about the Catholic Church I despised. We finally made our way to Morelia, but were still hours away from Zitácuaro. He ranted about the hierarchy of the Church and how the other priests disliked him because he was in the good graces of the Bishop. In fact, we even stopped by the Bishop's birthday party before he pointed out to other priests that he was surprised that they were not invited. Clearly the hierarchical order of the Church was constantly on his mind. It was not until in the afternoon the next day that we drove to Zitácuaro. We stopped in every village to visit the local church and slowly made our way through the area known as *Mil Cumbres*, or thousands of curves, having to stop once because I was getting sick from all the quick turns in the highway.

While the priest annoyed me, I must admit he had a brilliant plan. We arrived before the monthly meeting of all the priests in the town of Zitácuaro. Padre Klotz had arranged for us to speak with the priests and have whoever was in charge of the church where the migrants lived go with us to look for them. I thought showing up with one priest was going to be great, but showing up with two priests and the possibility that one of them had baptized your children or married you was certainly an amazing bonus. With the population being 83 percent Catholic, I figured the odds were pretty good that the migrants would know their local priest. Unfortunately, it appeared that none of the other priests were aware of our visit, and we started the meeting by me talking about why we were there. As I spoke I got the sense that nobody was really interested. When the priests looked at the addresses of the people, a few of them mentioned that it looked like they lived in Padre Juan Jose's parish. From the short conversation, it appeared that he was the loser and the other priests seemed happy that they would not have to deal with Padre Klotz or myself. Padre Klotz approached Padre Juan Jose after the meeting and asked if we could stay at his church. "My church is very poor, and in a poor neighborhood, it is not nice enough for you to stay there," responded Padre Juan Jose.

"It will be more than fine Padre, I assure you, and we would be honored," responded Padre Klotz. I knew that Padre Klotz would not take no for an answer, and one way or another Padre Juan Jose was going to be our host during our stay in Zitácuaro. We drove through the hilly streets of the city with over 130,000 inhabitants and made our way to the church not far from the center of town. Much to my surprise and satisfaction we were not even allowed to rest before jumping into Padre Juan Jose's car. We were finally off to look for the migrants. The first street was easy to find, being only a few blocks from the church. We drove down the street and Padre Juan Jose asked for the number. I told him the number we were looking for and we looked to the houses to figure out where we were.

"I do not know where that is," said Padre Juan Jose with a puzzled look on his face. We drove to where the street dead ended and realized that we were still a couple of hundred numbers off the mark. I was disappointed to learn that the house we were in front of was the last house on the street.

"I do not think that is a good address," Padre Klotz keenly observed after we had already set off in search of our next address. It only took Padre Juan Jose a few minutes to locate the next street and my heart started pumping when we found the house that matched the number on the documents. I was excited. As we exited the car we approached the bright orange house with a beautiful wooden door. I was expecting a much more humble looking home. A woman wearing a housekeeper's uniform answered the door.

"Hello, I am Padre Juan Jose, and these are a few of my friends, may I please speak with Delia?"

"Who?"

"Delia," Padre Juan Jose paused and looked at me.

"We are looking for Delia Vicente," I said.

"You have the wrong house, she doesn't live here," responded the woman.

"Well, maybe she lived here about a year ago and then left to the United States," I asked with a hint of desperation in my voice.

"No, I've been working here for fifteen years and the same people have lived here for much longer and there has never been a Delia Vicente here," she responded.

"Thank you very much, our apologies for the inconvenience," stated Padre Juan Jose.

With a pleasant smile the woman closed the door. We were sent walking back to the car. I looked down at the ground and could hear the voices of the people who told me not to come, that it would be a waste of time, and that most people probably gave the wrong addresses anyway. When back in the car, I told Padre Juan Jose of the next street, and he responded that he had never heard of it. He did know the *colonia* that was identified in the address. We drove around for nearly half an hour just looking for street signs and occasionally asking people if they knew where *Calle Redondo* was located. We got more than a couple of positive responses, but unfortunately each person gave conflicting directions. Padre Juan Jose again asked a woman walking down the road where *Calle Redondo* was, and she responded by saying that we were on it. The street again dead ended before we could get to the lot number we were looking for, but it appeared that the street might begin again above a small ridge. We drove around, and sure enough, finally found the street name and continued driving. We periodically slowed down to ask someone on the sidewalk what lot number we were at. When we finally got to the location, I saw that it was a small store, and I was disappointed that we had failed again. There were a few people sitting out front, and Padre Juan Jose asked if Mateo or Samuel were around.

"I am Mateo, and this is my son Samuel," responded an old-man who was wearing worn huarache sandals, dirty jeans, and a small cowboy hat. He spoke in a soft voice, and his graying mustache and calloused feet gave the impression of someone who had experienced much in his life. I was so overcome with joy that I went to hug Mateo and Samuel, and they looked at me like I was crazy. Here were a father and son sitting in their store the size of a small living room filled with less than $100 worth of sodas, chips, and candies who had been watching the cars drive-by and were all of the sudden met with strangers asking for them by their names. I am sure Padre Juan Jose sensed the nervousness coming from Mateo and Samuel, and he swung into action.

"I am Father Juan Jose from the church up the road and these are my friends who work in human rights," he began his introduction. His energy and enthusiasm seemed to come out of nowhere, and I was ready to fight for justice after he talked about the need to stand up against abuses and make a statement on behalf of all migrants. From the limited interaction, I assumed that he saw our presence as more of a nuisance, but he was on fire and reminded me of the liberation theologians I had read so much about and admired. "This rancher is mistreating all people who are crossing the border, it is not just yourself you are sticking up for, but every person he has ever abused, every person who leaves here simply looking for a better life, you represent all of them," Padre Juan Jose told Mateo and Samuel.

Mateo was very interested in what Padre Juan Jose was stating and would nod his head in agreement and repeat a few of the words that he had said. "Uh, huh, it's about more than us," stated Mateo as he sat on the steps in front of his small store.

"Someone has to stop this rancher, and I believe if you work with these people we will be able to find justice," Padre Juan Jose said, looking in my direction as if we had rehearsed the opening a dozen times. I took out some of the documents and went over other incidents where Barnett had abused people. I figured the best way was to put it in context to let Mateo and Samuel know that what happened to them also happened to other people. I thought that approaching them in their home settings, where they had a sense of personhood, they could think more about how they could do something positive for the sake of others. I imagined that when Consul Escobar interviewed Mateo and Samuel they had not only been belittled by Barnett, but also humiliated by the Border Patrol, thrown in the back of a van, and sent off like criminals to the processing center where they were searched, fingerprinted, and thrown behind bars. Of course they did not want to do anything then; they were probably at one of the lowest points of their life. They had sought a job to improve their lives and the lives on the ones they loved. Even though their labor would spur our economy they were treated as criminals. Here in Zitácuaro we weren't talking to abused migrants, but to Samuel and Mateo.

It was not until a few minutes later that the men introduced Sandra, Samuel's wife, who was also sitting in the storefront. Sandra looked no more than 18 years-old, and she and Samuel left all the talking to Mateo.

"What do you want us to do?" asked Mateo.

"Well, what do you want to do?" I responded.

"Whatever we can do to stop the rancher," said Mateo.

I went through a list of options from giving testimony, being available for a criminal prosecution, and also civil litigation. I gave a brief overview of the U.S. legal system, and one of the first questions they asked me was if they could do something even though they entered the country "illegally." I explained to Mateo that the Constitution protects everyone and most laws apply to persons and not only citizens. A common misperception in the country is that undocumented people have no rights. Of course they cannot vote or receive certain welfare benefits, but I explained that the legal system is supposed to protect everyone. I used the example that if undocumented people did not have rights, then Barnett could rape someone or beat them to death and not worry about law enforcement stopping him. I assured them that they have rights, but it was up to them to enforce their rights.

"We will do whatever so that this does not happen to anyone again," said Mateo. It was clear he also spoke for his son and daughter-in-law. I asked if they knew the others listed in the report, and Mateo told us person by person. He explained who was in the United States and who had returned to Zitácuaro. Mateo informed us that the young woman who was kicked, and a few of her sisters, were the only ones still in Zitácuaro. I asked if he could get everyone together to meet the next morning at the church. He told me he could make this happen. We got back in the car and drove back to the church.

The next morning I work up early and set-up the video camera on the roof of the church. I positioned the chairs perfectly so that each person who was interviewed would have the beautiful green hills of Michoacán in the background. I went downstairs to inform the receptionist that we were expecting visitors and to make sure we had meeting space. I was excited that everything was finally coming into place. Mateo, Samuel, and Sandra arrived just in time and with two others, Eric and Ana Maria, or Mari. Mari was dressed in her work attire with her blonde highlighted hair pulled back into a ponytail. Eric's hair was spiked up high and also contained blonde highlights. Both looked me up and down with a look of extreme ambivalence. There was no Eric mentioned in any of the reports, and I soon learned that he was a relative of Mari's. I started to talk and was quickly cut off by Eric. "What is it that you want them to do?"

"Well, I want them to do whatever they want," I said.

"And what do you get out of this? How much money are you going to make," asked Eric wasting no time in laying out his concerns.

"Well, there is no way I will get anything. Even if there is a lawsuit I am not a lawyer, and the organization I work for is a non-governmental human rights organization. We do not do things for the money, we...."

"So how is this going to affect Mari, if she wants to migrate legally someday, won't the government see this on her record?" asked Eric cutting me off mid-sentence.

"It is two totally separate systems and the immigration authorities will not know whether or not Mari or anybody else has filed a lawsuit," I responded to the question I was not prepared for.

"But they are already in the system, the immigration people took their photographs, their fingerprints, and know their names," said Eric. Mari sat back in her chair with her arms folded with an irritated look on her face. I could tell that from Eric's body posture that he was not going to let up anytime soon. "And what about the rancher, isn't he going to come after them if they do anything? I mean if you could find them, can't he?"

"Barnett is a very mean man, I live in the same city where he lives and of course I cannot promise you that he will not do anything, but I assure you that the safety of everyone here is my number one concern. But we also have to think about the safety of everyone else who is crossing the border, the rancher did not just do this once...."

"Then why don't you find other people, why does this have to be them?" Eric again interrupted me. I was starting to perspire as I was searching for the Spanish translation of the words I was trying to say and am sure I was looking like a bumbling fool.

"You see, I did a public records request," I began to tell the story going back to the beginning, but was having trouble explaining the legal concept of a public records request and FOIA request or even the difference between the Cochise County Sheriff's Office and the County Attorney's Office. I wanted to just shout, "Come on! Just trust me! I am a good guy, I got this fellowship, I could be making a lot of money, but I am here, seriously, I am a nice person, just take my word for it. I'll give you letters of recommendation, show you some awards, my transcript, whatever you want." However, none of the accolades from the privileged law school life were going to help me out in the hills of Michoacán. I kept on mumbling and Mari kept looking at her watch. Perhaps sensing how uncomfortable I was getting, Eric slightly backed off.

Eric explained, "Listen, I am Mari's brother-in-law, married to her older sister. Their parents died last year in a car accident and that is why the family was forced to cross the desert to try to make ends meet in the United States. I broke my leg and was unable to make the journey with them. As the oldest in the family, it is my responsibility to take care of them. I let them down by not being out there in the desert when this rancher did what he did, and I am not going to let them get hurt again." I had a better understanding of why he was being so protective. After all, it was not like he was asking unreasonable questions to the stranger who had just walked into their life unannounced to talk about a moment that everybody probably just wanted to forget. "What exactly is it that you want them to do?"

I knew I could not go back to the line of whatever they wanted to do so I just spoke frankly. "I am leaving Zitácuaro tomorrow because I have to catch a flight back home in a few days. I have my video camera set-up and would like to record their testimonies and am hoping that everyone is interested in pursuing a criminal action and a lawsuit against Barnett so this does not happen to anyone else."

"Why does everything have to happen so fast?" asked Eric.

"My flight is booked and I have to report back to my bosses. I only have another day to look for folks and then I fly back home," I stated.

Eric looked at Mari who remained in the same position with the same expression on her face, and she spoke the first words I had heard her say, "*No quiero meterme en problemas,*" and shook her head no. She did not want to get involved in problems, just as Consul Escobar explained.

Padre Klotz jumped in to try to salvage the situation, "but if you do not do anything this rancher is going to do the same things to others. Now is not the time to be selfish and think only of yourselves." Unfortunately, Padre Juan Jose was not in the meeting, and I tried to shut-up Padre Klotz before he insulted them anymore.

I asked Mateo what he thought, and he said that if Mari did not want to do anything then neither did they; it was a family decision. Everyone was kind enough to give me their phone numbers, and I promised I would stay in touch. After we walked out of the room, I was sure that nothing would ever come about. "Some people are just so selfish," said Padre Klotz after they had left the room. "Do you want to go play soccer with me and the other priests, we have this beautiful land."

"I think I just need to be alone right now," I responded. Padre Klotz stated he'd be back in a few hours and then we would leave. I walked to the center of Zitácuaro and sat in the plaza while people strolled by. I second-guessed every word that came out of my mouth in the meeting. I heard the doubting voices from back home; Consul Escobar stating that the migrants did not care about justice; Eleanor telling me it would be a waste of my time. I had the opportunity to help put an end to Roger Barnett's racist, violent actions. And I clearly failed.

I walked around the center of town for a few hours and then headed back to the church. Padre Klotz showed up with a big smile on his face and asked if I was ready to go. We got into the car and started our drive toward, the butterfly reserve that he had been talking about since I first met him in Ciudad Juarez. While it probably would have been best to use our daylight hours looking for the other people, after the morning meeting it was probably best to take a few more hours off anyway. The drive went by pretty quickly and we got out to hike through the El Rosario Butterfly Sanctuary. I thought I was in great shape, but the 8,000 foot altitude got to me quickly. The worst part is that we had yet to arrive at the entrance of the sanctuary. We finally climbed up to the entrance and read about how some hundred million monarch butterflies migrate from Canada every year to spend the winter months in Michoacán. "I wonder if they get their documents checked at the U.S.-Mexico border?" joked Padre Klotz while still gasping for air. "If humans could pass as easily as butterflies I guess you wouldn't have a job."

"That'd be fine with me," I said as I reached for my video camera to film the sign at the entrance. "Where's Rancho Escondido?" I asked a group of men who were waiting to see if we wanted their services as a tour guide. They explained to me that the "Hidden Ranch" was on the other way down the mountain toward the city of Angangueo.

"But the road is very bad, unless you have a truck it's difficult to navigate," said the dark-skinned indigenous looking young man that would soon guide us through the butterfly reserve. We hiked as much as our lungs could take and then headed back to Padre Klotz's small car prepared to drive up the mountain and around the other side to find the next people we were looking for, Abel Cruz Resendiz and Manuel Martinez. I knew it would not be easy to find them. Their addresses were simply listed as "Rancho Escondido, Municipio de Ocampo, Michoacán." I've never heard of a hidden ranch that was easy to find, and this occasion would not be any different.

We drove up the steep road we had already hiked past, narrowly fitting between the restaurant stands and tourist trinkets. It took us only a few minutes to get to the entrance of the butterfly reserve, and Padre Klotz and I just looked at each other and laughed when we realized we could have driven up here earlier and just parked. We knew we were leaving the tourist area when the bricks in the road were replaced by nothing but the dirt from the mountain. We continued driving up the mountain on a small, winding, and very narrow road, and I could feel every bump as our car went up the road. Off to one side, I saw the majestic mountains, and on the other was a great expanse of field and trees that made me feel as though I had traveled back through time. On more than one occasion, we got out of the car to inspect the holes in the road. We winced a couple of times when we misjudged how steep they were and heard the bottom of his car bang against the large mountain. Eventually, we came upon a large pickup truck and were forced to back-up because the road was not wide enough for both vehicles to drive past.

"Do you know were Rancho Escondido is?" asked Padre Klotz.

"You passed it already," stated the driver as he pointed to the direction in which we just came from. I had not seen a thing, and perhaps Padre Klotz and I were too busy worrying about the road to notice if any houses were on the side. Clearly, there were not any signs on the road, so we could not have missed any landmarks telling us to turn. We drove back for about fifteen or twenty minutes and saw someone walking on the side of the road. Again we asked where Rancho Escondido was. We were sent driving back in the other direction; this time we were told that it was about 25 minutes down the road. After finally finding a place to make a U-turn, we turned back around and wondered whether the man meant 25 minutes walking or 25 minutes driving. At least this time we knew where in the road to drive a little bit slower. After passing the spot where we had previously turned around, we ended up running into a group of young kids and teenagers playing on the road. When they saw us coming, two of them ran to a piece of string in the middle of the road and picked up the opposite ends. It looked as if someone could come and hang wet laundry on the rope but it was meant as a barrier to our crossing.

"Thirty pesos," demanded one of the older boys who came up to Padre Klotz's side of the car. As he fidgeted for change, he asked the boy where Rancho Escondido was. The boy pointed down below to a series of houses spread throughout the valley. "Do you know where Abel Cruz Resendiz or Manuel Martinez live?" The boy responded in the negative. We looked for a road to drive down toward, the houses and stopped at the first store we could find. It was a small house similar to the others we had just passed, only this one had advertisements for sodas on the outside walls. We thought this would be a good place to ask for the friends we were looking for.

"What are their last names?" asked the man tending the store as I was purchasing a small bag of chips.

"Cruz Resendiz or Martinez," I responded. He looked at the woman in the room who I was assuming was his wife.

"Well, it could be Hector's kid. Didn't he go to the United States about a year ago?" said the man.

"Hector, no. You are crazy, he is too young to have a kid that old. You are thinking of Saul," responded the woman. "But his last name is not Cruz Resendiz it is Cruz Sanchez."

"No, it is Cruz Resendiz," the older man responded, certain that he remembered the last name correctly.

"You should go down to where the school is and ask over there. This old-man doesn't remember a thing," said the woman as she laughed. I thanked them for their time and got directions to the local school that was further down the mountain. Outside of the school we saw a man with a cowboy hat getting ready to walk into a building that looked somewhat official. He smiled pleasantly and walked in our direction to greet us two strangers.

"I am Mike," he said in pretty good English as he reached out to shake our hands. "Pleasure to meet you." We told Mike about whom we were and what we were doing here. The pitch was getting routine, and it did not take long for Mike to agree to help us if he could. He invited us into his office and offered us drinks. He was the local mayor, judge, sheriff, and just about anything else you could think of. He gave us detailed directions to Abel's house and even offered to go with us, but we said that he was already being too kind and did not need to accommodate us anymore. We got back in the car and drove back up the mountain to get back on the main road and head further down toward Angangueo.

"There it is!" I exclaimed.

"Are you sure?" asked Padre Klotz.

"Yes, that has to be it. There is the two-story wall painted bright yellow right next to the basketball court, just like Mike explained. That has to be it." There was no sign of a road that we could use to drive to the house, so we left the car off to the side of the highway and decided to hike down the mountain. After hiking down the mountain and just in front of the basketball court we ran into a man stumbling toward us with a beer in his hand.

"Forgive me, forgive me," he was slurring as he walked in our direction.

"Is that Abel Cruz Resendiz's house?" I asked pointing in the direction of the two-story wall painted bright yellow. The drunk man turned around and responded in the affirmative. He grabbed me by the arm while slurring that he would walk us there. Padre Klotz was about 15 yards behind me and was obviously annoyed by the drunk who was confessing his problems to me. "You know that man behind me is a priest, you should confess to him."

"Padre, Padre," screamed the drunk man as he let go of my arm and ran toward Padre Klotz. "Forgive me, forgive me." A few minutes later we arrived at the house and saw a group of children playing out front. The drunk man yelled to one of the children to go inside the house to get their mother.

Before we arrived at the door, a woman with puffy hair wearing mismatching sweat pants and sweat shirt asked the drunk man who we were. "I do not know, but they are looking for Abel."

"Get out of here," she ordered the drunk. On command, he turned around and headed back to the basketball court. "How can I help you?" asked the woman. I started again with the pitch. The woman's body language and facial expression reminded me of Mari's earlier in the day, and I was now expecting the same result. After I finished speaking, the woman said, "Sorry, you have the wrong house, nobody by that name lives here, and I have never heard of the person you are looking for."

"Listen, we are not looking for trouble, we want to help Abel and all of the other migrants that are forced to go across," said Padre Klotz.

"I understand, but you have the wrong house, sorry I cannot help you," she stated before walking back inside the house.

"She's lying," said Padre Klotz angrily as we walked back toward the car. "I can't believe it, how could she just lie to us. You came all the way from the United States; I've driven all the way from Pátzcuaro. It's just not right to lie."

"Well I know one way we can find out for sure if she was lying or not," I said.

"How's that?" asked Padre Klotz.

About thirty minutes later we were again walking by the drunk at the basketball court, but this time we were accompanied by our new friend Mike. The children saw us coming and again ran inside to get their mother. She came back out, and when she saw Mike a look of disgrace came upon her face. Mike politely greeted Mrs. Cruz and explained that we were good people and that she could trust us. I am not sure how Mike came to that conclusion so quickly, but I was not going to argue with the kind words coming out of his mouth. This embarrassing moment could have been avoided if I simply would have taken Mike up on his original offer to come with us to Abel's house. Apparently, I still hadn't learned that trust needed to be built before any work could begin. Mrs. Cruz apologized and said that she hoped we understood that she was simply trying to protect her son; she had no idea who we really were and was quite sincere in her apologies. Nonetheless, Padre Klotz was still furious. He gave her a mini-sermon, but eventually let up, allowing us to talk about Abel. We learned that he was working in the United States but that Mrs. Cruz was not sure in what city and did not have contact information for him. There is one phone in Rancho Escondido. Abel occasionally calls that phone and then someone walks to Mrs. Cruz's house and summons her. She walks back to the phone and waits for him to call back. She mentioned that he planned to come home around Christmas time, and I could come back then to speak with him. She also mentioned that Abel's cousin, Manuel, was away working in another city in Mexico but would also be home during Christmas time. We chatted for awhile, and I played with Abel's children before we decided to head back up the mountain and make the drive down to Angangueo.

We arrived just in time for evening mass. Padre Klotz was nervous about securing a spot to sleep, as he had never met the priest before. He suggested that I get in line to eat the wafer and drink the wine, even though he knew that I had never been confirmed. He thought it would improve our chances, so I reluctantly got in line. I was not sure exactly what to do. I could see the priest's lips moving and people were saying something before he put the wafer in their mouth. Everyone was practically mumbling and I could not make-out what they were saying. It was finally my turn and the priest quickly mumbled something. A slight noise, an attempted mumble, came out of my mouth and I leaned my head in to eat the wafer. Before my mouth was able to savor the bland taste of cardboard, he drew his hand back and looked at me sternly.

"Amen," he said, as he looked straight into my eyes.

"Uh, amen," I responded. He put his hand forward and I hurriedly walked away consuming the wafer. Padre Klotz was able to secure lodging for us overnight in the most humble setting we had seen so far. We were taken above the church into what looked like a room used for teaching Sunday school and given two small folding cots. The priest apologized that there was no hot water and no heater. He also apologized for only having two small blankets for the absolutely freezing room. Padre Klotz suggested we keep our cots close to each other to stay warmer. I pretended not to hear him and set up my cot on the other side of the room. Still wearing my large jacket and the same clothes I had put on earlier in the morning, my mind began to wonder. Why was I in this freezing church, in the middle of nowhere with this priest that was annoying me so much, looking for people who did not want to be found? I thought about my friends who had just graduated and taken jobs with base salaries of $140,000 a year. They probably had just finished having a nice meal at a fancy restaurant in San

Francisco, Los Angeles, New York, or Washington, DC. Maybe they were driving around in their new car with leather seats and an in-dash navigation system on their way to a club, or perhaps they were sitting in front of a fireplace with someone they loved. Why was I here searching for "justice," trying to convince people who were struggling to eat and provide for their family, to do something more? Just then Padre Klotz started to snore.

I tried my best at taking a cold shower in the morning, and we were off to grab breakfast. I had been taking Padre Klotz's advice about eating as much as possible at breakfast because we would never know when we would be able to stop for our next meal. On our way to breakfast, I took in the beauty of the town that is located in a canyon and surrounded by heavily forested mountains. I was saddened to learn that a few years later the postcard picture-perfect community suffered deadly landslides, attributed to deforestation by some. Padre Klotz was in a good mood and said that if we kept moving forward something good was going to happen. This was the day, he could feel it. His optimism and upbeat nature perked me back up, and I figured we still had another day to keep trying. We drove out of the quiet, peaceful small town of Angangueo and went looking for another ranch-this one located somewhere outside of the city of Tuxpan. We were back on a paved highway and I was surprised that we actually came across a sign on the side of the road with the name of the ranch we were looking for. By now we had the routine down; if there was a person on the side of the road, I would talk to them if they were on my side of the car, and Padre Klotz would talk to them if they were on his side of the car. This time it was my turn. "Excuse me, do you know where I can find Gerardo Gonzalez Ferrer?" I asked. The person had never heard of him, so I got out and asked at the small store. As soon as I walked in the door and mentioned Gerardo's name, a giant smile came to the clerk's face. He provided me with directions to Gerardo's house that was only a few hundred yards down the highway.

At Gerardo's house, we met someone who said he was Gerardo's brother-in-law. He called him on his cell phone. We were then given directions to drive to where Gerardo was working and headed off to where he was cutting timber. Driving down the dirt road, we saw a pick-up heading fast in our direction; as we approached closer, we saw a hand coming out of the passenger side waving us down. We pulled over, got out of the car, and were approached by a large, light skinned man with a goatee.

"My name is Gerardo, pleasure to meet you," he said as he strongly gripped my hand. Apparently not many people drove this road, and he knew we were the ones his brother-in-law had told him about on his cell phone a few minutes earlier.

"So, are we going to do something to stop this fucking rancher? That son-of-a-bitch. I was just going to go to the border next week to file a lawsuit against him." I hadn't even told Gerardo my name yet but he was obviously ready for action. We headed back to Gerardo's house. His wife made us coffee and gave us cookies as we sat in his living room. "The way he was, you could just see the hate in his face, he was red, and his jaw was shaking, I had never seen someone with so much hate. I speak English and I could tell what he was saying, most people did not know, but you should have heard him, *You mother-fucking Mexicans, you pieces of shits, you have no right to be here! We don't want you here,*" Gerardo spoke Barnett's words in English and continued in Spanish.

"The hate in his voice, and all the women were crying, one of them begged to let us go. She was crying but he didn't care, he said his dog would bite her in the ass. And the young girl that he kicked, I think they were from Zitácuaro; it just was not right. After all that, we were robbed on the Mexican side of the border by Mexican gangsters, then we walk through the hot desert for a day and a half, then the rancher's dog comes out of nowhere followed by him. He jumped into the ravine like Superman. We were just resting in the shade because it was so hot, and he jumped down pointing his pistol at everyone and yelling. I thought he was going to shoot us all."

I asked Gerardo if I could film his testimony and he said sure, just get the camera and turn it on. For over half-an-hour he retold the story of that hot summer day, detail-by-detail, recounting everything written in the reports and giving even more information. "Then when the Border Patrol had us by the road I was telling them what the rancher did to us. He ran up to me, got right in my face and screamed, *'what did you say, what did you say?'* right there in front of the Border Patrol agent, this man did not even stop then." I asked Gerardo if he remembered being interviewed by the Mexican Consulate. He said yes and searched his memory for his name.

"Miguel Escobar Valdez," I inquired.

"Yes, that's him, bald-head, skinny man, I remember him. As a matter of fact I asked him to send me my wallet and I check the mail in town often, but it has never arrived."

"You mean, you gave him your address?" I asked.

"Oh yes, I gave him everything, my address, telephone numbers, I really wanted to get my wallet back. We were interviewed by everybody, the Consulate, the Sheriff, Border Patrol, detectives; I can't remember how many people we talked to. I have lived in the United States a lot, and I have been caught by the Border Patrol a lot. One time it took me twenty times trying before I finally made it. You should have seen my feet from walking so much in the desert. Blisters everywhere, for a while I didn't have skin on the bottom of my feet, but I knew I had to cross. I just cannot make enough money here to support my family; I have to do it for them, that is what kept me going. Every time they catch me it's just a couple of hours, they take your picture, do the fingerprints and then drop you back off on the other side of the border. But this time was different, they kept us overnight in the cell like animals and we had to interview with people all night long. If we had not met the rancher I would be working in the United States right now, but no, they kept us overnight and after everybody was sent back to the border they sent me to prison. I had to go to prison because of the rancher." Gerardo described how he previously had a deportation order. As a result of crossing the border again, he was committing a felony. The others had not been deported and were not criminally prosecuted. In Gerardo's mind, if it was only a routine stop by the Border Patrol there would not have been all the interviewing. Instead, he simply would have been dropped off in Agua Prieta like everyone else and given the opportunity to cross again. But because of all the attention, his previous deportation came up, and he was sent to jail. "So how do we go about stopping this rancher?" asked Gerardo.

"Well, the things I have been able to think of so far is to give your testimony on video so that the public will know what is actually happening, making yourself available for a criminal prosecution to potentially put him in jail, and filing a civil lawsuit so that the rancher knows that he can no longer do these things to people."

Gerardo did not need any long speeches. I could tell from the passion in his voice that he was sincere in wanting to put an end to the rancher's abuses. His energy and desire was certainly contagious. Padre Klotz was right, today was starting off on a much better note than any of the other days. The disappointment I felt the night before was already a distant memory as I sat in the living room of someone eager to stand up and fight for justice. "Whatever I have to do, if it means going back to the border, whatever, I am willing to do it," stated Gerardo.

With one more community to find, we said good-bye to Gerardo and his family and headed off to Maravatio. We had one address within the city limits of Maravatio and headed to the church to speak with the local priest. The narrow streets of the bustling city center were so filled that I was sure we were never going to find parking. To my surprise, Padre Klotz drove straight to the church and after a quick discussion with the security guard, the gate was lifted. We drove straight into the plaza and parked next to the church. Riding with a man of the cloth certainly had its privileges. Unfortunately, we were unable to locate the priest and headed out to the queue of taxis, hoping that one of them knew the address we were looking for. The taxi drivers were all confused and kept passing the address from one to another, hoping that the next person would know. None of them were certain, but one man toward the back of the queue thought he might have an idea. "I can't promise you anything, but I think I might know where it is." We haggled over the price for a good 15 minutes. Padre Klotz and I walked to the side to discuss it amongst ourselves.

"Well, what do you think?" I asked.

Padre Klotz folded his arms and raised his right hand to his chin. "It's hard to tell, but right now it's our only option. Maybe he doesn't really know where it is, but we should trust that he has the best of intentions."

We jumped into the taxi and took off. The taxi driver warned us that we were going to a bad neighborhood, but promised that everything would be okay. I gave a nervous glance to Padre Klotz, and he raised his hand as if telling me not to worry, everything would be fine. The horror stories of kidnappings and robberies that occur in Mexico jumped into my mind. When studying abroad a few years back in Mexico City, we were urged to never take taxis. If we were to take a taxi we were advised to act as if we knew exactly where we were going and the best route to get there. I started to sweat as the driver honked and weaved in and out of traffic as if he was in a rush to meet someone. Was I just perpetuating a negative stereotype about Mexicans? The question quickly jumped into my mind, and I remembered the countless discussions about similar topics in classroom settings and longed to be back in a room with a professor in the front. Padre Klotz could sense my nervousness and cracked a joke that I could not quite hear, but I laughed anyway. The driver would occasionally come to a halt, yell out the window to find out what street we were on and ask if anyone knew of the street we were looking for. We got a couple of affirmative responses and after about 30 minutes of driving we finally found the street. Unfortunately, similar to what happened on our first attempt in Zitácuaro, the number of the house did not exist. We made our way back to the city center, gave the driver a nice tip, and thanked him for his time.

The addresses of four people were listed as a *rancho* outside of Maravatio, so we decided to head back out to the highway. Unlike Rancho Escondido and Gerardo's *rancho*, this one was actually listed on the map that we had. As we drove on the highway, Padre Klotz asked me if I prayed in Spanish or in English. Figuring that "neither" would be an inappropriate answer at this time, the only thing I could think of was to answer "English."

"Well, let's say five Hail Mary's in hopes that we will find at least one of the people we are looking for." Shit, I was done for. Maybe I should have said Spanish and then I could have made the excuse that Hail Mary was the only one I did not know in that language. But then he probably would have had us do it in English anyway and I would have looked stupid twice. "Mumble, just mumble," I thought to myself. "Let him lead and listen close, as soon as he says something just say the same thing, you can do this."

Padre Klotz grabbed the rosary hanging from his dash and wrapped it around his hand. Then he began, "Our Father, who art in heaven, hallowed be Thy name. Thy kingdom come…." As soon as he started talking, my mind flashed back to me lying in a bunk bed as a small child and my mother holding her hands in front of her face and repeating the same words. "…Thy will be done on earth as it is in heaven. Give us this day our daily bread and forgive us our trespasses as we forgive those who trespass against us. And lead us not into temptation, but deliver us from evil. Hail Mary, full of grace, the Lord is with thee. Blessed art thou amongst women, and blessed is the fruit of thy womb, Jesus. Holy Mary, Mother of God, pray for us sinners, now, and at the hour of our death. Amen."

It was extremely difficult for me to contain the large smile that I wanted to express. I actually knew this one, but had no idea that I did. It came back instantaneously, and we repeated it four more times in sync. Padre Klotz put the rosary back on the dash, and we drove through beautiful green hills that reminded me of the scenic drive down Highway 280 from Palo Alto to San Francisco. We made our way to the *rancho* and started the same process again.

"Excuse me, sir, do you know where Jorge Perez Castro, Rigoberto Perez Torres, Rodolfo Torres Perez, or Octavio Perez Mateo live?"

"Who," asked the old man.

I repeated the names and he walked closer to the car. "Yes, I know them, but they are all working on the other side. Except Jorge, he lives up there," as he gestured up the mountain. "What you want to do is drive straight; when you get to the small store with a red door you take a right. You drive down that road for a little bit and pass the Campos's place. You'll know it is there place because there will be two dogs that came running out after you. Then you take a left. You drive past a green house, that's where Rigo used to live before they moved to where the Serrano's used to live. Then you go right. About four or five more houses down, no, I think it's about six or seven houses you will see another road that will take you up to where Jorge lives." Clearly we were going to get lost.

"Thank you very much for your time," we looked at each other hoping that the other would remember the directions and began to drive away.

"Wait! If you try to find it you will get lost, it is best to just go to the doctor's office right there. That is Jorge's sister. She can call Jorge to come down." Much easier. I guess the next time I should ask for the best way to get a hold of Jorge, as opposed to trying to find out where he lives. We got out of the car and walked to the doctor's office. Padre Klotz did the talking, as an attractive woman in her early thirties greeted us a few seconds after we walked into the building.

"Is he in some sort of trouble?" asked the doctor.

"No, we are searching for justice. This is my friend who came from the United States…." Padre Klotz began to tell the story I had heard countless times in the past few days.

"Oh, well he is in the back, let me go get him," stated the Doctor. "Jorge!" she screamed as she walked to the back of the building toward an open door. She walked outside and yelled his name again. We looked around the doctor's office and came to the conclusion that the animal food and products meant that Jorge's sister was a veterinarian. We could hear a conversation taking place in the back, but we could not make out exactly what was being discussed. Then, a tall, dark-skinned man covered in sweat walked through the back door. It was obvious he had been working hard. His pants were covered in dirt, and his tan boots showed signs of many hours spent outdoors.

"*Buenas tardes*, how can I help you?" said Jorge. I retraced the history of how two strangers showed up at his sister's office, and Jorge listened patiently. I asked him if he wanted to do anything, and Jorge's initial response was quite disconcerting.

"Well, I was in the country illegally and trespassing on his land," said Jorge as he leaned against the counter.

"Nobody has a right to treat anybody the way the rancher treated all of you," said Padre Klotz. "Human rights do not stop at the border, and even if you did not have the right papers to be in the United States, he had no right to do what he did. You were not trying to rob from him, just walking across the land." Jorge nodded. I could tell that the padre's words were sinking in. A story that Gerardo told me earlier in the day jumped into my mind. Gerardo talked about a couple of people from the United States that were riding bikes on the highway a few years back. He saw the Anglo couple riding and began to chat with them in English and invited them into his house for water and food. He showed them just how strangers should be treated.

"What would you do if we were walking back there and you saw us on your property?" I asked Jorge gesturing to the backdoor where he had just a few minutes ago walked through. "If we had gone back there first instead of coming in the front door would you have pulled out a gun and kicked one of us?"

"No, I would never treat anyone the way the rancher treated us," responded Jorge. "The hate that he had, you could tell he was a very angry man." We talked for awhile longer. I again asked Jorge if he wanted to do anything to make sure that what happened to him never happened to anyone else again.

"Well, what can be done?" he asked. I went over the options, and he agreed to be available for a criminal prosecution, be part of a civil lawsuit, and give his testimony on video. I went to the car to retrieve the video camera and set it up using his sister's building as the backdrop. Before going over the details of the day, the 26 year-old told me about recently graduating from college with his degree in chemical engineering. His whole life he had been in school. He earned good grades, but he could not find a position in Mexico where he could utilize his education. The only jobs that were available were for manual laborers, and those jobs were only open because the wages were so low they had forced others to migrate. Here was a chemical engineer hoping to find a job where he could make a decent living. Instead he ended up walking across the desert and probably would have ended up building someone's house or working in the kitchen where U.S. born chemical engineers were eating. At the end of the interview, I asked him if there was anything else he would like to say. Jorge looked into the camera and said, "Like we say in my pueblo, justice now."

There was no more time left to look for any of the remaining people on the list. We headed back to Morelia after gathering contact information for Jorge's friends in the United States. Instead of voyaging through *Mil Cumbres* we took the highway dotted with toll booths and were driving alongside the better off citizens in Mexico. During the week, Padre Klotz had certainly irritated me, but thinking back, his desire for justice cannot be questioned. Without him the trip certainly would not have happened. In all honesty, I probably never would have been able to find a single person. Early the next morning, Padre Klotz drove me to the bus station in Morelia. He wanted to drive me all the way to Guadalajara the next day for my flight, but I told him I wanted to explore the city before heading back to the States. We said our goodbyes and he promised to check in on the people we met. "I still feel really bad about the young woman and her family. I'll stop by to see them next time I am in Zitácuaro, but either way we found some people and everything will work out for the best."

When arriving in Guadalajara, I made my way to the hotel and set off to explore the city. I began the day eating outside of a restaurant in the plaza of the city center. Families and tourists took in the sunny day and enjoyed the music of the mariachis, while I tried to figure out what had gone wrong with Mari and her family. It did not take me long to realize that I had made an incredibly stupid mistake. After spending time talking with Mateo and his family, I just assumed that Mari and everyone else who showed up that day would be on board. I did not take the time to give more detail about myself, what the bigger problem was, and learning about Mari's current situation. They had absolutely no idea who I was and what my motivations were. And I had no idea who they were and what was important in their life. Instead of approaching them on a human level and letting a relationship develop, I was using them as objects to get at the larger problem. This was certainly not my desire. I mistakenly assumed that everyone who walked in the door was ready to sign-up and march ahead. I needed to give Mari and her family an opportunity to decide whether or not they could, or wanted, to trust me. Only after that could I work on explaining the larger issue and understanding what was important in her life. Maybe someone in the family was dying from cancer and everything else in the world was irrelevant at the time. Or, maybe they were preparing to cross next week and did not want the added burden. The myriad of possibilities went through my mind as I sat on the patio. I regretted relying on assumptions without first reaching out as a person. I decided to forget about the mistakes, and enjoy the rest of my time in Guadalajara. The next day, I flipped my passport at the airport and was ready to get back to work.

Return to Arizona

With at least a few people interested in going forward, I met with the people at the ACLU of Arizona to talk about a possible lawsuit. My flight from Guadalajara landed in Phoenix, and I went straight to the office to meet with Eleanor Eisenberg.

"How was your trip," asked Eleanor as I walked into her office.

"It was great, found three people who are willing to meet with the County Attorney and also want to file a lawsuit against Barnett," I responded. "How many plaintiffs do we need before we can file a lawsuit?"

"We, I hope you do not think the ACLU will take this lawsuit. We only sue the government, we do not sue private citizens," stated Eleanor with a quick response that sent my stomach to the floor.

"Oh, of course not," trying not to sound extremely ignorant of the ACLU's policies, though I am sure she could see the look of surprise on my face. Eleanor gave me the names of a couple of private attorneys she thought might be interested. I walked out of her office feeling like a fool. How could I have not known the policies of the very organization that I worked for? Of course, it did take me a few months to realize the ACLU had a national immigration project with offices based in New York and San Francisco. I guess I should not have been too surprised at my ignorance of the organization's policies. I decided to stay in Phoenix for a few more days to meet with people who might be interested in representing the people I had just met in Mexico. One of the names that Eleanor gave to me was former U.S. Attorney for the District of Arizona, Jose de Jesus Rivera. I was anxious to meet with Jose but was a bit apprehensive knowing that he was once a U.S. Attorney, a job which means you are probably putting a lot of poor people of color behind bars for drug or immigration offenses. I did some research and learned that he was appointed by President Clinton. I also learned he had even been one of the attorneys who prosecuted the Hanigans for their torture of migrants crossing through the Douglas area.

I quickly sent off an email explaining the work I was doing and on that same day received a response requesting that we get together for lunch on the following day.

I met Jose at his office and we drove in his SUV to pick up a couple of his attorney friends. Two other Chicanos jumped in his vehicle and we headed to grab some lunch. Jose reminded the other two about how they used to protest in front of his office encouraging the U.S. Attorney's office to prosecute the Hanigans. He laughed and reminded them that in their law school days they were *long-haired hippies*. Now with over twenty years of experience as lawyers, they reminded Jose of how they would have press conferences outside of the courtroom claiming that he was not doing a good enough job prosecuting the case. Here they were, decades later, taking a break from their private practice and reminiscing about their civil rights struggles. I could feel the passion in their voices as they described their battles. Over lunch, I told them about the public records request and my travels to Mexico. Jose asked if the ACLU paid for my travels, and I told him no. He said that the next time I wanted to go down to just let him know, and he would take care of the airfare. He thought he was too busy at the time to take the case as the attorney but promised to be of help any way he could. He even offered his house in Puerto Vallarta, Jalisco, should I ever need it. While I have yet to be able to find an excuse for work to take me through Puerto Vallarta, I did make good on his offer for a plane ticket back to Michoacán in December.

Before my next trip, I was in email communication with Tom Saenz, then the Vice-President of Litigation for the Mexican-American Legal Defense and Education Fund (MALDEF). MALDEF is a non-profit organization with a long history of bringing lawsuits on issues that would benefit Mexican-Americans and other minority groups. I had met Tom when he was visiting my law school through our Public Interest Program. I was looking forward to working with him as a legal intern for MALDEF before I had been awarded the position with the ACLU. Tom stated that

MALDEF might be interested in the case and to let him know how my next trip went.

Just before heading off to Michoacán, I was asked by Eleanor to make a brief presentation on my work to the board of directors of the ACLU of Arizona. I had no clue that the MALDEF connection would get me into trouble. While I knew that the far-right groups were anti-MALDEF, I did not expect the same vibe to come from what I assumed would be the very liberal-minded board of directors. I gave a brief presentation focusing mainly on the incident with Barnett. I then had my first experience handling questions from an anti-immigrant crowd. As soon as I finished, Alice Bendheim, a robust woman with hair as white as breaking waves, asked why the ACLU was subsidizing the work of MALDEF. She failed to see how the Barnett incident had anything to do with civil liberties. I was caught off guard as I was not anticipating any questions challenging my work. Instead, I simply assumed the board of directors would pat me on the back, and we would all go on our separate ways. The next question was asked by Dawn Wyland, a law student who would eventually become the interim director of the ACLU of Arizona. "I mean these people are illegal, they don't have any rights to sue anyways…don't they," asked Dawn. Dawn asked a question I hear often, not just from the anti-immigrant crowd, but from undocumented folks as well. While most Americans probably assume that undocumented migrants cannot turn to our domestic courts for lawsuits, I was surprised that someone who had already taken constitutional law and was on the board of directors for the nation's largest defender of civil liberties, would be so ignorant.

I explained to Dawn that with the exception of voting rights and certain welfare benefits, all persons within the jurisdiction of the United States are pretty much entitled to the same rights, regardless of whether or not you have the proper permission slip in your back pocket. The Constitution generally refers to "all persons," and does not make a distinction between citizen and non-citizen. As in "all persons are entitled to be free from unreasonable search and seizure." I went on to use examples that I have now used countless times. If the laws did prohibit undocumented people from turning to the courts, then if you knew someone was undocumented you could walk up to them, punch them in the face and not have to worry about being taken to jail or having to go to court for a civil lawsuit. Likewise, you could rape an undocumented person without concern for punishment from the judicial system. Thankfully, we live in a society where, at least in theory, all people are protected by the laws. Despite any answers I gave, the anti-immigrant tirade continued. People spoke about all the trash left by migrants in the borderlands and about the changing demographics of our state. It was nice to see a few of the board of directors as outraged as I was, but it was clear that the anti-immigrant crowd within this group was quite vocal. Finally, the night was over. Despite living my whole life in the Grand Canyon state, I was only beginning to understand just how bad the anti-immigrant sentiment in the state of Arizona was. Even the group that many demonize as being the defenders of undocumented migrants, the same group that has in the past stood up for the rights of Nazis to march through the streets, was leading the bandwagon of those against the rights of migrants to march through the desert.

    I had spoken on the phone a few days earlier with Ana Maria, or Mari, as she indentified herself when we first met, the young woman who was kicked by Barnett and sat so resistantly listening to me speak at the church in Michoacán. I was surprised when she told me that she had gone to the church a few days after I left to see if I was still there. She went on to mention that she had wanted to invite me to the local fair and was disappointed that I had left so soon. I told her not to worry, that I would be returning in a few weeks. I apologized for talking about work so quickly without first letting her and her family get a chance to know who I was as a person and the nature of my intentions. She concluded our quick conversation on the phone by stating that she was looking forward to getting to know me more. Not in the human rights context, but in a different way. I had a sneaking suspicion of what she was talking about, but put it to the back of my mind.

I decided to go back to try to see if I could find the other individuals who were held at gun point by Barnett. I also wanted to look for another group of people who had a similar encounter with Barnett a few months later. This group consisted of mainly people from the state of Tlaxcala. I figured I could spend a few days in Tlaxcala before heading back to Michoacán. I thought that this time I had a better understanding of how to proceed. I was surely not going to go straight in talking about lawsuits. I figured I'd make at least two or three separate visits before talking about the foreign system. While the actions of Barnett and his family deserved immediate attention, I learned my lesson from the first time. I would not swoop in from another country, pretending as if I already had all the answers and the migrants were simply props who needed to sign their names on the dotted lines.

I felt more prepared to meet with the group from Tlaxcala. They had a similarly horrific incident with Barnett. According to the public documents, the following occurred on June 5, 2004. Barnett spotted 15 "illegal aliens" on his property and detained seven of them. Eight were lucky enough to get away. When the Border Patrol agent asked Barnett whether or not any weapons were used during the detaining of the migrants, the report states the following: "He avoided the question and stated that these people were trespassing and should not be here." The seven migrants were then transported by the Border Patrol off of Mr. Barnett's ranch. They then informed the Border Patrol agents of the abuses that had just occurred. One man stated that while he was hiding in the brush, a man on an ATV approached and found where he was hiding. Grabbing him by the hair, he was kneed in the stomach. After being kneed in the stomach, he was placed on the front of the ATV. He was then driven through the pointy bushes, which resulted in visible lacerations on the man's arms. Another man stated he was lifted up by his shirt collar and was being strangled by Barnett or one of his posse members. Further stated in the report is a description of what happened to the one woman in the group:

> While she was hiding in the brush, one of the individuals, later presumed to be Roger Barnett, approached her with his gun in his hand. He stuck the barrel of the gun into her side, while grabbing her hair, pulled her up. He then pushed her towards the other UDAs [Undocumented Aliens].

According to the testimony of the one migrant in the group who spoke English, Barnett then approached the rest of the group while pointing his weapon at them and asked, "do you know what this is?"

One can only imagine having to walk through the desert for two to three days before coming onto Barnett's ranch. Undoubtedly, the group was already physically and mentally exhausted. The temperatures in July can easily reach over 110 degrees. For people who may have never experienced such heat in their lives, the journey must be even more miserable. Imagine having to face all of the horrors of the desert and then have something like this happen to you.

I had mapped out my agenda for the next ten days. I would spend one day in Mexico City, five days in Tlaxcala, and four days in Michoacán. A few nights before I was set to leave, I received an email from the director of a Tucson based non-profit. She told me that I should not go look for the people in Tlaxcala as she had already went. While she did not make contact with any of the migrants, family members she spoke with were very supportive of a lawsuit. I had sent her an email a few days earlier letting her know that I was returning to Mexico, and that I would let her know how things went. Apparently, she used the documents I had given her with the addresses to make an earlier trip without telling me. Not that I needed to be informed, but it would have been nice to have been able to share my mistakes so that they would not be repeated. But, such is the world of non-profits, what some have described as the non-profit industrial complex. There is such a rush to claim the victory on behalf of the organization, that often times the competition between groups can deter from the larger movement. I had assumed that this was simply a phenomenon I would experience in school, but that in the real world it would be different. This is one of the many examples that the "real world" contains the same drama. To some extent it makes perfect sense. In the non-profit world you will only continue to receive money from your funders if you show them measurable results. Thankfully, I was on a two-year grant and was not concerned about renewal. I could do whatever I wanted, but non-profits have to worry about their future. They need to receive recognition in order to garner future funding. The future funding is what results in paid activists putting their organization's stickers on people who show up at rallies, or having them hold signs with the organization's logos and then taking pictures of people. The picture with all the brown people, and the more children you can put in there, the better. It will certainly make a good lead picture on the report that is going to be delivered to the white funders.

Knowing the person who sent me the email, I was pretty sure that there would never be a lawsuit that came out of the incident. Sure enough, there has unfortunately yet to be anything. I changed my trip to make it one day in Mexico City and spent the rest of the time in Michoacán. One of the addresses of the people from the June incident was in Mexico City, and I thought I would at least try to pay him a visit. The director of the Tucson based non-profit had only went to look for the people in Tlaxcala, so I figured I would try my luck.

Heading back to Mexico

After arriving in Mexico City, it took me an entire day to simply try to figure out in what part of the massive city to begin looking for the street. While looking for a local library to find a detailed map of the city, I came across a street vendor who was selling an expensive book of maps. I thumbed through it briefly and made the purchase. I headed off to find a quiet place to look for the address. It ended up taking me longer to find a quiet place in Mexico City than it took me to actually find the street on the map. When people in the United States think about a busy, noisy city, they often think of New York. To me, Mexico City is like New York City on crack, and I am certainly an addict. From the moment you wake-up, you can hear the horns honking and the whistles of those trying to control the always crowded streets. I've been in taxis that make u-turns at intersections from the right-hand turning lane, and have been pushed off of subway cars by an old lady with a cane in one hand, and a small bag of groceries in the other.

I made my way to the outskirts of Mexico City. I got off at the last subway station. Not sure which direction to head, I initially went the wrong way but doubled back to find the street I was looking for. With no numbers on the houses, I started asking around to see if anyone knew where the family lived. After getting two answers that led me to the same house, I decided to knock. My heart started to beat and I kept repeating to myself, "don't say you want to do a lawsuit, don't say you want to do a lawsuit."

A woman appeared through the window from the second story of the building, "Buenas tardes," she stated looking at me with that cautious look you give when a stranger knocks at your door.

"Buenas tardes, is Jose here," I asked.

"He's working right now," responded the woman.

I asked if she knew when he would be back and she seemed to be getting even more nervous. "Who are you?"

I was anticipating the question but was unsure how to best answer. "I am from the United States and I work in human rights. I have these papers that have Jose's name on them and I came to ask him about them, could I show them to you really quick?" I did not want to have this conversation with her hanging out of a window and thought it would be more comfortable for the both of us if I could make it into the house. While I did not make it upstairs, I did make my way into the stairwell. I explained to Jose's mother why I had come down and showed her the documents that had Jose's name and his address. I told her I just wanted to talk to him to verify that what was written was what actually happened, and see if I could be of assistance to him in anyway. She told me that Jose had the next day off and I should come back then to talk to him.

I returned the following day, but no one answered the door. It was relatively early in the morning, about 10 a.m. I was hoping to talk to Jose and then take off to Michoacán. After grabbing breakfast, I returned to the house hoping that they were not answering the door because they knew I was the one knocking. The mother again appeared from the window explaining that Jose was called into work by his boss. I asked what time he would be back. She said she did not think he would be back, that occasionally he is gone for two or three days. I thanked her and walked to my car as frustrated as I could be. It was Christmas Eve and I knew that there was no way someone could get called into work and taken away from their family on both Christmas Eve and Christmas. I knew Jose was up in the house, and I wanted to walk back there and plead with his mother to just let me speak with him for a few minutes. Thankfully, I held off on my impressions and desire to begin begging. I instead decided to take off to Michoacán. I had gotten lost once on the way over, and was sure I would get lost at least once more trying to navigate through the streets of Mexico City. I decided that if I had time on the way back, I would again try to stop and see Jose before catching my flight back home.

I was trying to make it to the ranchos outside of Maravatillo, to spend Christmas Eve with Jorge and his family. I had spoken with both Jorge and his mother, and they were both very enthusiastic about my visit. They promised a large meal upon my arrival and I was dreaming of some home cooked Mexican food. Unfortunately, I got lost twice trying to get out of Mexico City and was held up in traffic for hours in the city of Toluca. Not wanting to arrive at Jose's doorstep late at night, I ended up spending the night in a hotel in Maravatio. I walked around the center of the small city that was filled with people. Street vendors were selling huaraches, sopes, fruit, candies, and anything else you might be craving. It appeared to be just another night. I did not get the feeling at all that it was Christmas Eve. There were no Christmas carolers, decorated trees, or stores offering holiday discounts. Nonetheless, I could not help but wonder what my family was doing. Where they were at, whether or not they were opening presents. As I walked through the streets, I felt alone, like a foreigner in a foreign land. I longed to be back on familiar territory with the family I loved and the celebrations I was accustomed to. Of course, I had the financial resources to drive back to Mexico City and board the next flight to Arizona. I could be back home on Christmas. I would even be able to wake-up early on the next day to go shopping for bargains. Even more importantly, I had the correct pieces of paper in my possession, by virtue of being born in a hospital that is one mile north of the U.S.-Mexico border. I thought about the stories from migrants in the interior who had wanted to go home upon hearing about the death of their mother or father, but were unable to attend the services because they did not have the paperwork to return to their family and community in the United States. I thought about Jorge's mother who said she has not seen her husband for five years. He is too old to again make the journey across the desert. He is essentially stuck in the United States.

I am glad my mother was understanding of me not being home during this holiday season. She knew that the migrants who do return home, more often than not, do so during the holiday season. This would be the best time during the year to find the people I was searching for.

Thankfully, the next day I was able to meet up with Jorge and one of his friends that had just returned from the United States. They drove me around in the jeep that was driven all the way from Chicago. The jeep was going to be given as a gift to a family member. But for now, the vehicle with Illinois license plates was driven around as the proud symbol of success in the United States. Jorge's friend was anxious to spend the money he had made. He was looking to contract with the most famous band in the region to play at their *ranchito* the following Friday. Before looking for the band, they drove me to meet with Rodolfo and Rigoberto. Jorge had given me their phone numbers earlier, and I had spoken with both men over the phone at their apartments in Chicago. I was happy to finally meet them in person. We chatted for awhile before they gave their testimony on camera and signed the paper work for the lawsuit. Everyone was in a good mood, surely happy to be back on the lands they grew up on, and spending time with their families. I was invited back for the big party and promised by everyone that there would be many *chicas* to dance with. I told them I would try my best, depending on how long I was in Zitácuaro.

I made my way down the curvy, mountainous roads. Just before the sunset, I came upon the hotel I had found on the internet. The listed price per room was 800 pesos and I somehow bargained down to 400 pesos a night. I woke-up in the morning ready to head into the city of Zitácuaro. I headed straight to Ana Maria's house, trying to remember the directions they had given me last time. I spent at least two hours looking for the house, but had no luck. I went to look for Eric, the annoyed brother-in-law, who I knew had a small stand in the center of town selling fruit. It did not take me long to come upon his small stand. As I approached, I could hear him barking at each person that was walking by.

"*Qué lleva, tenemos tomate, cebolla, naranja, qué lleva*," Eric called out, not just to anyone that would make eye contact with him or look at his goods, but anyone who was walking by. The words were familiar, but even more familiar was the tone used by the merchants with small stands. Each one you walked past, whether they were selling clothing, vegetables, or copied discs, had the same mantra-like hymn, undoubtedly repeated hundreds of times throughout the day. I snuck up on him from behind, grabbed an orange and asked how much.

He was getting ready to answer as he swung around and a big smile came upon his face. He gave me a hug and welcomed me back to Zitácuaro. Insisting that I take the orange at no cost, he pulled a plastic crate from underneath the stand for me to sit on. We spoke for quite some time. He occasionally jumped up to repeat his mantra to anyone who was looking at his produce. I was surprised when he apologized for being rude the first time we met. He again repeated the story of being the caretaker of the family, and I told him that I completely understood. I also apologized for starting off too quickly, and not allowing him and the rest of the family an opportunity to get to know me as a person. He invited me over for dinner that night and I gladly accepted. I told him I did not eat meat, and he told me not to worry. According to Eric, his wife's sister, Delia, makes the best *chiles rellenos* in all of Michoacán. I did not have the heart to tell him that I also did not eat cheese or eggs, so I just smiled and told him I was looking forward to it. Eric told me where I could find Mari and that she would be getting off of work at 3 p.m. I swung by the small store where she was selling meat and said hello. She was also happy to see me and told me to come back at 3 p.m. so that she could show me around town.

We started off with coffee at a local restaurant. It did not take me long to no longer see a victim of vigilante violence in front of me. Instead, I saw a young woman who liked to do aerobics at her local gym, dreamed of a life other than working at a meat shop, desperately missed her parents, and loved her family, especially her little nephews. She was quite funny, and would constantly repeat the words, "*a poco*." I began imitating her constant use of the words and soon we were just 22-something year-olds hanging out, having a good time and getting to know each other. We drove around town and she showed me the main sights in Zitácuaro, the large lake and the view of the city from the mountain top. Before we went to Eric's house for dinner, she invited me out to go dancing later that night. I had no interest in wanting to get into any kind of romantic relationship and was hesitant on saying yes. I was clear at the beginning that I wanted her and her family to get a chance to know me as a person before talking about work. I mentioned that I had a girlfriend on more than a few occasions. The truth was that I was single at the time. This was the only lie I ever told to Mari and her family, but I still do not regret making up a girlfriend. I also mentioned I had no shoes to go dancing, so of course our next trip was downtown to buy a pair of shoes. We then went to Eric's for the *chile rellenos* that were delicious in my mouth, but tore my stomach apart.

During dinner I was able to convince Eric to come out to the club with us. By the time the homemade flan was brought out, I was already feeling like a member of the family. It was getting late and I still needed to go back to the hotel and shower before getting our club on, so Eric and Mari walked me out. When we hit the corner where my car was parked, I saw Mari's chin drop to her knees. A young man was approaching. They held hands and chatted amongst themselves for a few seconds. I was as happy as could be. I waited patiently for the introduction and was ever so delighted to meet Mari's boyfriend. Of course, I did not mention to him that his name, or even a hint of his existence, was never mentioned during the day. Instead, I mentioned that Mari and Eric were taking me to a club, and I asked if he was interested in joining. He seemed very surprised that Mari was going out, but nonetheless accepted the invitation. A few hours later, he was buying me round after round of drinks. He turned out to be a super nice guy. He had just come back after working as a construction worker in Pomona, California. He was anxious to spend his money and show off to everyone how well he was doing in the United States. It was a long, but certainly enjoyable night. After shutting the club down everyone wanted to go find more alcohol and somewhere else to party. Well, I guess I could say everyone but Eric and myself. We were certainly ready for bed. My legs were tired from dancing and there was no Denny's to turn to, so I dropped everyone off and went back to the hotel.

Early the next morning, at least it was early for me, I called Gerardo from the hotel to let him know that I was in town. He asked if Mari and her family were still afraid to move forward. I told him we had not talked much about it. He asked me to just bring them over to his house and he would take care of everything. I went and found Eric downtown and told him that Gerardo wanted to meet him. He agreed to come along to Tuxpan, but Mari could not get off work.

It turns out that Gerardo is a master organizer. I mean this guy was brilliant. As soon as Eric and I walked into the room he started talking about how bad Barnett was, how he treated everyone worse than dogs, and that he had never felt so humiliated in his life. Gerardo emphasized that Barnett was being especially mean to the women, including Eric's family members. I could see the anger brewing in Eric's face as Gerardo described the incident. As Gerardo spoke, his words transported everyone in the room to the hot, dry desert of Arizona. We sat above the small arroyo watching Barnett scowl, curse, and point his weapon at everyone. Gerardo then talked about how there were other incidents similar to theirs, that he had seen the paperwork I had shown him. He mentioned that it was probably happening again as we sat there in the living room. It was only them that could stop the rancher, and it was time that someone stood up to him. Eric started in with some of the questions that he had asked me on the previous visit. Gerardo and I took turns answering, reassuring Eric that the Border Patrol would not take negative action against Mari or her family members.

"What have we got to lose," asked Gerardo, as he leaned forward almost falling off the edge of his couch and extending his arms. "If we win, we can stop this rancher from ever doing this again, and if we lose, so what. He already said that this is not going to cost us anything, that we will never have to pay for the services of the attorneys," said Gerardo pointing in my direction. "So what do we have to lose?"

"But do you think that legally this is a good case, that we can actually win," asked Eric.

Gerardo responded, "Why would he be down here during the holidays trying to make this case happen when he could be at home with his girlfriend and his family if it was not something we could win? Of course, nothing is ever certain, but what do we lose if we try? Absolutely nothing."

I could tell that Eric had become convinced. There was no need for further questions, he was ready to go. He then stated that he was never completely against the idea. He had told me during the previous visit that he needed more time to talk with the family, that I had come out of nowhere and everything happened so suddenly. Gerardo asked who else was left to meet with. I told him about Abel and Manuel who lived in Rancho Escondido. He said he thought he remembered them and suggested that we head up the mountain. I of course did not object, and the three of us jumped in the car. I parked in the same spot I did last time with Padre Klotz. We headed down the mountain toward the house with the yellow siding. We found Manuel and he and Gerardo began chatting. Manuel said he remembered Gerardo, specifically he recalled Barnett getting in his face when they were already in the custody of the Border Patrol.

Gerardo told the entire story, starting from the public records request and detailing my last visit. I do not recall speaking a word and instead would only nod when Gerardo would point in my direction. Manuel had a few questions, similar to Eric's. Gerardo answered them with ease. It did not take more than a half-an-hour before Manuel stated, "well, what do I have to lose," and signed the papers for the lawsuit. He then told us that Abel was currently working in the small town of Angangueo where the priest and I had stayed. Manuel gave us directions to the house where Abel was working. We quickly found the house and Gerardo repeated the same speech, with I nodding in accordance when required. We soon left with Abel's signature.

In a few days I went from only having the signatures of Jorge and Gerardo, to also having the signatures of Rodolfo, Rigoberto, Manuel, Abel, and promises from Eric that he could get Mari, Nancy, Delia, Juan, Sandra, Samuel, and Don Mateo to sign-on. I was a little nervous about him being so sure, but he stated that it was a family decision. After meeting Gerardo, he was sure how the family would decide.

I came to realize that migrants do not need an outsider to organize them. When given access to all of the relevant information, and a better understanding of their options, they can easily organize themselves. We need not simply look at oppressed people as victims; rather they should be seen as potential agents of social change who possess the knowledge of a better world and the willingness to fight for it. Or perhaps better stated, we need not look at the 'poor oppressed people' as if they need to be saved or organized, and should instead look for more ways to simply be chauffeurs.

There were still a few other people who I was yet able to make contact with. Don Mateo thought that one of his relatives, Francisco was back in town. The next day Eric, Don Mateo, and I made the hour and a half drive to Francisco's small *ranchito*. We had to stop a couple of times and ask for directions. Don Mateo had never driven there, having previously only taken the bus. We finally made it up to the small town. We found Francisco working hard on building a house. He bought the materials with the money he had made working in the States and was using his own labor to put it together. He stopped from his work to talk with us. Eric and Don Mateo took over Geraldo's role from the day before. Francisco caught on right away and did not ask very many questions. He then helped us locate the house of the other person from the small village, but she was working in Chicago, Illinois.

Before leaving, Don Mateo asked if I would be interested in meeting his relative who had a son who died crossing the border. In retrospect, I sometimes wish I had said no. I have been unable to forget the pain and sorrow expressed by this woman. In southern Arizona you hear about the numbers. They occasionally pop-up on the television screen, or appear in newspapers as if showing the weather. Another body found in the desert, three more bodies found in the desert, the recovered human remains from fiscal year 2011 in Arizona being 183, down from 253 the year before.

The numbers seemingly appear so often that occasionally you forget the real impact of each death. Perhaps it's the way the news covers the deaths, mainly as being another number and not much more. In the English media I have never seen any interview with someone's family members. As pathetic as the coverage is of the invasions of Iraq and Afghanistan, at least you occasionally see a mother, father, husband, or wife talking about how special their loved one was, and how much they are missed. But when it comes to the border, it is simply another number to be counted. There is no accompanying story to humanize the person who lost their life. The public is not given an understanding of the real impact of the militarization of the border. In this small house, no bigger than the size of hotel room, slept four people. The son had gone off to find work in the United States, hoping to build extra rooms for the family. He died of dehydration trying to cross the border through the Arizona desert. The mother did not find out until a month after he had left. He became just another number.

To cap off what otherwise would have been a very joyous day, she took me to his gravesite a few blocks from her house. After the months of organizing, trips to Mexico, phone calls, emails, and hours on the highway, there were now fourteen people who were ready to go. I had the phone numbers of one more person in Michigan and another person in Chicago. I would be lying if I said it felt good.

I decided to hang out in Zitácuaro for a couple of more days. The city, and especially the people, were becoming more enjoyable every day. I still crave the deep fried corn tortillas that are filled with salsa, onion, and cactus. It doesn't sound as tempting when written down, but trust me, the *huaraches* are delicious. I headed back to Mexico City on the 30th, hoping to again try to track down Jose. Though I thought it might not be worth the effort, I figured, what do I have to lose by trying. I could hear Gerardo's voice in the back of my head. I was met with the same response upon my stop at Jose's house, but his mother told me to come back the next day. She seemed in a better mood and even opened the door for me. I was hoping I would actually have some luck on the 31ˢᵗ. Sure enough, I did.

With a bit of sleep in his eyes, Jose came out of his bedroom. He greeted me with a pleasant hello. On my fourth visit to his house I had finally made it upstairs to the living room. We spoke for about 45 minutes. He complained about how terrible his boss is and I told him the same story that I had down pat by now. Though I wished Gerardo or Eric was with me, I seemed to be doing alright on my own. I explained to Jose that other folks who work in human rights had gone to contact the people in Tlaxcala but had yet to have any luck. He wished he could have been of more assistance on that end, but did not have the contact information for anyone else who was in the group. I again put the situation in context, showing him the public records documents of the other cases. I even showed him some footage of the interviews of the people from Michoacán. He asked what I wanted from him, and I said that I only wanted to see if I could be of service if he wanted to do anything to stop the rancher. He asked questions about a lawsuit and said he would be interested if others from the group could be found. He then said he would like to give his testimony as the others had. He wanted the rest of the world to know about what the vigilantes are actually doing. He retold the story and finished with excellent commentary, "[j]ust because we are not from there, it does not mean that we cannot exercise our human rights, rather we can exercise human rights everywhere."

Just after I finished recording Jose's testimony, the phone rang. Jose's mother brought the phone in to her son. It was Jose's boss and he was asking him to come into work again today, even though he had not had a day off in 13 days. He agreed, and on his way to work he dropped me off at the metro station. As much as he was complaining about his boss, it was clear that he had been at work all those times I had attempted to reach him. He offered to show me around Mexico City in the next few days, but I apologized explaining that I had a flight to catch back home the next day.

MALDEF to the rescue

Back home I quickly made contact with the attorneys at MALDEF. I flew to Los Angeles in early February 2005 to show them the video testimony. They decided to take the case against Barnett and filed on behalf of seventeen plaintiffs a federal lawsuit titled, *Vicente v. Barnett,* Case No. 05-CV-00157. I haven't heard a word about a lawsuit from the people in Tlaxcala, but I did use Jose's testimony in the documentary I co-wrote and co-produced, *Rights on the Line: Vigilantes at the Border*. In late March of that year, I brought a group of people from Michoacán to the border to testify in front of the Cochise County Attorney, Vincent Festa. It was quite a fun trip, bringing up Gerardo, Mari, Nancy, Don Mateo, Sandra, Samuel, and Francisco, but unfortunately it did not end up resulting in a prosecution. It was pretty clear at the outset of the meeting that Festa was not interested in pursuing any criminal charges. He began the interview with Mari by spending about a half an hour asking general questions about crossing the border, noting that he was just doing so out of his own curiosity. He did not even take time to interview all of the people who made the journey to testify. He ended up saying that he would not prosecute because it would just make a martyr out of Barnett, whether he won or lost. Festa thought it best to not draw attention to the problem in hopes that it would simply go away. This certainly made for a long trip back to Michoacán, but the route of a civil lawsuit was still wide open.

The work that MALDEF ended up doing on the federal civil lawsuit exceeded anything I had ever imagined. For local counsel MALDEF asked Jose de Jesus Rivera, the former U.S. Attorney for the District of Arizona who I previously mentioned paid for my airfare on one of the trips. Not only did the folks challenging Barnett have one of the strongest civil rights organizations in the country behind them, but they were also in Federal Court where their other attorney had formerly been the boss of the agency charged with pursuing federal crimes committed in Arizona. This certainly lent some credibility to the lawsuit, and I'm sure the presence of Mr. Rivera was known by U.S. District Judge John Roll. Judge Roll received much flack when he refused to follow Barnett's attorney's request to dismiss the case because undocumented immigrants did not have the same rights as U.S. Citizens. When he ruled against Barnett's outlandish claim it was reported that he received more than 200 phone calls in protest including threats, such as "we should kill him" and "he should be dead." Judge Roll and his family needed to have 24-hour security for a month, including Marshals guarding his home, screening his mail, and even escorting him to mass. On January 8, 2011, Judge Roll was tragically killed when he went to thank U.S. Representative Gabrielle Giffords for her support in backing his effort in getting a judicial emergency declared due to the high number of immigration and border control cases being heard in Arizona (a subject to be discussed later in this book). Some people initially speculated that Judge Roll was killed for his stance against Barnett, but later reports pointed more to him simply being in the wrong place at the wrong time when the shooter, Jared Lee Loughner opened fire in the parking lot of a Tucson grocery store.

The eight-day trial against Barnett began on February 2, 2009. When they entered the courtroom to testify they were not undocumented immigrants crossing the desert, instead they were "documented" plaintiffs standing up against Barnett. Even before the trial started, MALDEF had already secured U visas for some of the plaintiffs. U Visas can be given to undocumented immigrants if they were the victim of certain crimes and volunteered to assist in the prosecution or investigation of that crime. Since they all gave statements when arrested and even traveled back to the border to meet with the Cochise County Attorney's Office, they certainly met the criteria for being willing to assist in stopping Barnett. When all was said and done, MALDEF prevailed on behalf of several of the plaintiffs on the claims of assault and intentional infliction of emotional distress, with the jury ordering Barnett to pay over $77,000 in compensatory and punitive damages.

Instead of giving the plaintiffs the money the U.S. legal system ordered him to pay, Barnett chose to exercise his right to file an appeal. It seems lack of funds may have been an issue for the vigilante rancher as he asked the 9th Circuit Court of Appeals for his and his wife's attorney fees to be paid. Unfortunately for Barnett, on February 3, 2011, the 9th Circuit affirmed the judgment against Barnett and denied the request for attorney fees. Barnett appealed this decision to the U.S. Supreme Court but the nation's highest court affirmed the 9th Circuit's ruling in October 2011. With interest Barnett now must fork over $87,000. Another indication Barnett was hurting for money is the website www.helpingroger.com, which asks for people to mail checks or donate by credit card over the phone for the "Roger Barnett Legal Defense Fund." I guess all this lawsuit business cut into his hunting for immigrant funds.

Barnett's string of bad luck continued when a bill written by the Arizona legislature specifically for him could not even help him out. Arizona lawmakers were so enraged that undocumented immigrants were suing Barnett that in 2006 they passed a measure asking voters to change the state Constitution to forbid Arizona courts from awarding punitive damages to undocumented immigrants. It was put on the ballot as Proposition 102 and 74 percent of those who voted favored the initiative. Even though the law was written specifically with Barnett in mind, legislators later realized it would not help Barnett because it was not retroactive. So, less than a week after the 9th Circuit upheld the ruling against Barnett, the Republican lawmakers added an amendment to an unrelated bill making Prop. 102 retroactive to Jan 1, 2004.

After being rejected by the 9th Circuit Court of Appeals and U.S. Supreme Court, Barnett went back to U.S. District Court in Tucson, relying on the new law written just for him. However, in May 2012, U.S. District Judge Frank Zapata ruled that the retroactive law still did not apply to Barnett, citing that the law refers to a person's legal status when punitive damages are awarded, not when the incident happened. When they were awarded the damages, the plaintiffs either had U Visas, or were given permission to come into the country for purposes of the lawsuit. Judge Zapata also called into question the constitutionality of the law, but stated it did not apply because the plaintiffs had legal status.

In a press release following Judge Zapata's ruling, Tom Saenz, MALDEF President and General Counsel, stated, "The court's decision ensures that no wrongdoer can escape accountability by targeting the most vulnerable immigrants for attack. MALDEF looks forward to collecting from Barnett the recompense he owes the plaintiffs." There is no doubt MALDEF will not rest until the money is turned over.

It was a pleasure to meet Ana Maria, Gerardo, Samuel, Sandra, Mateo, Adela, Nancy, Francisco, Abel, Manuel, Jorge, Rigoberto, Rodolfo, Octavio, Juan, Sara, and Eric. I have great memories of spending time at their houses and traveling with them to the border (I won't mention who ended up running up a big bill on pay-per-view movies when we stayed at the Hilton at the Mexico City Airport) to meet with the Cochise County Attorney's Office. With the help of many good-hearted people along the way, these individuals stood up against the vigilante rancher who terrorized hundreds, maybe thousands of migrants and put a stop to his vicious actions. In retrospect, it was a pretty crazy idea to go look for them. Thinking back now, I realize that I was pretty foolish and ignorant just to buy an airplane ticket and head south. I guess sometimes it pays to be foolish and ignorant and follow your heart.

CHAPTER FOUR

Choosing Death

The lawsuit against Barnett was filed on March 4, 2005. This was three days before MALDEF thought the statute of limitations was going to expire on the unlawful imprisonment cause of action. I was happy to hand the case over to the attorneys at MALDEF, because as soon as I got home, there was another battle to fight.

That day, I returned and shifted my focus toward organizing against the Minuteman Project, which was set to begin in less than a month. When I first heard of the Minuteman Project I simply dismissed it as another Chris Simcox ploy. I assumed he was doing the same thing he does every couple of years. I was sure the result would be the same: lots of rhetoric and hardly any people would show up. I knew that the Barnetts and Ranch Rescue were the real ones to worry about and decided to keep my focus on them. But postings on White Supremacists websites quickly changed the strategy. On websites such as Stormfront and White Revolution, I read about racists wanting to come to the desert to "arrest illegal invaders" and "clean up our country." The following is an actual quote I found on Stormfront:

> Stopping that invader of our country will be the highlight of my white nationalist carreer [sic]. When my comrades and I are standing over an illegal we bagged and tagged in a citizens arrest I will finally see some sort of action that allthough [sic] miniscule has changed the course of our nation for the better, not some dumb flyer drop, or some secret meeting, but action. Not only will this program have a great morale [sic?] effect but

I can guarantee that if we are successful there will be a huge propaganda effect.

I knew this was not just going to be Simcox and a small handful of senior citizens. Here were a group of people, including White Supremacists, who wanted to come to my community. This is the land where my ancestors have lived for generations, since before the land "belonged" to the United States of America and probably before the land "belonged" to Mexico. They were not coming down for a vacation. Rather they were coming to hunt people who could possibly be my relatives. They were trying to stop people from seeking to improve their lives. This disgusting action demanded a strong response. This was not a time for a press conference or to start a petition drive, but a time to take to the desert. At the bare minimum, I thought there needed to be people following the Minutemen. I decided to recruit people to stand between armed individuals filled with hate and those they wish to place all of our society's ills upon, with no government protection. I thought the possibility of violence was highly likely. However, I reasoned that violence was less likely if people were out in the desert with video cameras.

The purpose of the legal observer project was to deter abuses, document the actions of these individuals, and highlight the real tragedies that occur along the border. The time was long overdue for a direct intervention into the human rights crisis on the border. Perhaps someday we will live in a society where no human being will have to face death and hatred in pursuit of work that this country requires. Until that day comes, the experiences of undocumented migrants crossing the U.S.-Mexican Border needs to be highlighted in order to demonstrate the fact that this is one of the grossest human rights violations in the history of the United States. Hundreds of people die annually in the desert and the American public chooses to turn a blind eye.

Instead of highlighting the human rights tragedy, the Minuteman Project sought to call attention to our nation's "porous" borders and lack of enforcement. Co-founder James Gilchrist heard Simcox speaking on a right-wing radio program and contacted him with the idea of calling for volunteers to come down to the border in April of 2005. At the time there was very little focus on the border in the Arizona news, much less in the national media. For whatever reason, the Minuteman Project became a media sensation and news outlets from across the globe gave free press to this very small group of right wing individuals. While Simcox has been doing citizen patrols for some time, and others had done similar ploys in Arizona and California, the idea of the "Minuteman Project" took off and became an international sensation seemingly overnight. Simcox and Gilchrist provided interviews across the world and warned of the impending doom if the government did not take immediate action against the immigrants entering the United States.

As opposed to being outraged about the deaths, the general sentiment of the public is similar to that of the vigilantes. People's perceptions are rooted in fear and misunderstanding; it is this attitude that gives rise to the Minutemen. Not all are evil racists, but undoubtedly I knew some would show up. It is important to note that the purpose of the legal observer project was not to demonize any one individual or group. Rather, I hoped that people could see the Minutemen not so much as enemies, but as victims. This of course was one of the main reasons why legal observers were unarmed and pledged to adhere to non-violence even if attacked by one of the White Supremacists. As much as possible I wanted the emphasis to be on the struggles of those crossing, not on the hate groups patrolling.

I had no idea how many people would volunteer. At the beginning, I thought it would just be myself and my cousin David. And that is only because I was not going to tell him where we were going.

The Legal Observer Project was modeled after the Black Panther Party for Self-Defense and Cop Watch. As the Black Panther Party for Self Defense took to the street to protect community members from police brutality and state violence, legal observers took to the desert to stand up for human rights and protect migrants from possible violence at the hands of vigilantes. As opposed to being armed with weapons for self-defense, legal observers were armed with video cameras and the power of nonviolence. I wrote a brief legal memorandum to the Cochise County Sheriff explaining to him how the actions of the Minutemen Project would result in unlawful imprisonment. The concept is not difficult to grasp, that is if you are trying to understand, which of course the County Sheriff Larry Dever was not trying to do. Imagine you go to a restaurant tonight and you have a great meal. Though happy with your food, you get the sneaking suspicion that the cook, busboy, and dishwasher are undocumented immigrants. So you pull out your cell phone and call up ten of your friends to meet you in the alley of the restaurant. Everyone hides in the alley, waiting for the workers to leave. When they come out, you surround them with your weapons drawn and "suggest" that they wait until the Border Patrol comes to determine whether or not they are in the country legally. You can of course change the scenario to have the vigilantes sitting in front of a church or walking through a park. Or if you like, walking through the desert of Arizona. Regardless of the location, the law is crystal clear; private citizens are in no circumstances authorized to detain other private citizens for alleged violation of civil immigration laws. Would you really want private citizens to be able to stop whomever they think is undocumented? I certainly do not. I am sure my dark skin would result in me being stopped quite often. I already have enough racial profiling to deal with from the Border Patrol.

In addition to sending an email requesting volunteers, a press release was sent out informing the media that the ACLU of Arizona would be training legal observers to monitor the Minuteman Project. We received limited coverage in local papers. But, the news quickly spread to the far-right wing groups and White Supremacist websites. Subsequently, we began receiving death threats and harassing emails and phone calls. Apparently the threats were both more numerous and severe than typically received by ACLU affiliates. A few weeks before the Minuteman Project was to begin, this fear prompted discussions about whether to proceed with the Legal Observer Project. I was told to call an attorney who was very active in the Civil Rights Movement to get feedback as to how to proceed. This individual served as counsel to Martin Luther King Jr. and was beaten by White Supremacists while doing work in the South. Needless to say, he is an extremely intelligent and courageous person and a man I greatly admire. Unfortunately, my phone call with him led to a series of conversations that I wish had never happened. I talked to this attorney about the Legal Observer Project, and he thought it sounded more dangerous than the type of work he had done in the South. In his mind it would be equivalent to civil rights activists following the Ku Klux Klan around while they went out "Night Riding." Night Riding is when Klansmen went out in packs to search for African-Americans to beat. He also mentioned that his situation had been safer because what African-Americans were attempting to do was 'legal.' The legality of their actions gave them protection of the federal government, whereas here the Minutemen are simply mimicking the actions of the federal government.

Pressure to abandon the Legal Observer Project continued to mount. In fact, the ACLU of Arizona State Board discussed canceling the project. I was not invited to the Board's discussion but later learned what they were planning. Instead of the project, they proposed a candlelight vigil. They appointed me to organize the vigil and promised to travel to the border to participate. I could not believe they expected me to organize a prayer session. A few days after the State Board meeting, I participated in a conference call along with the Executive Director of the ACLU of Arizona, and two high-ranking attorneys at the National ACLU. I learned that the civil rights attorney I spoke with called the national office to inform them of his concerns. I prepared for the conference call by making a long list of the precautions planned to minimize the possibility of violence. Unfortunately, I did not get a chance to share the list (much less otherwise defend the project) before the decision was made by three white people, living and working far from the border, that the Legal Observer Project was to be cancelled. They were afraid of harm to the volunteers and me.

I had already spent a great deal of time thinking about how to proceed if the Legal Observer Project was cancelled. I asked to take vacation time, but was told that I did not qualify for it because I had not yet been employed a year. I then asked for a month off. The response was that I was already too affiliated with the ACLU for the project to be seen as anything but an ACLU action. The only options left were to quit or start buying candles. After being informed of the project's cancellation, I spent a lot of time sitting on the roof of my house looking out at the border fence that separates Douglas from Agua Prieta. I spoke with Padre Cayetano Cabrera, the priest earlier mentioned who runs the migrant center in Agua Prieta, my good friend Xavier Zaragoza, and our favorite waitress at Denny's, Sarai. I weighed the pros and cons of quitting and finally came to the conclusion that I should quit my job to run the Legal Observer Project. I submitted my letter of resignation and hoped that it would be possible to run the project without the financial and logistical support of the ACLU.

As soon as people knew that the project was moving forward despite the loss of the ACLU's wavering support, additional assistance poured in to fill the void. An independent silk screener in Tucson, Dwight Evans, offered to donate t-shirts. Derechos Humanos/Alianza de Indigenas Sin Fronteras offered to sponsor the project, and my professors at Stanford worked overtime to get cameras and radios donated while simultaneously lobbying the National ACLU to reconsider their decision. At the same time, the American Friends Service Committee of Arizona agreed to sponsor the project. Also, a group of state legislators sent out a press release saying they would be traveling to the border to serve as legal observers and would continue to support the project. Finally, Ira Glasser, in whose honor my fellowship had been named, intervened to advocate on my behalf.

I was convinced that the action was necessary but was still hoping someone would find a better alternative that would not put anyone in harm's way. Unfortunately, this did not happen. Perhaps I could have been described as bull-headed, illogical, and unwilling to compromise. In retrospect, you might be able to still say the same thing. What can I say? I was convinced that the project needed to happen. If it was me crossing the desert, I would hope that people of privilege would stand-up and follow the Minutemen in order to minimize the chance of myself getting beaten or killed. Plain and simply, we possessed the opportunity to be of service to our fellow human beings who, because of the geographical location and economic conditions they were born, lack such a privilege. The logic was very simple but the pressure to not do it was enormous. Throughout my life, I had never been much for succumbing to peer pressure. I saw no reason to start now. I had gotten this far following my heart and figured it was best to simply continue to move forward.

Over the next week, I spent as much time trying to resolve this issue as I spent actually organizing the project and recruiting volunteers. Just a few days before the Minuteman Project was to begin, and after numerous conversations and the advocacy of many individuals, the ACLU of Arizona agreed to once again sponsor the Legal Observer Project. Unfortunately, the complications did not stop there. The issue of messaging became very contentious; the ACLU of Arizona State Board wanted the Legal Observer Project to be seen as a 'neutral' endeavor. The board wanted to publicly state that the purpose of legal observing was to protect the First Amendment rights of the Minutemen and prevent physical abuse of migrants. There was criticism of the project in the local newspaper by a non-profit that advocated on behalf of migrants and border communities. There were also accusations from people within the ACLU affiliate that I was seeking martyrdom. In response to those reacting negatively to the Legal Observer Project, I wrote a lengthy description of the purpose of legal observing a few days before April 1st and will share a short excerpt here.

"…If a Minuteman volunteer says hello, legal observers will respond with kindness and sincerity, but there will never be an opportunity for political dialogue. At all times Minutemen will be treated with the respect and dignity that human beings deserve, but we are not under the illusion that we can convince them that what they are doing is either illegal or immoral.

Let us not be under the illusion that the Minutemen are the real problem. While imminent violence from a volunteer who strays from the Standard Operating Procedures is certainly an immediate concern, the focus must also be on our failings as a society.

We cannot simply dismiss the Minuteman volunteers as evil racists. They are individuals who see their society changing, transforming into something different than what they once knew. Spanish language radio and television stations are now more available than they ever have been on the airwaves.

Supermarkets are filled with items from Latin America and Spanish language billboards are appearing everywhere from Georgia to Minnesota. People of color are assuming some of the highest positions in our government. Some have called it the 'browning' of America, and many fear this change.

It is the misunderstanding and fear within our society that we must seek to overcome. This victory cannot come about from a county attorney or by placing a few individuals in jail. While preventing abuses and seeking immediate remedies is important, we must also denounce our larger failures as a society.

Legal observing is also an opportunity to make a statement to the world. Just as Cesar Chavez communicated his message through his actions, so are we. Mr. Chavez communicated his discontent with and LOVE for the world by self-sacrifice: picketing, fasting, and pilgrimages.

It is in this spirit that legal observers are willing to make the self-sacrifice of following Minutemen into the desert. Our legs and arms will be cut by the sharp brush, the sudden movement of desert animals will make our hearts quickly race, the relentless sun will burn our skin and give us great thirst, and the nearby armed, angry individuals will certainly be daunting.

Yet, our suffering will not be one-tenth of what the average migrant experiences. The land in Cochise County is super saturated with the blood, sweat, and tears of people from Latin America. Our minimal suffering is an acknowledgment of the suffering, a way to ask for forgiveness for living in a society that allows such a situation to occur.

It is extremely dangerous. But, not as dangerous as being a migrant. Legal observers will return to Douglas to sleep [and] to enjoy a nice meal; most migrants are in the desert for three to four days.

For the last ten months I have been listening to migrants' stories as I volunteered at a shelter in Agua Prieta, Sonora, Mexico. Every day I hear about how they walk until their shoes are torn and their feet are swollen with blisters. I have heard stories of legs cramping up to the point where one can no longer walk, about people becoming so dehydrated they begin to drink their own urine, of being robbed in the desert, of being beat for not having any money to turn over, of being threatened with pistols by vigilantes while being circled by vicious dogs and being told you were a worthless Mexican who is not wanted in the United States.

The suffering is real and it has occurred for too long. I have often asked myself how migrants can overcome so much adversity, where do they find their motivation? More often than not their motivation is love, mainly the love of their family. The U.S.-Mexico border is one of the greatest tragedies ever written, filled with danger, emotion, passion, and love. It is now time to close out this tragedy and recognize that we need not make human beings suffer anymore.

I for one cannot sit by as more migrant beatings take place. This tragedy is currently playing out in my backyard. I was born in Douglas and many of these Minutemen will be patrolling around the Paul Lime factory where my grandfather worked for so many years, also serving as the [local] President of the United Steelworkers of America, AFL-CIO.

In the grand scheme of things, America has nothing to worry about. America is a land that is supposed to be based on principles and ideologies, not skin color or language. The ideas of democracy, justice, and freedom should be our common bonds.

Someday this will be seen as one of the worst human rights abuses in the history of the United States. This fact will only become common knowledge when individuals are willing to stand-up and demand they be treated with respect and dignity. That movement will come about and be led by someone who crossed the border without the proper documents.

Until that movement begins, we cannot simply say this is too dangerous and come to the conclusion that this is one of those circumstances when it is best to do nothing. This is one of those circumstances when people must choose between the lesser of two fears. The fear of sitting at home and doing nothing and the fear of suffering for your fellow human being.

Legal observers are choosing to suffer for their fellow human beings and it is our hope that we prevent abuses and raise awareness of the current plight of migrants."

The day before observing was to begin I drove to Tucson to buy supplies for the volunteers. I loaded up on lawn chairs, two-way radios, video cameras, flashlights, food, water and, very importantly, bug spray. Searching for night vision goggles, I walked into a firearms store for my first time. I was also curious about the price of a bullet proof vest. I asked one of the men behind the counter if they had night vision goggles and bullet proof vests. At this point, all eyes in the room turned to me. Here were a bunch of heavily armed, tattooed white people looking at me quite suspiciously. They asked if I was military and I said no. Then they responded that they could only sell bullet proof vests to military or police personnel. I quickly walked back to my car and it was finally starting to dawn on me what I was actually about to do. My concerns about anything the ACLU of Arizona would say or do were no longer relevant. I was only concerned about the safety of the volunteers I had encouraged to come down and the migrants who would be crossing, oh, and myself.

CHAPTER FIVE

Legal Observing Part I

Truth be told, the first weekend of the Legal Observing Project there were probably more members of the media than there were Minutemen. The excitement did not occur until well after the media members had left and forgotten about the crazies in the desert. This is not to say that there was a lack of drama during the first few days. While the Minutemen claimed that they would only protest in front of the Border Patrol stations the first weekend, it was clear that the gun-toting folks who came from around the country were getting anxious. I heard from reporters that volunteers were getting upset with the leadership of James Gilchrist and Chris Simcox and wanted to head immediately to the desert to catch some Mexicans.

On April 2, we heard that Minutemen had set up posts along Border Road, about a twenty-minute drive from Douglas. I drove west on Highway 80, passing Cochise College and the baseball field where I had spent so much time, and turned off toward Border Road. The gravel turns into a dirt road just past the Paul Lime Factory, the plant my grandfather retired from, and heads southwest to the border. In my car were a camera crew and my two good friends from law school who came down for the first weekend to legal observe, Matthew Liebman and Jason Tarricone. We came upon the first group as the road began to parallel the seven strands of barb wire that signify the U.S.-Mexico border. I saw a group of four people, all wearing side arms standing outside of their truck and as we drove by, one woman proudly waived her American flag. Patriotism will make you do some crazy things, and this was certainly one of them. I slowed down the car so that the clouds of dirt that the tires were kicking up would not be so large. We made our way over a small hill, and I saw groups of two or three vehicles stationed about 100 yards from each other. It was strange to see so many people in an area where I normally visited to enjoy the quietness and solitude of the Sonoran Desert. One of the Minutemen's stations was set up right next to one of the water tanks put out by the humanitarian group Humane Borders. It was clear that no migrants would benefit from the water in the big blue jugs this month. I could see the Minutemen inspecting the jugs and shaking their heads in disbelief that someone would actually want to help the migrants. It was not a surprise to later find the jugs vandalized. I kept driving, and for a moment, I thought the line of big trucks with out-of-state license plates was going to go on forever. But it did not take too long to drive by the last outpost. I realized that there were only about ten stations, totaling approximately 40 people.

I got out of my car and saw an older white man with a Yosemite Sam-like moustache, looking through his binoculars into Mexico. Holstered on his hip was a gun with a very large barrel. It felt like a throwback to the Wild West days. It was still pretty difficult to understand why on earth someone would feel so passionate to drive across country to stop people from crossing the border. But as the month went by, I would get more than my fair share of answers from the Minutemen who came up to either yell at us or engage in friendly conversation.

But at that moment, it was time to get all of the legal observers in the desert and make sure they were safe. Each team of legal observers was equipped with a radio that ran off of receivers on nearby mountains, and I relayed to the rest of the volunteers to meet me at the side of Highway 80 so we could set up out in the desert. This was it. Time to see how the crazies with guns would react when we hiked behind them and sat in lawn chairs fifty yards or so from their positions. Just after announcing the legal observing, I stopped in unannounced to Simcox's office to let him know what we were going to be doing and to go over ground rules. I caught him and his crew off guard but Simcox was quite pleasant. He told me to expect nothing but courtesy from the Minutemen and he welcomed extra eyes and ears in the desert, even noting that our presence would simply make his group look bigger and deter people from trying to cross in the first place. Apparently, he had not done much studying on border policy. Academic and government studies have repeatedly shown that presence in one area simply diverts traffic to a different area, never completely stopping people from crossing the border. We exchanged cell phone numbers and promised to call each other if either of us saw one another's volunteers acting inappropriately. He had heard about threats that I'd received, I did not ask how, and offered his own security detail for me. I politely declined, but was thankful to have his phone number. I would end up using it on more than one occasion.

I met a group of 30 legal observers by the side of Highway 80. We joined together for final instructions before heading into the desert. The group mainly consisted of students from Prescott College and their ever-present Professor Randall Amster. Just as I was preparing the volunteers, Eleanor Eisenberg pulled up and quickly approached the circle. After I was finished talking she pulled me aside and began complaining about my choice to have a certain person do a television interview on a Latino-themed program about the Legal Observer Project. I explained that I chose this person because I knew she would do a great job. However, it was obvious that Eleanor was upset that I did not ask her to appear on the show. Eleanor went on to say that she had decided to accept my letter of resignation, and I reminded her that I had already rescinded that. She then said that it would be best if I just went back to school. I told her that we could talk about that later, at the moment I was concerned with the safety of the volunteers about to be sent to sit behind the Minutemen.

"One more thing," Eleanor said in a tone that signified I was not going to like what was coming next, "you cannot talk to the media, if there is any media out there I will talk to them. When I am not here you just have them call me on my cell phone. I'll make sure to leave it on." I had heard about Eleanor's performance a few nights before on the Lou Dobbs show where she adamantly defended the Minutemen and said the legal observers would be out there to ensure the Minutemen's First Amendment Rights were respected.

"Are you saying that the ACLU is taking away my First Amendment right to free speech?" I asked.

"Only the government can take away your First Amendment rights, the ACLU cannot," responded Eleanor.

"Eleanor, I am going to do what I have to do, and you can do what you have to do," I stated as I began walking back to my car. The thought of Eleanor controlling all of the messaging was frightening. People were coming out to the desert to put their lives on the line to protect migrants and to make a statement about the human rights tragedy on the border. What if something was to happen to them? Would we tell the media that they were hurt while protecting the Minutemen's First Amendment rights that nobody was trying to take away?

By the time Eleanor made it to the border, I was speaking with Hernan Rozemberg, a reporter with the San Antonio Express Newspaper. The legal observers were set up in their positions and no problems had been reported yet. Then the sun started to set, and you could feel the entire atmosphere changing. As soon as the sun disappears, the desert turns from a warm, open land where you can see for miles, to a cold, dark area where you can see as far as you can extend your hand. Each small noise in the bushes sounds like a rattlesnake or a crazy vigilante sneaking up from behind. As the sun was descending, the anticipation was growing. Would migrants suddenly storm across the line and be met with the gunfire of the Minutemen?

We stayed out for quite some time but nothing happened. The next day we discovered another Minutemen outpost after hearing from reporters that there were two different areas where the Minutemen were setting up, the Naco line and the Huachuca line. We headed to the Huachuca

Mountains to try to find the other line, leaving one group of legal observers back on Border Road, or as the Minutemen were referring to it, the Naco line. About a 45-minute drive from Douglas, the Huachuca Mountains lie just south of the city of Sierra Vista. Matt, Jason, and I drove around the small path that leads up the mountain but did not have any luck. We tried a few different small roads that lead up the mountain until we found one that was being completely blocked by a plump man with Missouri license plates. We knew that we had found the area we were looking for.

The Huachuca line was the opposite of the Naco line in many ways. First, the geography. Whereas the Naco line was pure desert, the Huachuca line was up in the mountains and was filled with large trees with plenty of shade and temperatures were much cooler during both the day and night. The other interesting difference was the types of Minutemen at the different lines. It appeared that the Minutemen sent all of the older folks to the Naco line, to sit in the sun with their lawn chairs and not have to worry about moving around. On the Huachuca line were more of the G.I. Joe Minutemen; those really looking for action and trying to create an atmosphere of war. It should not be hard to guess where the Minutemen sent the media members. The newspaper photos were of older people out in the middle of the desert and not camouflaged men. It was a brilliant public relations move; lead the media to believe that you are simply a bunch of harmless old people who are sitting out in the desert knitting, while the volunteers who are really looking for action are miles away hiding in between trees, looking to recreate Vietnam.

The Minutemen fooled the media into thinking there were never any White Supremacists who actually participated in their border activities. David Holthouse, an investigator for the Southern Poverty Law Center, had proven them wrong by infiltrating the Minuteman Project and going on patrol with a group of White Supremacists. Holthouse later told me that every time the ACLU volunteers would drive-by they would say, "[h]ere comes the ACL-Jews." Interestingly enough, Holthouse was not the only person to infiltrate the Minuteman Project. While the Minutemen claimed to be doing extensive background checks, to weed out White Supremacists and other unwanted volunteers, a simple Internet search using Google would have revealed David Holthouse's employer. Another person who used her real name, and was amazingly not discovered, was Deborah Girard. Deborah Girard is certainly not a household name, but is one Chris Simcox should remember. Girard is the federal agent who ordered Chris Simcox to get face down on the ground and arrested him after he lied to her and said he was not carrying a weapon. During one of Simcox's earlier missions, well before the Minuteman Project, he was caught on federal park land, where it was prohibited to carry a weapon. Instead of telling the truth, he decided to lie to Agent Girard and as a result was prohibited from carrying a firearm by the federal government for three years. So much for the "extensive background checks" done by the Minutemen.

The first weekend had come and gone with legal observers only receiving a few racist remarks and some overt threats. One of the legal observers, Beth Sanders, was approached by one the Minutemen and asked if she locked her windows at night. Beth was also informed that it was very easy to find out where she lived and that she ought to be careful. Meanwhile, the Minutemen were alleging to reporters and documentary film makers that the legal observers were intentionally interfering with the Minutemen's activities. According to the creative mind of one Minuteman named Gary, I had escorted 200 migrants around the Minutemen's Huachuca line. Legal observers were also supposedly using bird calls to signal to the migrants the location of the Minutemen and making loud noises late at night. It was beginning to remind me of my time working with elementary school kids.

There were certainly a few school-yard bullies out on patrol. One night just after sunset, we heard reports that station eight was holding a group of migrants along the Huachuca line. I was in a car by myself, driving behind two other vehicles with legal observers. The two vehicles in front of me accidentally passed the turn-off for station eight and I was the first person to arrive. I jumped out of my car and ran over to where I saw a small flashlight pointing toward the ground. It was already completely dark and I could not make out what was happening underneath the trees. To be safe, I turned my video camera on and began recording while I walked toward the light. As I approached, I could see a small group of people sitting down and a few men standing around them. Since the video camera was not picking up the images I began speaking so I could at least have audio recorded. The Minutemen did not like the fact that I was recording and demanded that I shut the camera off. "Turn, that god damn camera off," demanded one man.

"Sorry, sir, we are on public land and I have a right to be filming. I am just documenting what is going on here…"

"I said turn that god-damn camera off," repeated the man as he walked in my direction. The video shows the light of the flashlight coming in my direction and then all of the sudden the light disappears. The man had turned off the flashlight and used it as a weapon to try to knock the camera out of my hands.

"You cannot do that to me. What do you think you are doing?" I asked the man. I noticed that one of the other Minutemen in the crowd was the Huachuca line leader, James Chase. Chase had earlier in the day told us a story about ninja turtles who carry drugs through the Huachuca Mountains and concluded his saga by requesting that we come to him if any of his volunteers got out of line. He promised that he would not let happen what he saw in Vietnam and his men would behave well. So I took him up on his promise, "Jim, you saw what he just did, that's ridiculous, you can't let your volunteers be acting like this." Jim remained silent, and the man with the flashlight walked back to the group as I phoned the County Sheriff and then Simcox. The other legal observers arrived just as I was making the calls and when the Sheriff showed up the Minutemen made up a grand story that I ran up to them and was shoving the camera in their face, but that no one had ever touched me.

The Sheriff and County Attorney's Office did nothing, just as they had done nothing with previous vigilante incidents, and just as they would do nothing for the rest of the month. It was no surprise, but at least it was documented and nobody could say that there were no incidents of violence from the Minutemen. This does not keep them from alleging the exact opposite. After receiving the reports from the County Sheriff's Office months later, I learned that the man who hit me with the flashlight was Joe McCutchen. McCutchen had been outed by the Anti-Defamation League and the Southern Poverty Law Center for his connections with White Supremacists organizations. A fine southern gentleman from the state of Alabama, McCutchen is one of those characters you figured the Minutemen's excellent background checks would have prevented from joining.

The freaks come out at night

Pretty much all of the action took place at night. It made sense; night time is when migrants generally walk as they spend the day time resting and hiding from sight. Night time was also when the craziest of the Minutemen were out on patrol. There was so much tension and paranoia in the air that it is difficult to describe. Listening to the Minutemen's radio transactions and walking around the area really gave me the sense that I was on a battlefield. The Minutemen all used two-way radios that can be purchased at any super market. All we had to do was buy our own and then hit the scan button. Every time they would communicate with each other we could hear what they were saying. It could be hours without hearing anything, and then all of a sudden, there would be a tense voice whispering, "Charlie, behind the wire, repeat, Charlie behind the wire." The Minutemen had taken to using "Charlie," a term from Vietnam referring to the enemy, to identify migrants. We would figure out what station the report was coming from then put beanies over our heads, gloves on our hands, and step out of the car to put on an extra jacket before hiking around to find the location. More often than not "Charlie" turned out to be a cow or some other animal.

In order to ease some of the tension that occurred at night, my friend Scott Kerr suggested walking up and down the line during the middle of the night to say hello to the Minutemen. He reasoned that if migrants ever actually did approach, the Minutemen would be less likely to be surprised and do something crazy because they had already experienced someone coming out of nowhere and approaching them. I worried that we might give the Minutemen an excuse to pull the trigger at 2 a.m., but I trusted Scott. Scott was a member of the Christian Peacemakers Team, and as such, had experience going around the world to places of conflict to try to minimize the possibility of violence. He had been in Iraq, Palestine, Colombia, and Chiapas (Mexico). Because he had so much more experience I let him walk in front of me. At the first stop we ran into my good buddy Mitch Geiger. Mitch was a young guy, about my age, and was the line leader that night. By now we were pretty comfortable with each other, and to be honest, I was beginning to think he was a pretty nice guy. This is not to say I completely let my guard down. I remembered the 180 degree turn from James Chase and always kept this in mind. "Did you guys come over for some coffee?" asked Mitch.

"No, thanks, I am already pretty well wired for the night, just giving the legs some exercise," I replied. He offered to accompany us on the journey down the line but we said we would be fine. As we walked through the brush I could hear the occasional car driving by on the highway. It would still be a few minutes of walking before coming to the next station. The silence of the night was broken by the sound of a big dog barking. I started to run back when Scott yelled out that we were just legal observers out for a walk.

"You should be more careful out here, this ain't some picnic," replied a man's voice from the direction where the dog was barking.

"Sorry 'bout that," said Scott. "We're just out here stretching the old legs, that's all. How you doin' tonight?"

"I am fine," replied the man sternly and abruptly, giving me the indication he was not much in the mood for conversation. As we walked past his station I noticed his license plates were from New York and realized that he was the Minuteman that had driven all the way from the East Coast along with his Doberman Pinscher.

As we continued our walk down the line things would continue to get crazier. Our breaths coming out as puffs of smoke in the cold desert night were a direct contrast to earlier in the day. Just a few hours before, I was searching for shade to cope with the ridiculous heat on Border Road. At the next station, the Minuteman had barricaded himself in and was surrounded by trip wire. "Excuse me sir, if I cross over one of these wires, will a bomb go off?" asked Scott.

"No, but it'll make a loud enough sound that the whole line will know it, so do not do it," responded the man.

"So how's it going tonight?" asked Scott.

"It was going just fine until you showed up," the Minuteman replied. Taking that as our indication to keep walking down the line we moved along. The branches beneath our feet cracked, and I could not help but just start laughing.

"What's up?" asked Scott.

"I just can't believe all this. It's like one of those fantasy baseball camps that old people go to, except this is for war. Your chance to relieve your glory days, give yourself a ridiculous name like Cobra, Jackknife, Casanova, and play on your walkie-talkie using jargon that you learned back in the military. You get to camp out in the middle of nowhere and have the leadership tell you what to do, and on top of that there is the feeling that there is a real enemy."

"Yeah, it would be comical if there weren't real people coming across the border, ay," said Scott. That was certainly the truth. If someone set up a camp and charged the same price as the Minutemen so that a bunch of white men could leave their families and gather around in circles and make homophobic, racists, and sexists remarks it would look just like the Minuteman Project. They would of course also have to label the sleeping quarters, bathrooms, and cafeteria using military sounding names. For instance, you could not say you were going back to base to use the restrooms, you have to go back to use the latrines. You would also have to hire a medic to drive around in a camouflage jeep, seemingly bought from the set of MASH, to hand out meals-ready to-eat (MRE's). Of course, in this fantasy camp you would probably have to pay Mike the Medic to do this, but here in southeastern Arizona, they had some crazy guy doing it for free.

Before reaching the next station, we saw a bright flash of light come out of nowhere. Actually, Scott saw it a lot better as it was directly aimed at his eyes and he was temporarily blinded. "Holy cow!" yelled Scott. "How many watts is that thing, man that must be a spotlight." The Minutemen were laughing and stated that they had brighter lights if we cared to see. "No thanks, I'll take your word for it," replied Scott. As we walked into the small camp we could see, well at this point I could see, three men standing around, one of them dressed in full military fatigues, complete with polished black boots strapped tightly around his ankles and his dark fatigues tucked into them. He was a skinny white guy, with a shaved head and sucked in cheek bones that made him look like a Timothy McVeigh clone. We chatted the men up for awhile. The Timothy McVeigh clone kept quiet, and looked angry throughout our conversation. It turns out that one of the other men was not a Minuteman but a member of another border watch group, American Border Patrol. He proudly boasted that he had been coming up here for years, way before the Minutemen. He sounded like one of those people you talk to who used to follow a popular band before they became famous and now was upset that they were mainstream. He wanted us to know that even before it was cool to hunt for people he was already doing it. I left my cookies back in the car, or else I would have given him one. He had a van equipped with a large antenna on top and there was so much video equipment inside it looked as if it belonged to a television news crew. He looked more like a guy who was prepared to chase tornadoes. Out of nowhere, little McVeigh spoke, "I am sick of this talk, I am going to go hunt me some illegals!" Sure enough, off he marched into the dark with his pistol strapped to his waist. The last image I remember seeing of him that night was his backpack bouncing up and down as he headed up the mountain.

I saw little McVeigh out a few times, but as the days went by it was becoming obvious that the Minutemen's numbers were dwindling. But who was left? In addition to little McVeigh, Mitch was still around and so was Doberman guy. Ninja man, James Chase, was still present, and there was also another scary character that would come back every night, "martyr man." I had first seen martyr man a few days before when he was standing over a small ravine dangling a microwavable burrito that was hooked on the end of a fishing line. He was holding the fishing pole as a Minuteman in the ravine was pretending to be an "illegal immigrant" and jumping up and down trying to grasp the burrito. Martyr Minuteman was making his own little video to pass the time during the day. When he was not busy filming he spent a lot of time bothering the women legal observers. He was rude, obnoxious and frankly quite annoying. As one legal observer, Karen Lutrick, observed he was similar to many Minutemen in that he lacked social skills and you could tell it was difficult for him to interact with people of the opposite gender. He thought himself a comedian and claimed to have his own television show in California. One afternoon after the burrito filming he explained to me some of his strategies.

"You see, with the women it's easy. Man, I have so many women I do not know what to do with them. If you come with me to the bar tonight, any bar you pick, I guarantee we will leave with women," he told me. I had already explained to him for about the eighth time that our policy prohibited us from engaging in political conversation but that we could listen to anything they wanted to tell us or would be happy to talk about any subject other than politics. The first time I told him this a few days ago he went off on a mad rant about diseases, welfare, and crime and then stormed away. Apparently today he had either taken his medications or was simply in a better mood so he had decided to share with me his secrets tricks for seducing women.

"So here is what you do," he explained after I told him I would not be going out to any bars tonight. "You just treat them like shit, I mean be real mean to them. For awhile they'll hate you, call you all kinds of names and everything, but after a while they think that you don't like them and it becomes a challenge for them. You see, they are like, 'why doesn't he like me?' Then they do anything you want in hopes that you'll start liking them. It works every time; I mean they'll do anything." I was afraid he was about to get a little more graphic so I tried to change the subject.

"So why are you still here, I mean if you could be at a bar picking up women, why are you sitting out in the middle of the desert?" I asked.

"Well, I'll be going to the bars in just a minute, but I am not leaving here until I have myself on camera getting shot at by some drug dealers or coyotes," responded martyr man with his eyes widening and the grin on his face turning him into a demonic cartoon character. He began to act out his dream scene in front of me. He used his hands as pistols to simulate the bad guys shooting at him and then stated, "Bang, bang, and then I am going to be over here," he ran a few yards away and the hand he had used as a pistol was now holding an imaginary video camera. "And it's going to be just like that movie The Matrix, you know when he is dodging those bullets, that's what I am going to be doing," he added while moving from left to right. "I am going to be famous, oh yeah, I am not leaving here until that happens, and I'll just be living out here." I really wanted to think that he was just joking, that he was about to throw in a punch line, or maybe even just say he was kidding. But that did not happen. Instead, after acting out his dream scene, he walked over to the legal observers in the car said goodbye, and then walked back to his vehicle.

There were Minutemen even stranger than martyr man. There was the woman who would always be at a post by herself. I never saw her speaking to anyone, and when we walked by her, she would hurriedly grab her binoculars and look in our direction. She would stare at us for awhile and then just as suddenly as she rushed for her binoculars and stood up, she would return to her chair overlooking a small arroyo. Then there was bow and arrow guy who would get out of his car with his face already freshly painted and ready for action. I was never quite sure why he carried a bow and arrow with him, or why he would paint his face if the purpose was simply to report to the Border Patrol when he saw someone he suspected was undocumented. Despite the dwindling number, the war atmosphere continued to grow.

Encounters with immigrants

I was grateful that we did not see a lot of migrants. We had informed everyone we knew about the whereabouts of the Minutemen and there were human rights workers and Mexican government officials informing migrants on the other side of the border. I am sure these communications were the main reason people were not crossing in these areas. Of course that did not mean that there were no migrants crossing whatsoever. One night after on patrol along Border Road, my father and I were driving back into Douglas when on the side of the dirt road I saw two people. I stopped the car and got out to speak with the two individuals.

"Hello, how are you?" I asked in Spanish.

"I am okay, but my friend has broken her ankle and she cannot walk anymore," responded the man in his late thirties. The woman was sitting on the ground unable to stand up, and I asked what they wanted to do. The woman and man simultaneously said they wanted to go back to Mexico and then the man asked if we could call the Border Patrol. While calling the Border Patrol on migrants is not my favorite activity, it was a request from a migrant, and I was set on following the rules of not giving anyone a ride. In retrospect, it probably would have been easier for them if I had either just given them a ride to the hospital or back to the border, but I took out my cell phone and made the call.

"You guys are lucky, do you see that light over there, those are the Minutemen," I said motioning to the light in the Minutemen's RV a couple of hundred yards down the road. "Have you heard of the Minutemen?" I asked.

"Yes, the racists," responded the man. "People told us they were out here, but when you are hungry and you need to find work, what can you do? I was just getting ready to start walking toward that light too." We waited with them until the Border Patrol came and then continued on our way back to Douglas. They were not even half a mile into the United States when they had to abandon their journey. It reminded me of a story of a woman who died right on Border Road; she had just crossed into the United States and could no longer take the heat.

We would encounter migrants in worse situations later in the month. It was around 11 p.m. on another cold night along the Huachuca Mountains. There were four of us driving in a car searching for what we believed to be other Minutemen sites. Their numbers were getting so low that we assumed they were moving their people to positions further into the mountain, but it turns out they were not getting many volunteers. Driving down the dark, dirt roads felt like the beginning of a scary movie when we picked up on the radio that the Minutemen had two people detained on the side of the highway. I turned the car around and headed back to the highway where we noticed a car parked off to the side of the road and a group of men congregating. I parked the car down the road and Alex, Janey, Stacey, and I jumped out and headed toward the scene. A Minuteman walked straight toward us, walked right past me and then Stacey turned her flashlight on, shining it straight into his eyes. "Could you please turn that off?" scowled the Minuteman. I turned around and saw a hate-filled look coming from Stacey, and I knew what she had just done was on purpose. I shook my head and noted to myself that this was going to require a conversation with Stacey later on, and I heard Janey telling her that we did not need to be doing those kinds of things and now certainly was not the appropriate time.

As I crossed the street I heard a voice yell out, "Who goes there?"

"How are you doing gentleman?" I responded.

"Just fine, who are you?" responded James Gilchrist.

"Legal observers, how about you?" I asked. "We heard you got two."

"Well, we didn't get anybody, but there are two gentleman sitting there on the side of the road," responded the ever witty Gilchrist, who a few weeks earlier had taken language off the Minutemen's website about "surprising illegal aliens" and "suggesting" they wait for the Border Patrol, in response to a letter I wrote to the County Sheriff outlining how these actions could constitute false imprisonment. We walked through the small crowd of men that looked as if they were tailgating after their team's victory. There was definitely a vibe of celebration coming from the group of armed white men as they stood around and observed their captives sitting on the ground.

I got down on one knee to be at eye level with the men sitting down and told them who we were. After asking if they were alright, one of the men responded that he was fine but that his friend was not doing so well. Alex went back to the car to grab some blankets, food and water while the men recounted how they ended up sitting on the side of the road. They had been separated from the group and had been walking for the past four days and without food for the last two days and without water for the last day.

The man sitting to my right spoke, "My feet, I can't move them anymore, I mean they have just given out on me. And then I have this pain in my stomach." With his right hand he grabbed his stomach and winced while leaning his head forward making sounds of a grown man dealing with serious pain. Stacey began asking the man questions about his health while the other man was telling Janey why he had decided to come across. The two men were obviously in no state to keep walking and were simply waiting for the Border Patrol. Neither reported any abuse from the Minutemen. Even so, I still consider this one of the most horrible nights of my life. Here were two human beings in front of me in obvious pain. They were freezing cold and in need of food, water, and serious medical attention. But this was of no concern to their fellow human beings, the Minutemen, standing around them. Instead, they were simply enjoying the moment of the "capture." To see my fellow human beings suffering was painful, but to see how the Minutemen enjoyed witnessing the suffering made the situation even worse. Seeing the actions of my fellow countrymen made me ashamed to call myself a United States citizen. Can a flag and political boundary really mask concern for humanity? Is it right to say that because you were not born within the same space that I was born, or you don't have the same passport that I have, that you are therefore worth less as a human being? People waive the red, white, and blue flag and talk about freedom and liberty, but mainly as empty concepts with no meaning. What about the phrase, "All human beings are endowed by their creator with certain inalienable rights and among these are the right to life, liberty, and the pursuit of happiness?" People will say this on the Fourth of July while somewhere along the U.S.-Mexico border, many have gone days without food and water and are near death. While hiding underneath the brush pursuing their happiness and exercising their liberty, their lives are being pursued by well-armed and well-funded federal agents trying to kill their dreams. This is the United States of America that I have seen on the U.S.-Mexico border.

I do not mean to say that all United States citizens are cold-hearted people only concerned about what they perceive to be their own self-interest. In fact, I met 150 of the greatest people I've ever met in my life out there in the desert, my fellow legal observers. They came from all over the country, from New York to the state of Washington and were from extremely diverse backgrounds. We had seasoned human rights activists who have been all over the world standing up against abuses to local community college students engaging in their first political action. There were attorneys, pilots, law school students, college students, state legislators, homemakers, professors, nurses, salesman, and retired folks. It was an honor to stand out in the desert with such quality people who were willing to put themselves in harm's way to assist their fellow human beings and make a strong political statement about the tragedy on the border. Most of the time we were not intervening between migrants and Minutemen or being hit with flashlights, rather we just sat around and talked to each other. There were even a few romantic connections made between legal observers. No doubt to some people it was just boring, but boring was the goal. Most days the legal observers would sit in the desert or in the mountains and talk to each other, perhaps waiving at the Minutemen when they got their binoculars out to look in our direction. This was a good day in my view, because it meant the legal observers were safe and no migrants were assaulted or psychologically abused by the Minutemen.

Lessons from observing

However, there were other days when volunteers had to deal with Minutemen that just did not know when to stop. One of these days was a Sunday, and a group of five legal observers were being harassed by two Minutemen, Cindy Kolb and another woman with a mullet haircut. I do not mean to dehumanize "mullet woman" by not giving her a name; we simply used mullet woman so much that it stuck and to be honest I do not think I ever knew her real name. I don't think I need to give a physical description of mullet woman, as you can get a sense of what her hair looked like. Earlier she had claimed to be a lobbyist from Washington

D.C. with many contacts with senators and representatives. She did not dress the part of a big-time lobbyist; in fact she looked more like someone you would see shopping for clothes at Wal-Mart. She carried around with her a fairly large camcorder and this afternoon appeared to be assisting local Minuteman supporter Cindy Kolb in harassing the legal observers. They were getting straight in the faces of legal observers and being quite aggressive. "Do you support illegal activity?" mullet woman would scream as she put the camera straight into the face of legal observers. They took turns battering the legal observers with questions as if interrogating them underneath a bright light in a windowless room. "Do you support drug dealers?" she screamed. Moving from one legal observer to the next she would switch questions, "Do you like that fact that women are getting raped? Do you condone women getting raped?" It was a textbook case for legal observers on how to act when being harassed by the Minutemen, and these legal observers were doing great. I've actually used the video of this incident recorded by legal observers during non-violence trainings. With a pistol holstered to her hip, Cindy Kolb took out a letter she had written and begins reciting it in front of the camera with the legal observers in the background. As she mispronounced my last name and complained about something or other, mullet woman got tired of filming her and went back to getting in the faces of legal observers. Even though she was told repeatedly that legal observers can not engage in political conversation, she persisted. By this time, a crowd of armed Minutemen had encircled the legal observers and were enjoying watching mullet woman's and Cindy's antics, furthering increasing the tension.

 I was over on Border Road and when I heard what was going on, I started driving in that direction. Well before I got there things grew worse. Mullet woman was obviously frustrated that she could not draw a charge out of the legal observers, and during one of her rounds of questioning she grabbed one of the legal observers arms and shook it violently while screaming, "uh, do you, do you support illegal activity, answer me!" By the time I arrived, about a dozen Minutemen were out in support of mullet woman and Cindy and I walked over to Gilchrist to inform him that the Sheriff's Department was on their way. At the base of the densely forested mountains that the immigrants had to cross, a battle took place. Me and my camera versus the infamous James Gilchrist, yelling at the top of his lungs with all his soldiers behind him. I told him what happened, and he threw his hands in the air and laughed, "What? Is this a joke? If I shake your hand are you going to sue me? This is ridiculous. Or better yet, here shake my hand Ray, and then I'll sue you," said Gilchrist extending his hand. Without hesitation I barked right back, "why don't you go right ahead and do that. I think I have a few attorneys behind me as well." We laughed later as he obviously forgot we had a full force of attorneys behind us, and he was probably thinking he was just threatening another "Mexican." To a man who sees nothing wrong with getting a bunch of armed folks together to hunt for Mexicans, I should have expected that an assault of this caliber would seem insignificant to him. He went off on a rant and was only interrupted when Al Garza, one of the infamous Hispanic Minutemen, jumped in to try to tell me about his Second Amendment right to carry a weapon and the fact that he fought for the right in Vietnam. With a deep voice and a loaded firearm holstered on his hip, and looking every bit like he intended to use it, Al's rant had nothing to do with the situation at hand, but it seemed like one of those speeches he probably practiced in front of the mirror just waiting for the next time he saw me. However, before he could get to whatever his closing line was going to be, I raised my voice and started to get in their faces.

"What do you want to do? You want to sue me, you want something else, go right ahead, I've had enough of the both of you!" I began walking toward the both of them and I heard my father calling my name, saying that one of the legal observers wanted to talk with me. I had lost it, and was tired of their bullshit and all their talk. It was probably about my seventeenth day spending 16 to 20 hours a day out following the Minutemen.

Even before April 1st I could not remember my last day off. This on top of all the drama from the ACLU of Arizona, I was clearly in need of a break. I had certainly just engaged in conduct that I spent hours training my legal observers to avoid. I regained my cool, and as I was walking away from Gilchrist I told him, "Simcox was right about you." I am glad Gilchrist did not ask me to clarify my statement, because I am not sure what I would have said. I was simply trying to put it in Gilchrist's mind that Simcox was talking bad behind Gilchrist's back. Truthfully he was, and anytime I had a chance to play the two off against each other I did. Not that those two egos needed any intervention. As fate would have it, they did not even last the entire month together.

Before the month was out, Gilchrist headed back to California and took with him the name of the Minuteman Project. I was excited to get a call from a reporter that the Minuteman Project was ending early, only to discover that it was a falling out between Simcox and Gilchrist while in fact the crazies would stay in the desert. James Chase also ended up getting kicked out by Simcox and would head to California to start his own patrols, later having his old Vietnam buddy Gilchrist by his side. The Minutemen tried selling the split as Gilchrist moving on to focus on interior operations and going after big corporations while Simcox continued to focus on the border operations. The truth of the matter was that their egos had collided. Simcox did not like the fact that Gilchrist was getting all the notoriety when he had been the man in the desert for years and Gilchrist did not like the fact that Simcox was a control freak who wanted all of the credit.

The Minutemen's numbers were dropping. There were some weekends when the legal observers well outnumbered the Minutemen. The rest of the month was relatively quiet with only a few minor incidents to deal with and, thankfully, we did not see the Minutemen catch many more migrants.

A long month comes to an end

There was still the whole issue of the ACLU of Arizona to deal with, which was showing no sign of letting up. Eleanor was after me to come up to Phoenix to meet with her, but at the time I was a little busy, to say the least. Eventually we agreed to meet at a restaurant in Sierra Vista, not far from the Minutemen's Huachuca line. Carolyn Trowbridge, one of the ACLU Board of Directors members and a veteran legal observer, stepped in as moderator as we each laid out each other's grievances. Eleanor was hurt that I laid out all the details of how poorly I was treated by the ACLU of Arizona in my resignation letter, the fact that I was working out of the laundry room in my grandfather's $19,000 house, that I had to use my own computer and printer, bought my own desk from St. Vincent DePaul, used my grandmother's old sewing chair as my office chair, took out credit cards to pay for video equipment, paid for my own trips to find plaintiffs, among other issues. I noted that she should have been embarrassed and told her I was tired of being criticized for doing exactly what I wrote in my fellowship proposal that I was going to be doing. Eleanor knew that following the vigilantes and defending the rights of migrants were the principal objectives of the fellowship as she helped me write it. In fact, what we emphasized in the fellowship is that we were going to show how U.S. immigration policy is racist. The problem for Eleanor was that she never showed the proposal to any of the board members. Eleanor had heard that ACLU Executive Director Anthony Romero had given me the options to go to any other ACLU affiliate I wanted to, move to New York or Oakland to work for the ACLU's National Immigrants Rights Project, or take the money and go to another organization. I told Eleanor that I would make my decision at the end of the month but for now I was going back to sit behind the Minutemen.

During the last week, people were asking me where I was going to go on vacation when the Minutemen left. I guess it was obvious to just about everybody that I needed a break. I was riding with a priest who volunteers with the Christian Peacemakers Team (CPT). He was one of those old people you look at and think to yourself, this person looks like they have been around the block more than a couple of times, probably best to listen closely to what they have to say. The priest told me a story about how volunteers for the CPT often feel guilty leaving an area such as Palestine because the people who live in the area are unable to leave, and they work so hard that they burn out. He stressed the need for human beings to be able to step back and realize their limitations, the need to not take all of the problems of the world onto their individual shoulders. The advice was certainly well timed. Sitting out in the middle of the desert, there is a lot of time to think. I often thought to myself that this is the land where people die; this is where they walk and are cut by the brush, where they are bitten by snakes, beaten by vigilantes, and robbed by bandits. This beautiful desert is where it all happens, and all I do is sit behind a bunch of crazies all day when I should be doing something more. I had no idea what else that I could be doing, but it always felt like what I was doing was never close to enough.

I was re-energized the last weekend when forty legal observers showed up to follow the Minutemen. We sent those who had already been trained to set up posts behind the Minutemen in the desert. I began yet another training in the office that the ACLU of Arizona was now renting in downtown Douglas. I got a call on the radio that the Minutemen were no longer out in the desert. I made a couple of calls to reporters, and it was confirmed: the Minutemen were finally leaving Cochise County. I apologized to the volunteers who had driven from all over the state but was certainly happy to drive out to Border Road and see it free of Minutemen.

Manuel signing up for lawsuit against Roger Barnett as Gerardo looks on.

Myself, Eric and the others from Michoacán at a hotel in Agua Prieta, Sonora prior to meeting with the Cochise County Attorney's Office. (Left to right) Samuel, Sandra, Mari, Nancy (standing), myself, Eric, Don Mateo, and Francisco.

The young baby and mother who I met during the Minutemen's last day of patrolling in April 2006. The young baby had been carried through the unforgiving Arizona desert for three days before coming upon the Minutemen.

Young girl walking along the border fence in Nogales, Arizona.

Giving an interview in El Paso, Texas, following a press conference.

Javier Perez and myself in front of the Minutemen's headquarters in Hachita, New Mexico. This was one of the times they shined their headlights directly at us, hence my wearing sunglasses in the middle of the night.

Looking into the desert after the Border Patrol took away the baby and others who the Minutemen turned in after their three day journey.

Water bottle found in the desert outside of El Paso, Texas.

Chapter Six

Out of the Desert and into the Interior

After the Minutemen went back to their homes, finally Douglas was back to normal. For a month there was an invasion, not only of armed white people, but also journalists from around the world, activists in support of migrants, and legal observers. In my small little town there were reporters from Korea, Germany, France, Italy, the United Kingdom, and just about every major media outlet in the United States. As enjoyable as many of the interactions with journalists and activists were, it was nice to be able to walk back into Chef's or the Grand Café and enjoy a meal where the only outsiders walking in were Border Patrol agents.

The problem was that I was not sure how long I was going to be staying. I desperately wanted to stay in Douglas, but the reality was that this was going to be nearly impossible. Working under the ACLU of Arizona was not an option, so I was set to take a trip to Texas to meet with Will Harrell, Executive Director for the ACLU of Texas. I had no real intention of becoming a Texan, but Will drove a hard bargain. Will cut his teeth in the human rights area as a young attorney aiding the far-left toward the end of the civil war in Guatemala, in the mid 90s. As such, he was obviously a strong advocate for migrants' rights. We spent a few days getting to know each other, as I stayed at his condominium by the river. Anyone who knows Will Harrell knows that a few days with him means a lot of time to get acquainted, and not a whole lot of time to sleep. The Steven Seagal look-a-like took me out on the river on his engine-powered canoe, and I could tell he was at peace on the water. He asked about the drama with the ACLU and I came clean. He promised that in Texas I would not have to worry about anything like that, and I could set up my office in El Paso and keep running the way I was running. He promised a pair of cowboy boots and to always have my back, and that was all I needed to hear. In Spanish there is the phrase, *"me cayó bien,"* which I cannot find a decent translation for so let's just say that I knew he was someone I would enjoy working with. He still has not come through with the boots, but he has bailed me out more than a few times.

I spent a few days packing my stuff and drove out to El Paso to look for a place. Having to leave Douglas was rough. I was living with my grandfather and enjoyed being able to see my uncles, aunts, and cousins on a regular basis. Plus, there is just something special about D-town that is hard to describe. Life slows down when you enter G Avenue off highway 80. The once bustling downtown area that catered to those who were making money from the Phelps Dodge mine retains the character of an old mining town. I remember being a kid sitting in the back of the car while my parents drove down G Avenue after the long drive from up north and looking to the benches on the side of the road where my Tata Memo, my dad's father, would always be sitting. It seemed no matter what time we got into Douglas, there he would be sitting with one of his friends, perhaps telling the story about him being awarded a Purple Heart for his service in Korea or striking against the Phelps Dodge Company. Despite the absolute invasion of government agents in Douglas, it still has that small town feel that family and values are more important than portraying an image of wealth and status. While the water and soil remains polluted from the times in which the mine was operating, it is the people that make Douglas a special place. I was saddened to leave D-town and was nervous about starting from scratch in a new city.

Thankfully, I had Claudia Guevara, a recent graduate of Boalt Hall

Law School at the University of California at Berkeley, working with me and she began to immediately set-up operations in El Paso. I did not have much time, as I was set to be in New York for six weeks to edit a short documentary about the Minutemen. At a meeting in Philadelphia about the documentary I was making with Witness and the American Friends Service Committee, it had been decided that the coverage of the Minutemen was so poor that a short documentary highlighting the reality of the Minutemen needed to be made. I had plenty of footage from my interviews with vigilantes and from legal observing, so I was ready to start.

During the week I sifted through over one hundred hours of footage and spent days at a time looking at the interviews shot with the vigilantes. It was at times overbearing to listen to them talking about the invasion, the imminent destruction of the country and the forthcoming bloodbath. These really were the people who want to be at the front lines when a war begins and they were not shy about sharing their hatred and radical views.

On the weekends, I would fly back to the border to assist with groups who were organizing against the Minutemen. The Minutemen were expanding their operations to Southern California, so I flew to San Diego to meet with the legendary immigrants' rights activists Claudia Smith and the ACLU of San Diego, to set-up a legal observer project. Other weekend trips included Houston, Austin, Brownsville, and Albuquerque.

Facing a mixed audience

The production of the video was almost finished and I was invited to present it at a migrants' rights conference in Phoenix. It would be the first public screening and I was anxious to get feedback from community members. I was not quite prepared for everyone who ended up showing up. The screening was set for six in the afternoon, and only about 40 people remained from the conference that had over 100 participants. About five minutes before the screening was scheduled to start, I was trying to assist the technician in setting up the DVD. We were having quite a bit of difficulty, and as I had my back turned to the audience I heard someone say, "Oh my God." I turned around to see a group of Minutemen marching in the room, one behind the other. With the person in the front carrying a large U.S. flag and some members wearing bullet proof vests, I was surprised that they were not kicking their legs high in front of themselves in unison. I had never been in a room where the tension increased so quickly. Just a minute ago we were joking about the Minutemen messing with the projector, and now there were migrants' rights activists and Minutemen sitting side-by-side. Someone ran up to me and asked what I wanted to do, and the only thing I could think of was to continue figuring out how to get the video to play.

I was initially going to speak briefly after the screening and then take questions, but I decided that it was also best to say a few words before beginning the film. As we continued to try to fix the technical problem, I searched for what was best to say. After spending a month in the desert and hearing countless Minutemen ramble on, I knew they would make an effort to control the debate even before it got started. I wanted to make sure this was not the case while at the same time not letting the Minutemen think they were putting fear into anyone. I also wanted to ensure that everyone else in the room would respect what they had to say. I knew I had to be kind, but not so nice that the Minutemen thought they could walk over me and everyone else. I had to be tough, but not so tough as to seem like I was trying to be antagonistic, since people on both sides were on edge.

With the technical problems resolved I picked up the microphone to address the crowd. I gave the general background on the film, explaining how it came about and mentioning that it was still not a finished product. As I scanned the room, I recognized most of the people from the migrants' rights community and also just about every Minuteman. There was my buddy Mitch, as well as his friend Jim, David, and Laine. Jim is featured prominently in the film and I was wondering how he was going to take his portrayal. For those who have seen the film, he is the one in the middle of the desert waiving his finger in the air while asserting his right to carry a gun. I went on to emphasize the need to respect everyone, regardless of their opinion and where they stand on the issue. The words coming out of my mouth were not simply meant to decrease the possibility of violence, they were sincere. I remember as a child my father emphasizing that no matter who a person is, what they say should be valued and respected. Whether it is a homeless person on the street or the president of a country, everyone has life experiences and something to share with the rest of the world. I briefly described the legal observer project and the emphasis on non-violence in order to respect all human beings. I then transitioned into talking about the plight of the migrants and how it would be a better world if everyone would treat each other with dignity and respect. The folks from the migrants' rights community began to applaud and I could tell the Minutemen were feeling that the comment was directed straight at them. One of the Minutemen raised his hand to speak and I announced that now was not the time for questions and answers but that I would be taking questions after the screening. I turned around to start the film and Jim yelled out, "Ray, hey Ray…."

Before he could finish what he was saying, I politely cut him off, "hey Jim, how is it going buddy, I promise you I'll take questions after this, just hold on a few more minutes, thanks." I did not for a second want any of the Minutemen to think they could come in and control the debate. They were certainly welcome to be there, but were not going to control the night. The easy part was over and I sat to the side of the audience to gauge their reactions to the different scenes. It appeared everyone was engaged the entire time and as the film was wrapping up I was trying to figure out what to say before taking questions. I wanted to re-emphasize the earlier point about respect without sounding preachy, while at the same time setting the tone for the questions and answers. I did not know whether to expect shouting matches to start immediately after the film was over, and was hoping people would at least wait until the question and answer period. Would I be heckled and cut off mid-sentence? My mouth was dry and I was searching for something to drink. No matter how small the audience is, every time I have to speak in public, I get nervous. I was so shy as a child that I did not even like to order food at restaurants. Some people love being the center of attention and having the microphone in their hands, but I prefer to be the guy who walks in late, sits in the back, and leaves early. But that night the microphone was in my hand, and it was up to me to figure out how to keep this from becoming a riot. Truth be told, I do not remember exactly what I said, but I do remember that I spoke from my heart. I am not one for saying things just to make people happy, and I was not about to start that night. I just said what I felt and decided that I would react as best as I could to whatever happened next.

I do remember how I concluded my little speech; it's the way I do it every now and again when I think there might be a handful of antagonistic folks in the crowd. I don't like doing it like this, but in certain cases it has to be done. "Now we have come to the part that everyone has been anxiously waiting for." I was pleased to hear a slight laughter from the crowd. "Questions and Answers. But let me remind you that this is question and answer time, it's not questions and answers and comments and opinions, no, just old-fashioned questions from you and answers from me. You see I have a big-ego, if you have not noticed already I made a movie and put myself in it, that is a good indication that I have a big ego," I said stating the obvious. "With all due respect to your brilliance, I did not fly five hours from New York to listen to your opinion, but would be more than happy to answer any question you have for me." Of course a true dialogue requires listening from both parties, but I was not in the mood to listen to anybody's rants and wanted to maintain control so things did not get out of hand. I added a disclaimer, "Now, I'll promise you an answer; it might not be the correct answer, but it will at least be an answer." A few more laughs from the crowd, and the tension was somewhat dying down. "Oh, and one more thing. Unfortunately we cannot go on all night because I have a dinner reservation at my favorite Ethiopian restaurant, so my apologies if we cannot get to all of your questions," I added before mentioning that I would take one question from the migrants rights community and one question from a Minuteman supporter and keep going in that order. Again, if you do it the other way, it becomes such that the right ends up monopolizing the time trying to ask question after question. The first question from the migrants' rights people was a softball and it did not take too much time to answer. By this time I was anxious to see what the Minutemen would come up with. I was surprised to see that Jim was not raising his hand, as he was so anxious to speak earlier. The first question came from Laine Lawless and she made some wild allegation about me inserting a white power chant after a J.T. Ready speech at one of the Minutemen's rallies, and I assured her that she was mistaken and there were no white power chants in the film. There were a few rumblings in the audience and I quickly went to the next question, which was another softball.

Back to the Minutemen again; this time there were a couple of hands to choose from, and I took an old man wearing a cowboy hat. He stood up and the room fell dead silent. I was hoping he was not going to ask me to face back-to-back and take ten paces. You could hear the anger in his voice and see the frustration in his face as he began to ask his question. Much to my surprise and probably to the surprise of most migrants' rights people in the audience he was railing against NAFTA. The North American Free Trade Agreement (NAFTA) is a trilateral trade bloc agreement between the U.S., Mexico and Canada. NAFTA began on January 1, 1994. For a moment, I thought he was a migrants' rights activist pretending to be a Minutemen because he was throwing me another softball. His focus was on NAFTA's negative impact on American workers, and I picked up right where he left off. "Well sir, I think that is an excellent question, NAFTA has not only had a negative effect on working people here in this country, but also in Mexico. I volunteered for a year at a migrant center and I cannot tell you how many people I met who said they used to be corn farmers in Southern Mexico and just could not make it anymore. You see, what happened with NAFTA was that the Mexican markets were open to competition with the big U.S. companies that are subsidized by the government and also heavily mechanized. So what you had were small farmers in Mexico having to all of a sudden begin competing with these giant corporations who were using the latest in chemicals, fertilizers, farming techniques, etc. Overnight the price of corn dropped as the U.S. companies entered the market and were able to undercut the Mexican farmers who were living in a protected economy for years. So they were left with no options but to leave their farms and migrate to the United States."

The old-man stumbled a little bit and said, "Well, I did not know that the Mexicans were against NAFTA too."

"Well, not all Mexicans. NAFTA is another example of the wealthy helping the wealthy. It benefited the rich in both countries but hurt working people in both countries," I responded. "Of course what the rich people want is for working class folks to keep fighting each other so they do not have to worry about us. The old "divide and conquer," but here it's, keep divided and keep oppressed. I'm sure they love to see working folks trying to stop one another from improving their lots." I wondered whether the last line went over the heads of the Minutemen in the audience.

I took a few more questions that in time would become routine. Minutemen asked about security and the economy and those were easily dealt with. Before you knew it I had talked enough to finally deserve some Ethiopian food. There were still hands in the air, but it was getting late and we called it a night. Afterwards Jim, Mitch, and a few others came up to shake my hand, and I actually left in one piece. Walking to my car I noticed the police in the parking lot and was glad that they did not have to come into the room that night.

The Minutemen and migrants' rights activists did not stick around to strategize how to reshape or destroy NAFTA, but I think it was a rational dialogue about the issue. I am not as ignorant as to think that any person in the room changed their mind about their previously held beliefs, but at least the event did not erupt into a brawl. This would not be my last time speaking in front of a mixed audience.

Minutemen-Texas Style

I was able to finally get back to El Paso, but pretty much only long enough to put a few clothes in the closet and repack the suitcase. It seemed just about everyone wanted to hear about the Minutemen. Who were they, what did they look like, did they really carry guns? At a presentation at the University of Texas School of Law there was another appearance by the Minutemen. This time it was a group of characters I had never seen before, and despite being outnumbered about eighty to four, they still did a pretty good job of grabbing a lot of attention. I repeated the same refrain as my talk in Phoenix about only taking questions, but this did not stop one of the resilient men in the back.

He was patient throughout the talk and I called on him to be the first person to ask a question. I knew he was a Minuteman; they are not difficult to spot in the audience. They are the ones with sour faces who look as if they are about to explode with anger. They rarely smile at jokes and never nod in accordance when there is an argument made in favor of migrants. "I am a Minuteman," the man standing at the back of the room began his question. The entire room turned in his direction with the announcement. The talk had come close to being cancelled after the word spread that the Minutemen would be in attendance, and the administration feared a violent attack. Thankfully, he did not pull out a gun and instead he kept talking. "Illegals are not only bringing drugs, violence and lawlessness across the border, they are also bringing with them diseases that had previously been eradicated. These diseases walking across our border are a health threat for the entire nation. There has been an increase in Tuberculosis among other….," stated the man.

"My apologies for cutting you off sir, I do not mean to be rude, but I did request that you ask a question, now, do you have a question to ask or should I go on to the next person?" I asked.

"I am getting there, I am getting there. So my question to you, representative of the ACLU, is the ACLU in favor of bringing diseases across the border that will hurt the American public?" he finally asked.

I turned to Will Harrell who had driven me over from the ACLU of Texas's office and asked, "Will, didn't we at the last ACLU staff convention pass a resolution in favor of increasing diseases in the United States?" The entire room broke out in laughter, except for the Minuteman who had asked the question. "My apologies sir, I do not mean to make light of your question, but let me begin by saying that these are not diseases coming across the border, they are human beings. They are brothers, sisters, mothers, fathers, sons, and daughters. But you bring up an important point, which is the use of the fear of diseases. Now if you go back and look at previous anti-immigrant movements in the United States, you will see the exact same argument. There was a fear that the Chinese were going to contaminate California and the Irish and Italians were going to forever destroy the East Coast. Today, I often hear from Minutemen folks about the fear that migrants from Latin America are bringing across diseases. I have done the research and the best I can tell you is that there is no valid scientific evidence to support these arguments. When you mention the increase in diseases, which study are you referring to?"

"Well, uh…, um, I read it from a Congress person," said the man, stumbling over his own words. He could not remember which congressperson, probably Tom Tancredo, so I asked him to get back to me with the study and I would be happy to take a look at it.

I took a few questions from other audience members and called on another Minuteman who had his hand raised for quite some time. With silver hair and a whitening beard he was pretty rude during the talk, trying to yell at Will for a few minutes. "You make a pretty convincing moral argument," he began, "but realistically, there just are not enough jobs here. Now do not get me wrong, if I was in their shoes I would be doing the same thing, but our economy can just not sustain all of the people who are coming over."

"That is a great question, and I can tell you that many people express that exact same sentiment," I stated, validating his point which I am sure he was not expecting. "But, I think we have to stop looking at migration as charity and look at it for the reality that it is. It is not as if God said, 'United States of America you have 80 million jobs and no more, so you better figure out whom to give them to.' No, that is not how our economy works. Instead, as people come into the economy they end up expanding the pie and creating more jobs, expanding different markets. The worker needs somewhere to wash their clothes, needs to buy food, rent an apartment, buy clothes, etc. etc. All of this spending means more revenue for other industries and more jobs. That is why we say the pie expands and other sectors continue to grow as well. If it was not for the working people coming over here our economy would not be as strong as it is, and we would not be able to go all over the world and kill poor people of color. In truth, as a nation we are probably getting more bang for our buck, so to speak. If you think in economic terms, children are an investment. We pay a lot of taxes so they can have an education so they will be more productive when they are older. We pay for schools and parks, and in addition to that children get to enjoy the roads, stoplights, and highways, all without contributing to the economy. A very large economic investment that in time will be paid off when they are working adults paying the various taxes adults pay. For the migrants who come across the border to work, we get the benefit of having an additional tax payer, without ever having had the burden of that person as a child."

The next question in the audience piggybacked on the economic discussion. "Is it not also true that if it was not for undocumented migrants our social security system would not be functioning? People who use false social security numbers put all the money into the federal system and never see anything in return," stated one of the law students.

"I agree with you totally. It was Alan Greenspan, the economic guru, who said that immigrants, even undocumented immigrants, contribute more than their fair share of taxes to our economic system. There is a wealth of studies out there that detail the economic impact of migrants and the overwhelming majority shows a net benefit for the economy. Now certainly there are some that will argue the opposite; it seems numbers can be manipulated to the highest bidders liking, but the vast majority of studies come out in favor of migration being a positive force for our economy." When it comes to migration the facts and studies are pretty clear. But I have learned that those are just the facts while the reality is you have to deal with the perception as it exists in the public, no matter how far from the truth those perceptions might be.

The Minutemen who asked the first question in the back had his hand held up high. As a matter of fact, he did not even bother taking it down when others were asking their questions or when I was responding, it was just stuck in the air as if he was unable to move it. I looked in his direction and told him that I would first take questions from those who have not yet had a chance to speak and then go back to him. He finally dropped his hand and I took a few more questions before calling on him again. He was polite enough to not interrupt, but I was certain that he was not listening to a word anyone else was saying and only waiting for his next chance to speak. I felt I was having one of those conversations where while you are mid-sentence you can tell the other person has already stopped listening and is just waiting for you to pause so they can begin speaking.

I called on the man in the back, and as previously, every head in the room turned in his direction. "Well you have not talked at all about security, you know like what if Osama Bin Laden wanted to come across the border; there just are not enough Border Patrol to catch everyone who wants to come across the border. This is not about racism, it is about safety. Isn't it possible that Bin Laden could come across the border?" asked the Minuteman. Once Osama Bin Laden has entered the conversation I know the talk is almost over and the Minutemen are running out of questions to ask.

"You are right, for all I know Bigfoot could come across the border and we might never know about it," I responded. "It is within the realm of possibilities that a terrorist could come across the border. But is it likely? I think not. If you read the 9/11 Commission Report you will see the type of threats that we are up against. Look at all the terrorists from 9/11. None of them crossed through the Arizona desert. They all came in quite comfortably on airplanes with the proper visas. Now ask yourself this question: say you are a terrorist leader and you want to attack the United States. Do you recruit someone who does not have any criminal background and has enough studies and finances to get a proper visa, or do you just pick some random person off the street and put them on a plane to Latin America? The 9/11 Commission Report describes these "clean operatives" that we are up against. They have enough resources and time that they do not need to send anyone through the desert with the fear of being caught by the Border Patrol or dying of dehydration. So why are we going to put thousands of Border Patrol agents in the middle of the desert on the southwestern border when all of terrorists from 9/11 arrived through airports? It is like having a large cut on your arm and deciding to put a knee brace on your leg. It is simply illogical. Speaking of terrorism, let us not simply assume that the only ones who can be terrorists are brown people from the Middle East. I guarantee you that the next terrorist act on U.S. soil will not be by someone from abroad but will be a homegrown terrorist. Just like the Oklahoma City bombing. If we see this anti-immigrant climate continue to escalate and the federal government does not respond with more militarization of the border then there will be a large attack by a Minuteman or one of their supporters. I guarantee that is the next step, I've heard it time and time again; we have been abandoned by our government. They are not going to listen until there is bloodshed, etc. etc." The Minutemen in the audience certainly did not like this prediction.

After the talk, a few people came up to ask a few questions, and I saw out of the corner of my eye that the Minuteman from the back of the room was walking in my direction. Security was watching the crowds filtering out the back, and the man's quick pace in my direction signaled to me that he was on a mission. He stood behind those who had lined up to talk and I noticed that Will also noticed that the man was not too happy. As the man with neck-long hair and glasses approached, Will stood perpendicular between myself and the Minutemen, as if a referee ready to ask us to touch gloves and get in on. As the Minuteman began to speak, his voice was shaking, and Will positioned his legs into some pseudo karate position. The man reiterated his concern about diseases and hoped that I would not catch any diseases while working with migrants. I think he was being a tad bit facetious, but I shook his hand as he extended his right arm. "Thanks for the concerns, but I have been working with migrants for quite some time and I am clean as can be. I really think that everything is going to be alright and you really have nothing to worry about. Life is good."

He still had not let go of my hand, and I could see in his eyes the hatred and anger and his entire face was shaking. "Well, I hope nothing happens to you, out in the desert too. I hear it can be pretty dangerous," he responded finally letting go of my hand and walking away.

Another month out in the desert was just around the corner, and I headed back to El Paso to begin focusing on the month of October. It had been six months since the Minutemen patrolled in Arizona and now they were planning on running a month-long operation in the four southwestern border states of California, Arizona, New Mexico, and Texas. Legal observing in California was already being organized by Claudia Smith and the ACLU, and they hired a hard working man named Juan Gallegos to coordinate the operation. In Arizona there was nobody, and I was sure I was not going to be invited back, so my intention was to cover New Mexico and Texas.

CHAPTER SEVEN

Return to the Desert

The majority of my time was spent away from El Paso, but thankfully Claudia Guevara had done an excellent job in recruiting volunteers and doing research to find out where the Minutemen were going to be. We sent out emails calling for volunteers and worked with the local MEChA (Movimiento Estudiantil Chican@ de Aztlan) groups to hold trainings on local university and community college campuses. Many Minutemen-types like to use MEChA as an example of a far-left organization looking to reconquer the Southwestern United States, based on the organization's founding documents that were written during an entirely different era. The two-hour trainings now consisted of showing the film as well as a more in-depth explanation of what to expect and non-violence training.

By joining listservs —electronic mailing lists— and meeting with media members and government officials, Claudia had figured out that there were going to be two different Minutemen groups that we would be able to observe. The first would run operations east of El Paso and was led by a man named Shannon McGauley. Shannon moved to El Paso for the month of October and never had much success recruiting local volunteers, and instead had relied on volunteers from outside of El Paso. While he claimed to have been an original Minuteman volunteer in Arizona, he had a falling-out with Simcox and his operation was not at all associated with the Minutemen's operations in Arizona. Shannon had told Simcox to stay out of Texas, and despite the El Paso City Council passing a resolution against civilian patrols, Shannon moved down to the border anyway. He had made friends with the Ivey family who owned property along the Rio Grande River and set up patrols amongst the pecan trees.

The second group of characters out of New Mexico were affiliated with Simcox. The group was being led by none other than the Commander of the 1st Brigade New Mexico Militia, Bob Wright. Bob was very active with the Minutemen back in Arizona and sported a green military hat with a short bill in the front that covered his cleanly shaven head, which gave him his radio name of "Chrome Dome." Old Chrome Dome certainly fit the mold of the commander of a militia group. His bushy moustache sat on a face that looked like he would be happy to order you to drop and give him twenty.

We began by covering both groups, with Claudia taking volunteers to the Fabens area east of El Paso and myself making the hour and a half drive into the boot heal of New Mexico to follow Chrome Dome and his posse. Claudia did not have much luck as every time she found the Minutemen they would pack up and head back to the Ivey's ranch where they could not be followed. At least the Minutemen were on notice that they were being watched and did not feel as if they could roam around El Paso County and do as they pleased. One evening I decided to go out with Claudia to try to find roads where we would be able to observe the Minutemen on their property. It was late at night, and we were driving along the levees just north of the border in an area that many had told us was the most heavily used region of the border to cross drugs. I was hesitant about being in the area so late at night by ourselves, but Claudia was calm and in control. A four-wheel vehicle was needed to maneuver around the unpaved roads, and we got out of the vehicle to see if we could find anything. My heart was thumping and every instinct in my body told me to get back in the car and drive away, but then I looked over at Claudia, and she was simply looking through the night vision goggles to see if she could find the Minutemen. She is certainly one of the most courageous people I have ever met. Even though we did not find the Minutemen that night, we returned home safely.

Given that Shannon and his crew would run and hide every time we saw them, we decided to focus most of our energy on Chrome Dome, though occasionally we would still drive around the Fabens area. This is not to say that we did not think that Shannon and his crew were dangerous characters; in fact Claudia came upon pictures of them on patrol proudly boasting their high-powered assault rifles and shotguns. One reporter who spent a night with the Minutemen also commented that they seemed pretty trigger happy but that a great deal of their time was worrying more about us than the migrants.

I was always a little torn about that, especially in New Mexico and Texas. That month we would see fewer than five migrants and only a few more Minutemen. In other words, it was extremely boring and we felt like we were part of the Minutemen's fantasy game. I wondered if we were not out there whether or not many Minutemen would have just decided to go home. This is not to say that there were many of them out there in the first place, but at times it was extremely ridiculous. They finally caught on to the fact that we were listening to their radios and would make rude, childish remarks. When following a caravan of Minutemen they would encourage us to follow and would add comments such as, "why you staying at the back Ray, is that how you like it. Huh, you like it in the back?" This is not to say that all nights were fun and games.

It was getting close to midnight on a weekday night and the Minutemen were heading in from their night patrol. I was quite surprised, as normally they stayed out all night, and we had only been out for a couple of hours. I thought it was some sort of trick, so I decided to follow the caravan back to the headquarters in the extremely small town of Hachita. I mean small town as in not having a store, gas station, or a single stop light. There was one vehicle, a small RV that was having difficulty getting out of the small dirt road and back onto the highway. The clearance on the truck was quite low, and he could not find an exit point. I decided to turn on my brights so that he could have a better view of the land he was trying to drive over, but he simply drove in the other direction. By this time, all of the other Minutemen were long gone and probably halfway back to the headquarters. It took another ten minutes or so for him to get onto the highway as my fellow legal observer and I, Morgan, chatted away.

We began following the RV, and before I knew it, he had slowed down to about 40 miles per hour. It was obvious that he was looking for me to pass him, but I thought it might be some sort of trick, so I continued to stay behind him. Besides, I was not in a rush to get anywhere. It seemed as if it took twice as long to get back to the headquarters and when we arrived we saw all of the vehicles parked in front of the Hachita Community Center. However, instead of stopping to park alongside his friends at the headquarters, the RV kept driving down the road and ended up taking a right as if heading back to the highway.

"You think we should follow him?" asked Morgan.

"I don't know," I responded. "It looks like they are up to something, but since there are more of them here; let's wait to see if any of them move." Sure enough, a few minutes later they began to move, and they were moving faster than I had ever seen them. The Minutemen ran from outside of headquarters and jumped into their vehicles. Each person backed their car up and pulled back into their previous parking positions but this time with their headlights facing the highway.

"What are these crazies doing?" asked Morgan. I had no answer and had never seen the Minutemen do anything like this. We were directly on the other side of the highway pretty much in the middle of all of the vehicles. Just as the last car backed into position, all them turned on their headlights, including the brights. The desert turned into daylight, and I temporarily lost my sight. All of the sudden Morgan yells that there is someone walking our way. I still couldn't see but turned the car on. What seemed like minutes later, but was probably only a few seconds, I saw someone standing in front of the car.

"What the fuck is going on?" I asked Morgan. I back the car up at an angle in hopes of driving away, but the person in front of me moved so that they were again in the middle of my path. I backed up again and tried to move the other direction, but he followed in suit. I could go in reverse no further, and we were stuck in the middle of the desert, encircled by a bunch of crazies with guns. No cell phones worked in Hachita so there was nobody to call. I recognized the person in front of me as Gary and I rolled my window down. "What are you doing Gary?" I asked him.

In a monotone voice with his narrow eyes looking straight at me he asked, "what did you do to the old man, Ray?"

The old man, what old man was he talking about? "Gary, I did not do anything to any old man, I have no clue what you mean," I responded.

"What did you do to the old man Ray?" repeated Gary in the same monotonous tone. I was waiting for a bunch of zombies to appear from behind him asking the same question, but I was in no mood to wait around to see what was going to happen next.

A little bit firmer this time I answered Gary, "Gary, you are standing in front of my car and I cannot leave, this is called false imprisonment, get out of my way, I want to leave."

By now, my sight was completely back, and I could see that the legal jargon had snapped him out of his little trance. He stepped to the side and as I was driving away, he began to yell, "we are going to find out what you did to the old man Ray, trust me, we will find out what you did and you will pay."

"Alright Gary, have a nice night," I replied as we drove to try to find the nearest Sheriff's vehicle to report the incident, which of course would result in Gary claiming he was never standing in front of the car.

The next day I would discover from the Sheriff's officers that the Minutemen were claiming that I had threatened the individual driving the RV and he was in fear for his life. In fact, the Minutemen alleged that he was so afraid that he decided to stop volunteering and returned home. I told the officers that I had no clue why they would be afraid, they are the ones with all of the guns and we are the ones committed to absolute non-violence. It seems that being young, brown, and male was often sufficient enough to intimidate the Minutemen.

More Minutemen games

I was expecting something the next day, but it would take a few nights for the Minutemen to seek retribution for their comrade who was forced to go AWOL. At 1 a.m. Papa Bear, another wannabe drill sergeant who stands just over five feet tall, announced over the radio that he was leaving the formation and going to set up a different outpost. Given that the announcement was made at exactly 1 a.m. and that this was something brand new, I already suspected that the Minutemen were up to something else. I was in the car with Javier Perez, a young college student and activist who had been hired by the ACLU of New Mexico to assist with the legal observing. A few minutes later we heard Gary's voice over the radio, "It appears it is not working, the ACLU is not following you, repeat, the ACLU is NOT following you." With one swift announcement Gary shed light on why the rest of the night would simply continue to get crazier.

"Doesn't the idiot realize that we are listening to everything they are saying?" asked Javier.

"Seriously, Gary can't be that dumb," I responded. Then I thought for a few seconds. "Well, maybe he actually is, or maybe it is just all part of their plan to make us think they want us to follow him so that we won't follow him."

"Ray, we are talking about the Minutemen here," said Javier as we sat in the car where we spent every night as if police officers on stake-out. "They are not that smart to think something through like that." Javier was right. Even though the Minutemen had three days to conjure up a plan, I was certain that Gary had just blown everything. I could just imagine the Minutemen in their cars looking at their radios and cursing Gary for being such an idiot. "I guess they think that we think that Papa Bear is so important that we will just follow him wherever he goes."

There was no radio traffic for a few minutes and eventually Papa Bear returned and drove straight to Gary's truck. I am sure there was a nice chewing out going on and then Papa Bear announced over the radio that it was time to head back to headquarters to restrategize. We followed the caravan back to the headquarters and parked in the same spot where we had the night before when Gary had blocked us in. The only difference was that the car was parallel to the highway so that we could no longer be blocked in by somebody standing in front of us. Inside the Community Center, which was actually an empty hall that looked like it had not been used for years, the Minutemen were circled around, and I could see Papa Bear giving orders and other Minutemen occasionally chiming in.

"I got an idea," I told Javier as I started the car and drove down the highway. "Let's go park behind the building on one of the side streets where they cannot see us, and we'll see if we can get them to think that we decided to head home." There were fewer vehicles than normal, with Chrome Dome's and a few other people's vehicles missing. If there was someone who was looking to trap us in and have their way, I was sure it was going to be Chrome Dome, and I certainly kept this in mind.

We waited and eventually saw the caravan of vehicles heading back out toward the area where they were previously patrolling. Instead of following the caravan we kept our lights off and stayed in place. Almost immediately over the radios we heard Gary's voice, "Does anyone have a visual on the ACLU?"

A few seconds of silence and then someone responded, "that's a negative, they must have gone home thinking we were staying in for the night."

Then Papa Bear chimed in, "God dammit Gary, they would have followed me to the cemetery if you just had not said anything!" Their plan was getting a little clearer.

Javier and I looked at each other and Javier joked, "Do you want to go take a drive to the cemetery and say hi to Chrome Dome?" Within ten minutes the Minutemen caravan returned back to headquarters with Chrome Dome and a few other vehicles not far behind, presumably having come from the cemetery. So I had two choices at this point. One, just drive home and let the Minutemen think that we actually did drive away earlier. Or, I could drive back and sit in front of the headquarters of the Minutemen. The latter would obviously be rubbing it in and the adult in me said to just drive away. Javier and I discussed it for awhile and we decided that we should go back to sit in front of the headquarters. You know, just in case they planned on going back out again.

We pulled up to our normal spot in front of the Minutemen's headquarters, but they were already inside. We were basking in our victory of avoiding who knows what. Though it was probably nearing two in the morning we were wide awake. It had taken a few days, but my body was now accustomed to sleeping during the day and following the Minutemen from sunset until sunrise. The Minutemen had stopped patrolling during the day long ago and when the sun was up, we would make use of a donated RV that we parked in a lovely hippie-artist community, just outside the small New Mexican border town of Columbus. Though I figured the Minutemen were done patrolling, I was not quite prepared to take the 40 minute drive along the highway that runs parallel to the border. We had been sitting outside for about fifteen minutes before someone finally came outside to retrieve something from their vehicle and noticed our presence. Seeing us sitting in my car across the small two-lane highway, the Minuteman ran back inside to retrieve his fellow conspirators. Out came Chrome Dome, Gary, Papa Bear, and the rest of the bunch to see if it was really true. I rolled down the window and smiled my sheepish grin that has gotten me in trouble many times before, and I am sure will get me in trouble many times in the future.

"Fucking little prick," grunted Chrome Dome before turning around and walking back into the headquarters.

The "spy" from the ACLU

The next night the games continued, at least that was the impression that the Minutemen were under. This night it was only Claudia and I on patrol and we had our vehicle north of the highway while the Minutemen were set up in intervals approximately 300 yards away from each other on the south side of the highway. I had told Claudia all about the adventures from the night before, and we were waiting for round two, but thus far it was a normal, boring night. The sky was well lit by the moon and the multitude of stars. Only the howls of the coyotes occasionally broke the silence. I was stretching my legs and walking up and down the highway when we finally heard the Minutemen over the radio.

"This is station four for Gary," said a nervous voice.

"This is Gary, go ahead station four," responded Gary.

"There is someone walking in my direction, and I cannot tell who it is, they are coming straight at me," shook the man's voice as he was searching for a response as to how to act.

"Is it a group of people, can you tell how many there are?" asked Gary.

"No, it is just one person and he is coming straight at me, he is right here, hold on….hold on," said the man at station four. Thirty seconds of silence was followed by another transmission from the man. "I could not quite understand what this person is saying, but I think he is asking for water."

Gary hurriedly responded, "Turn your lights on and get out of there, that is not an illegal, that is the ACLU and you are being set up. Illegals do not come up to you and they travel in groups, turn your lights on immediately and leave. I repeat it is the ACLU and you are being set up, leave now." The only thing Claudia and I could do was look at each other and laugh. We scanned the desert to see where a pair of headlights were going to come on and then drove straight in that direction. The scared Minuteman's cloud of dirt was still in the air when we got out of the car to speak with the person who has just come out of the desert.

The young man was crossing with a group of people and they had stopped for a few minutes to rest. He fell asleep, and when he awoke, he found himself thousands of miles from home in the middle of a desert he had never crossed before. The young man was only nineteen years old and was crossing the border for the first time. He was not traveling with friends or family members, and no one in the group woke him up before they continued on their path. We explained to him the situation with the Minutemen, but all he seemed worried about was what his next step was going to be. Should he keep walking north? Which way was north? Who should he call when he made it to a city? The coyote had promised to take care of all the transportation all the way to Florida, where he knew friends and family members were working. He could not remember which city in Florida, but was sure the coyote knew where to take him. He was unsure on where he was going and absolutely clueless about how to get there. The look on his face was one of utter helplessness. In retrospect, he was not really doing anything wrong. He left home because the jobs were not paying well enough there, and he was coming to find work in an economy that would benefit from his assistance. As I have heard hundreds of times from Minutemen and migrants' rights activists, he was just doing what any of us would do if we were in his position. So why on earth should he be forced to be in a situation that felt like one of those horrible nightmares you have where you wake-up sweating and thanking the heavens that it was all a creation of your mind? He was braving the cold night with only a small sweater and the humane thing to do would have been to put him in the car and give him a ride to Tucson where we could re-strategize from there. But these are not humane times, this was the year 2005, and we were in the middle of the desert along the U.S.-Mexico border.

We could still hear the Minutemen chatting on the radio about the person being an ACLU spy and that was obvious by the fact that we were having a conversation off the side of the highway. There was conversation about the urgent need to get our license plate number, even though this was the same vehicle I had been driving all month and would certainly be parked in front of their headquarters again the next day. One brave soldier volunteered to do the recon and get the license plate and he drove up from behind, but his old eyes were having difficulty reading the small letters. As he was transmitting over the radio the incorrect license plate number, I walked up to the side of his door and simply read him the correct one, which he then transmitted over the radio.

He finally drove away, and we were again left to wonder what to do. My excuse for not giving him a ride was the following. A few nights before, we were approached by a highway patrolman as we sat in front of the Minutemen's headquarters. We told him what we were doing and he thanked us for being out there to keep an eye on the crazies. I was caught off guard by his compliment, and it was clear that we were not in Cochise County. He went on to tell us about how the week before one of his fellow officers pulled over a vehicle that a Minuteman was driving. The officer approached the vehicle and asked him if there was anyone else in the car and he responded no. The officer then shined his light in the back and saw someone in the back seat. He took the Minuteman in for questioning and it turned out that he had picked-up the migrant along the highway and was alleging that he was taking him into the city to give him food and water. As the sheriff's deputy stated, "I have no idea what he was really planning on doing with that guy in his backseat, but I do know that there is a whole lot of empty desert out here." The Minuteman was being investigated, and the possible charges ranged from kidnapping to transporting. We were trying to get media attention and an investigation going, and the timing of us being caught with someone in our car would certainly not bode well.

We went over the possible options. He could keep walking or wait for the Border Patrol to come by and turn himself in. Walking was not much of an option as he had no clue where to go and did not know the next step to take once he arrived in a city. It seemed the best thing to do would be to find the Border Patrol and return to Palomas, the border town on the Mexican side, where he knew he could eventually reconnect with the coyote.

It is easy to sit here now and regret not having done more. I can still see his light brown eyes that gave the look of confusion. His short black hair covered his head that had probably been shaved about a month ago and his sideburns were the same length going just below his ears. In his left ear, he had a silver earring and his chin sported a small amount of facial hair. The drive would not have been that far and we probably never would have even passed a Border Patrol vehicle. But instead, we did nothing but wait alongside the highway. That was not the last surprise that we would come upon in the desert that month.

The war comes to the border

For the next five days it was extremely boring, and we passed the hours engaged in conversation with only the occasional break to listen to the Minutemen's radio checks. We were taking out a new group of volunteers and by the time we arrived at the Minutemen's headquarters the vehicles were all gone. This night we had driven all the way in from El Paso and came down from Interstate 10, so we had no idea whether the Minutemen were out in their usual spot. As usual, the empty highway was only lit by our headlights as we headed east on the small highway. We slowed down to the speed limit around the areas where the Minutemen usually pulled off, but there were no vehicles. We kept driving to see if they moved further east, and I scanned the desert to the south. From the passenger seat I thought I saw something. "Man, I must not be getting enough sleep or something, I thought I just saw a tank back there," I told Claudia and one of the new volunteers. "The Minutemen do not have tanks do they?" I asked Claudia. In the rear view mirror I could see one of our new volunteer's face in the back freeze with terror and I turned to the back, "I am just joking, there aren't any tanks out here." Everyone giggled. We continued to drive down the road and we all looked to the right.

"What the fuck, that is a tank," I screamed about a half-a-mile down the road.

"Stop messing around Ray," said Claudia.

"No, I am dead serious, go back there, I swear to you it was a tank, it looked like two of them, right there on the side of the road," I told Claudia. "How did they get tanks?" Sure enough we drove back and there they were just off the side of the road, two large dark green camouflaged tanks sitting in the middle of the desert right off of the small highway. We drove further down the road and the tanks were set up almost identically to the Minutemen, in essentially what were the same spots only a few miles to the east.

It turns out the tanks did not belong to the Minutemen, but instead were in the possession of Uncle Sam and the Marines who were assisting the Border Patrol in spotting migrants. While the military is prohibited from apprehending migrants, there is a history of military forces assisting the Border Patrol in spotting migrants, with their role supposed to be similar to the Minutemen's stated position of solely observing and reporting. However, there is a tragic history in the use of soldiers for such operations. On May 20, 1997, Ezekiel Hernandez was murdered by a U.S. Marine near the Texas-Mexico border. The Marines were working with the Border Patrol under the project Joint Task Force Six, hoping to assist stopping drug dealers. Instead they ended up killing the 18 year-old U.S. citizen who was out herding goats.

For the rest of the month we would see the Marines driving along the small highway in their tanks, turning the small city of Hachita into what looked like some Third World nation that the United States had come to liberate. With their heads popped out of the top of the tanks, all that was missing was the picture of a marine giving a child a lollipop or holding them at gunpoint.

I remember stopping late one night and seeing a group of about 20 migrants being held approximately 30 yards from one of the tanks. I slowed my car and was going to get out to talk to the migrants when someone in complete camouflage came running over with a very mean scowl on their face. Before I could explain myself I was told by G.I. Joe to, "get the hell out of here." This was no Chrome Dome or Papa Bear, this guy was the real deal. Seeing as he had the tank and the guns I decided to drive along.

The demeanor of this individual was something I had not experienced even with the Minutemen, though they often times come quite close. With his military fatigues, guns, tanks, and other high-powered equipment he was not simply playing war, he was in a war. The fact that he was on U.S. soil and was only a few miles from a city made no difference to him.

Say what you want about Border Patrol, but at least their primary training is not to kill. I have run into plenty of rude, racists, and angry Border Patrol agents, but for the most part I have not sensed from them that they think they are in a war zone. Timothy Dunn points out in his book *The Militarization of the U.S.-Mexico Border, 1978-1982* that the doctrine of low-intensity conflict has come home. It was plenty clear that night that he was right.

The vigilantes have been crying for military forces on the border for quite some time, mainly making calls for the National Guard. I knew the political climate had reached ridiculous proportions when Arizona Governor Janet Napolitano, a Democrat, called for putting the National Guard on the border a few months later in her annual address to the Arizona State Legislature.

Her call for placing the National Guard on the border was an ill-designed attempt to gather points for her political career. As a Governor with high ambitions to become a national political figure, she was exploiting the increased paranoia and fear related to our southern border. The impact of Governor Napolitano's call for the National Guard goes beyond bad border policy and demonstrates how our society is quick to see aggressiveness and possible violence as a solution to just about any problem. Whether it is the military-industrial complex or the prison-industrial complex, we are quick to use punishment or force as a tool of social control. There are over 2 million people in U.S. prisons and jails, per capita we incarcerate more people than any country on the planet. We spend billions of dollars on border-related expenses and now have more sensors, fences, armed agents, helicopters, and cameras on our border then we ever have in the history of our nation.

Imagine walking through the desert and coming upon tanks and the G.I. Joes? The cans of tuna and bottles of water would certainly be no match for the heavy artillery found in the tanks.

Day after day we would see the tanks rolling down the highway and the Minutemen saluting the soldiers with joy every time they passed, until the month finally came to an end. Viewed in the terms of a battle, the far right was certainly victorious. It felt like we were in some fascist dictatorship with the military running the country, and I was hoping to see mass resistance to the military force but no such protests developed. It would take a few more months before the atmosphere would begin to shift.

CHAPTER EIGHT

The Beginning of Mass Mobilizations

I was again relieved to be done with the Minutemen. During October, my entire existence consisted of Papa Bear, Chrome Dome, radio checks, Marines, and junk food. I do not remember turning on a television and only occasionally picked up a newspaper. For most everyone else, it was simply another month, only difference being the stores were filled with bargains on candies and children's costumes for Halloween.

The traveling began in early November with the premiere of the documentary at the East Los Angeles Film Festival. I was extremely fortunate to have a $1,000-a-month travel budget that accompanied my move to Texas. Additionally, I was fortunate to have many speaking engagements paid for by universities.

On one of the university trips, I headed to Grinnell College in Iowa at the request of Professor Luis Fernandez. Luis is a friend and legal observer who had spent a few weekends down in Douglas.

I enjoy speaking with students, the energy and passion to make the world a better place is still quite alive on universities around the country. Students are for the most part free from mortgages, car payments, and the monotony of a full-time job. As such, they can focus on thinking critically about the world around them. People are still in the process of making life decisions that will reshape society and also are heavily involved in the day-to-day organizing within the immigrant communities.

But what I enjoy most about trips to universities are the opportunities to visit with the migrant communities in the local areas. Most community groups lack the resources to fly someone across the country, and it is great to be able to combine visits to local groups with the talks given to super privileged students. Luis drove me through the cornfields of Iowa to a small town that seemed to be hidden amongst large stalks of the same corn that probably resulted in many people having to migrate. It was early on a Sunday afternoon. We drove by a church where I had to do a quick double take. Here we were, in the middle of nowhere, and I was looking at a bunch of Mexicans wearing cowboy boots and cowboy hats. It felt just like driving by a church in Agua Prieta after mass had been let out. We were a little early for the meeting, so we stopped off at a Mexican restaurant near the center of town. The items on the menu were all familiar, as were the products being sold by the register. It was almost like being back at home. The only difference was that we were in the cornfields of Iowa.

We made our way over to the meeting and there were about twenty people in attendance. The meeting was held in Spanish, and I began with an overview of my work and then reviewed the new piece of legislation that had just recently been introduced in the House of Representatives, H.R. 4437, also known as the Sensenbrenner Bill (The Border Protection, Anti-terrorism, and Illegal Immigration Control Act of 2005). People seemed most upset at the part of the legislation that would make it a felony to be unlawfully present in the United States and a felony to assist someone who was in the United States unlawfully. A strict interpretation of the bill would have classified priests and social workers as felons for assisting undocumented migrants. The small group was beginning to become visibly angered, here were people who were simply scraping by day-to-day to improve their lives and the lives of their loved ones and the government was about to label them and their friends felons. To show how the grassroots were organizing to fight back against the Minutemen and against this piece of legislation, I read a list of actions that were taken by community members in the past couple of months. "We can thank the crazies for waking us up and requiring that communities come together," I said in Spanish. "The time is long overdue to come together and show the rest of the world that we are not afraid and we will not sit back and take these kinds of abuses. It has been a pleasure to spend time with you today and I look forward to adding actions that you take to the list of actions across the country. I am glad to know that even in the cornfields of Iowa community members are standing up for their rights and demanding justice."

I was set to speak at a couple of other universities in Iowa, and was a little nervous about how the crowds would react to what I was saying. I remember walking into the room at Iowa State University and seeing a sea of white. The only other person of color in the room was the professor who escorted me through the door. I did not know whether the audience was pro-Minutemen, pro-migrant, or simply curious about the issue. Would they simply see the relatively recent increase in migrants to Iowa as a threat or as a necessity of a changing economy? I was anxious to hear how the audience would respond, but was concerned that I might get booed off the stage, or ridiculed before I was done speaking.

I made it through without being booed and opened up the floor for questions and answers. I still could not tell how the audience was leaning, and I did not make any announcements about taking only questions or alternating between opposing views. For the trip to Iowa, I had done even extra research to be prepared to answer even detailed questions about national security, economics, and recent legislation. Like a fighter who runs for miles, lifts weights, and spars before the title fight, I read the latest reports, reviewed the seminal books, and scoured newspapers and magazines for the most recent articles.

I took the first question from a person in the back of the room. "I just do not understand, I mean it all seems very simple," began the man. "People from Mexico want to work and we need workers. Here in Iowa, the children do not want to work in the fields anymore the way their parents did. They want to go to college. Even those who do not go to college would prefer to work in fast food or something, but nobody; I mean nobody wants to be out there in the fields anymore. Why not just open the borders and make things easier for everyone? People will not have to die in the desert like you spoke about, employers will not have to worry about racial profiling their workers, and it would just be easier all around. It's not like if there were not any jobs here people would still keep coming. Why do we not just let the market decide when all of the jobs are taken? If there are no jobs then people will stop coming."

Despite all of my preparation, I was at a loss for words. I had been stumped. His question set the tone for the rest of the debate, and I was consistently surprised on just how liberal the folks in the audience were with respect to immigration. There were no vile responses to the man's question; nobody looked at him like he was a fool. If that question had been asked at a similar forum in Arizona, there would have been members in the audience who clapped vigorously in support and others who would have verbalized their disgust before even half the words he spoke left his mouth. The debate was much less polarized and leaned much farther to the left than I would have ever imagined. Of course, it must be kept in mind that this conversation was still taking place on the campus of a university, and not at a community center near where white residents were dealing with the changing demographics. I guarantee you it would not be difficult to find a newspaper article that has quotes from Iowans complaining about the increase in migration. After all, the mainstream media profits from such controversy. Even if it took knocking on one hundred doors to get an anti-immigrant response, I am sure a story would not be published without the "opposing view."

The question of "open borders" is far off the political map in Washington D.C., but is discussed at every community event I have been to across the country. At a meeting with a community based group in San Francisco called *Deporten La Migra* (Deport the Border Patrol), local residents spoke passionately about their right to cross borders to find work. With a sense of frustration and passion in her voice, the woman stated, "How come an American (U.S. Citizen) can go to Mexico whenever they want and enjoy the beautiful beaches, and we have to suffer so much to try to get here? I have seen it with my own two eyes, they go down there and have a good time, and we treat them with respect and dignity, and why? Why, well because they are human beings. But when we come here, do we receive the same kind of treatment? No, no I tell you. Even though we wash their clothes, clean their houses, mow the grass, work in the restaurants, they treat us like less than human. I ask you, where is the equality, where is it at? Am I less human than them? I will stand before you here today and say no, no I am not, I am human too." From Iowa to California, New York to New Mexico, Seattle to Minnesota, I have consistently heard the same message coming from migrants. While some would like to believe that the workers are only machines who perform labor, in fact they are human beings with the ability to rationalize and can use their life experiences to critique the world around them. Some would like to tell you that migrants are voiceless, and it is the role of the privileged activist to give them a voice. I wholeheartedly disagree with that. I certainly do not see my role as giving a voice to the voiceless. The migrants are already yelling at the top of their lungs, repeating almost precisely the same messages without the assistance of any public relations firm giving them sound bites. If anything, I see my role as giving an ear to the earless, to those who benefit from the sweat, suffering, and deaths of migrants while hoping that they simply remain workers to be exploited.

It's no easy task to push people to think of a world that threatens their privileges. Most U.S. citizens take for granted their birthright privilege of being able to travel freely throughout the rest of the Americas. While there is still the travel ban to Cuba, all someone has to do is board a flight to Cancun and purchase a ticket to Havana, no Border Patrol or vigilantes to worry about. For people to think that such a privilege should be extended to their darker skinned neighbors to the South is heresy. Migrants and advocates point to a system similar to the European Union where Latin Americans, beginning with the North American partner of Mexico, can freely cross each other's borders for work or vacation.

While for some that is difficult to comprehend, there was also a time when it was difficult to comprehend a Union without slavery, an extension of the vote to women, or African-Americans marrying Caucasians. The wheels of change are slow. But, a simple glance at the changes that have occurred in the past couple of hundred years reminds us that the country as we experience it now will someday be drastically different.

How such drastic changes occur is the subject that individuals have dedicated their lives to studying. Such change often begins with those at the grassroots level demanding radical change. A taking to the streets to create the tension and conflict necessary to snap people out of their comfort zones. While giving a presentation to an immigrants' rights class at Stanford Law School, I was asked just how such change would come about. While sitting in a black, Aeron chair that cost more than all of the furniture in the room where I used to facilitate the human rights discussions with migrants, I responded that there needed to be mass mobilizations with undocumented people taking to the streets to demand their rights.

Immediately upon making that statement hands shot in the air and one woman blurted out, "There is no way that is going to happen. Undocumented people are so afraid, they already live in the shadows and are even afraid to call the police. You expect them to openly take to the streets in massive numbers, which is just not possible for them. Maybe for you, but to ask people to risk everything like that is just completely unrealistic." Her opinion was seconded by another student, and keep in mind that was a class that focused on immigrants' rights, and as such is supposed to be training the next generation of lawyers to defend immigrants. It was apparent that those in the ivory tower were in need of some seriously large binoculars to see what was really happening in immigrant communities.

I showed up at a rally in Phoenix in early January 2006. While I was still concerned about being lynched by the ACLU of Arizona or Minutemen if I was caught back in Arizona, I would frequently return to see family. I was hoping for a couple of hundred people and was shocked to see over 4,000 in front of the Arizona State Legislature. For similar rallies in college we were overjoyed if one hundred people showed up, and I was thrilled to be able to walk through the crowd and not know a single person. These were not the full-time activists who met in coffee shops; rather these were construction workers coming from the jobsite covered in sweat and dirt. There were restaurant workers who carried their aprons in their hands and young babies being pushed in strollers. The atmosphere was not one of fear, and nobody was hiding in the shadows. ¡El pueblo estaba presente!

I also made time to meet with a disgruntled Minuteman on this trip to Phoenix.

Chris Simcox exposed by his own Minutemen

This Minuteman and I had corresponded over email a few times and he asked to meet in person the next time I was in Phoenix. Naturally I was a little leery of his request. But I would always tell the Minutemen that if they wanted to meet somewhere else than the desert, I would be happy to talk politics with them. Though I was not sure of the nature of the meeting, I was intent on keeping my word. Plus, this Minuteman had been respectful to me and other volunteers while on patrol, and had attended the film screening a few months back. To be safe, I told a few people who I was meeting with and at what time, and that I would call them after a few hours. We met at a local Applebee's and the Minuteman was sitting down when I walked in. "I bet you were not sure if I was going to be alone or not," the Minuteman joked. "No need to worry, I left my gun at home. Plus, the Minutemen probably want to hurt me right now, just as much as they want to hurt you. And after we are done talking today, they'll probably want to hurt me more."

The Minuteman's comments eased my nervousness, and we went straight into the details. "I've been kicked out," said the man with a sense of anger and disappointment you feel when someone you trust turns their back on you. He went on to explain that he had made inquiries into the Minutemen's finances and apparently Simcox was not too happy about that. He stated that Simcox was hardly out on patrol anymore and that none of the resources were being put to the operations in the desert. He had requested more radios, port-a-potties, night vision goggles, but had received none of the equipment. "I do not understand," said the Minuteman, "I have seen with my own two eyes people hand over checks for thousands of dollars. About a month ago I saw someone give a $15,000 check. People donate the money thinking that the money is going to be used for operations in the desert, but I am telling you, it ain't getting out there. I'll tell you where it is going though, straight into Simcox's pocket." The Minuteman mentioned Simcox's new sports utility vehicle and talked about his recent marriage to a woman 20 years younger than him. "The guy has just lost it, well, if he has ever had it together. He's a nutcase, total ego-tripper." He was already halfway through his beer as I continued to sip on mine. After his repeated requests for equipment fell on deaf ears, he decided to approach some of the other Minutemen with his concerns. As soon as Simcox found out about this, the Minuteman was told to return the databases he was managing and informed he could no longer go on patrol. "Oh yeah, let me tell you something else, not only is Simcox a dirty thief, but he lies through his teeth. He keeps saying there are 4,000 people that are signed up to patrol for this April. Bullshit, I was the one managing the databases and there are not even six-hundred names that we have. Whatever he tells the media they just print it, even though it is complete lies." Included in the less than six-hundred names I am sure were hundreds of activists who signed-up simply to keep informed of what the Minutemen were doing. I know every time the Minutemen would send out an email my inbox would be flooded with people redirecting it my way.

I was able to put this Minuteman in contact with a local news station that was investigating the Minutemen. When the piece finally aired there were Minutemen bashing Simcox left and right. The disgruntled Minuteman had connected the reporter with others concerned about Simcox pocketing the finances, and one of the people bad-mouthing Simcox was Joe McCutchen, the man who had last April hit me with a flashlight. The reporter then drilled Simcox about the allegations leading him to squirm in his seat as if being scolded by an angry parent. His answers to the questions were not only evasive; he directly refused to open the books to show the public what he was doing with all the money.

A movement takes shape

While the Minutemen were continuing to fall apart from within, the migrants' rights community was continuing to organize and mobilize. I attended two different national conferences, one in Chicago and the other in Tennessee, of groups trying to come together to combat the growing anti-immigrant sentiment. Activists spoke of Minutemen chapters forming as far away as Maryland to harass day laborers standing on street corners looking for work. By far the worst stories continued to come from Arizona. The state legislature was passing draconian anti-immigrant legislation, and Minutemen's activities were a weekly occurrence on street corners and in front of day labor centers. Discussing the problems were simple, but mapping the solutions were difficult. There was a large split between those wanting to focus energy on a grassroots movement to get people in the streets and those wanting to focus on messaging that would resonate with the people in the middle. While the immediate effects of the meetings were committees that never met, and new email listservs that were rarely used, historic mobilizations were just around the corner.

I continued to travel around the country and at each location people would stand-up with great passion and a sense of urgency that something must be done to stop HR 4437, the previously mentioned federal legislation that sought to make felons out of undocumented migrants and those who assisted them. To use an old cliché, H.R. 4437 was the straw that broke the camel's back.

A detailed timeline of all the xenophobic and racists actions that preceded H.R. 4437 would be too great to list here, but the more recent developments provide a good context. Let's start with the Minutemen. Essentially, they were a bunch of white people with guns who went to the border to stop brown people from coming across. But the Minutemen also became a symbol within the Latino community. Your racist boss who forces you to work overtime without pay was a Minuteman. The salesperson who followed you as if you were a thief about to put a pair of jeans under your shirt and run out the store was a Minuteman. The judge who sentenced your child to a juvenile detention facility while giving probation to the white child for the same act was a Minuteman. In other words, all of the injustices faced because of your country of origin or skin color could somehow be labeled as having been caused by *los* Minutemen. Of course, such injustices have existed for centuries and the label was the only recent encapsulation of a racist society.

While symbolically the Minutemen are emblematic of a much larger problem, the simple act of white people going to the border with guns to keep out brown people was a large slap in the face for the Latino community. The actions and rhetoric of the Minutemen then emboldened pseudo-journalists such as Lou Dobbs and Sean Hannity to ratchet up their anti-immigrant rants and was another large slap in the face. As local radio hosts across the country followed suit, local and state politicians were quick to capitalize on the growing anti-immigrant sentiment. State legislatures introduced anti-immigrant bills and Democratic Governors of Arizona and New Mexico declared states of emergencies. Because these actions were coming from government officials they could no longer be dismissed as simple slaps in the face. The power of the state resulted in them being more like strong blows to the rib cage that suck the wind out of you and force you to keel over. Then came the strong right hand that landed squarely on the chin, H.R. 4437. This one piece of legislation making its way through the revered halls of Washington D.C., was the House of Representatives legitimizing the hateful rhetoric and racist actions taking place across the country. The anti-immigrant crowd expected a knockout that would result in immigrants being carried out of the ring and back to the countries they came from while asking for "*no más*." But instead of going down for the count, communities fought back.

Such a reaction was certainly not something that I foresaw happening so quickly. While speaking at Harvard University in late February, I was asked how it was possible for me to remain optimistic while the atmosphere against migrants seemed to be increasing every day. "It's true," I responded. "The anti-immigrant sentiment is really getting out of control. Unfortunately, I think it is going to get much worse before it gets any better. But, we must remember that the darkest part of the night comes before the sun is going to rise. And it will get darker; there will be more vigilante violence, more anti-immigrant hysteria at the local level, and more ridiculous bills in front of state legislatures and in Washington D.C. But it is impossible for me to give up hope because I have seen the faces of too many migrants. When you have seen someone who has just been sent back to Mexico by the Border Patrol after almost having died in the desert, and you look into their eyes and they tell you that no matter what they will find a way to get across and find work, then you know that the sun will eventually rise. As much hate as the anti-immigrant folks have in their hearts, there is much more love in the hearts of migrants. Just the other day I heard word that activists in Chicago are expecting 15,000 people to attend a rally on March 10th. When I hear about actions like that, then I know there is hope for change." Earlier in the day I had been walking through Harvard Square attempting to cope with the frigid weather while wearing two large jackets, gloves, a beanie, and a scarf. For a moment my mind took me away from the snow-covered grass and historic buildings to the Huachuca Mountains back in Arizona. I knew migrants were at that very moment walking through the cold weather that has given many hypothermia. I had spent a good deal of time the past couple of months in extremely cold weather, and had many times longed to be back in the desert. While bundled-up at the Sundance Film Festival in Park City, Utah for the premiere of the documentary *Crossing Arizona*, I thought about being back home where I could walk outside wearing a pair of shorts and a t-shirt. The cold weather in Chicago and Iowa made me curse myself for being away from home during the months that made the ridiculous summer temperatures somewhat tolerable. For whatever reason, it was not until earlier that day that I had remembered that crossing the border is deadly year-round. Night-time temperatures in the desert and mountains routinely drop well below freezing.

The cold temperatures in Chicago must have seemed irrelevant to those who took to the streets in protest on March 10, 2006. Out of a summit in mid-February in Southern California, came the idea of marches in local areas against the previously mentioned H.R. 4437. Chicago was the first city to pull off one of the mega marches. While I had previously heard estimates that 15,000 people were going to participate, organizers put the actual turnout at over 100,000 people. This was the largest street rally in Chicago since 90,000 people, many immigrant workers, took to the street on May 1, 1886 to demand an eight-hour workday. Similar to the current migrants rights mobilizations; the seeds of the eight-hour workday movement were planted many years before. In 1791, carpenters in Philadelphia went on strike for a ten-hour work day. As early as 1817, across the Atlantic Ocean, Robert Owen was calling for "eight hours labour, eight hours recreation, eight hours rest." It was not until 1938 that the Fair Labor Standards Act came into law giving many working people the eight-hour workday.

Undoubtedly, historians will point to the mass mobilizations that took place after Chicago as a central turning point of a movement that will similarly take decades or even longer. While previously thousands had taken to the streets in Philadelphia and Washington D.C., the Chicago rally gave greater momentum to efforts across the country. Before the end of March there would be massive rallies on the streets of Milwaukee, Phoenix, Los Angeles, Denver, Cleveland, Columbus, Ohio, Detroit, and Nashville. Students in Los Angeles walked out of school and marched to City Hall, resulting in across the country repeating their actions.

While I would have loved to have been able to focus my energy on the upcoming marches in April, it was time to begin turning my attention back to organizing the legal observer project. Almost six months had passed since last October, and the Minutemen were preparing for another month long patrol. I traveled to Bellingham, Washington, to assist Rosalinda Guillen and her crew in starting a legal observer project and then made my way back to El Paso to begin preparations for another long month. Little did I know that I would soon find myself on familiar territory.

CHAPTER NINE

Back to Arizona

Why would I go back? After the wasted hours, big headaches, and censure, probably the best thing to do would have been to stay as far away from Arizona as possible.

But I knew that the splintered Minutemen group was going to have the majority of its resources focused on Arizona. With New Mexico militia man Bob Wright threatening to knock out Simcox the next time he saw him, and the Minutemen's headquarters being placed in Scottsdale, Arizona, I knew the Minutemen would shuffle the majority of their volunteers into the state that has been likened to Civil Rights-era Alabama.

The group of legal observers who clandestinely had been observing the Minutemen as they harassed day laborers in Phoenix for the past five months decided that they were going to run a legal observer project on the border. They approached Alessandra Soler-Meetze, the new Executive Director of the ACLU of Arizona, and asked if I could return to Arizona to run the program.

Not surprisingly, the previous Executive Director had left her position soon after the controversy from the first Minuteman Patrols in April 2005. What was surprising, however, was that the virulently anti-immigrant State Board then chose to hire a young Latina from Florida to head the ACLU of Arizona. I met with Alessandra in early March, and while she did not have much of a handle on how bad the anti-immigrant sentiment was in Arizona, she was very sympathetic to migrant issues. To my surprise, she agreed with the request from the legal observers and invited me to come to

Arizona to coordinate the legal observer project a week and a half before the Minutemen were set to arrive. She clearly had no idea what the implications of her invitation would be.

I packed my clothes, two-way radios, and video cameras and headed west on the Interstate 10. With the help of the great activists in Tucson and students from Grinnell College, I was able to find a small house in Three Points, Arizona, only minutes from the Minutemen's headquarters.

On April 1st, I sat in the Three Points Community Center and prepared for the legal observer training at 2 p.m. A glance at the clock revealed that it was already 2:05, and I realized I was still alone in the room. I wondered if the fact that the media attention had died down significantly meant that no volunteers would come out. Perhaps potential volunteers thought that the idea of legal observing was exciting last year, but they had done their duty for migrants and now were more focused on other endeavors.

The different scenarios raced through my head. Maybe there would only be a few legal observers and this time a thousand Minutemen really would show up. My heart started pumping, and I could feel my throat getting dry when the door opened and in walked seasoned legal observer Leila Pine. Leila was shortly followed by a group of sweaty, crunchy, and energetic students from Prescott College. Just as he had done the year before, Professor Amster had loaded the small liberal arts school's van with enthusiastic students and driven down to the border. The energy from the college students and veteran activists who followed soon filled the room.

I gave a quick overview and sent a group of eight legal observers out to wait outside of the Minutemen's compound well before they were scheduled to leave for their first patrol. It did not take long for the Minutemen to start causing trouble. Legal observers had not been out of their car for fifteen minutes when they were approached by two documentary filmmakers from Mexico. A young, heavyset woman described what had just transpired. She and her partner were filming a caravan of Minutemen cars as they exited the compound. The young filmmakers heard tires screech and looked over their shoulders to see a car in reverse heading toward them. A Minute-woman got out of the car and began screaming at the filmmakers that they had no right to film her license plate.

The filmmakers explained that they were not filming license plates, but the procession of cars, but the head of Mothers Against Illegal Aliens, Michelle Dellacrose, was not listening. I first saw Michelle at a Minuteman rally in front of a Home Depot in Phoenix, Arizona. Legal observers quickly gave her the name 'Bouncy Lady' because she jumped up and down incessantly, yelling toward the cars passing by that 'illegals' are destroying her community. She hollered and moved around as if someone had spiked her double espresso with crack. Apparently, the Minutemen did not find her too fun to hang around with and legal observers stopped seeing 'Bouncy Lady' for a few weeks. Then a new anti-immigrant group calling itself Mothers Against Illegal Aliens was born. Or perhaps I should say that a woman calling herself Mothers Against Illegal Aliens began to be more vocal.

On this day, it appeared that Bouncy Lady had once again drunk her strong dose of caffeine, and she was laying into the two young filmmakers. Dellacrose's ranting drew the attention of the crowd, and soon there stood seven armed Minutemen behind her as she belittled the filmmakers and demanded that they erase the footage they had taken. The filmmakers originally refused to erase the tape, but after being surrounded by seven armed men they felt intimidated and complied with Bouncy Lady's demands.

I finished the training at the community center and arrived to see journalists from as far away as Germany and Spain waiting for interviews. The media presence was nothing compared to the year before, but nonetheless, there were enough journalists to be quite annoying. Another group of people looking for a quick sound bite for a story they pretty much had written before they even came out to the desert.

The media waited while we called the Pima County Sheriff's Department to file a report. Sheriff's deputies would eventually arrive, but no action was taken. While the law student in me quickly saw the Minutemen's threats and intimidation as a crime, the Sheriff's Deputies saw no basis to issue a citation. Certainly threatening and intimidating is a more serious crime than crossing a line in the desert without the proper permission slip in your hand, but today the latter garnered all the attention. Chalk this up as another one of the many incidents of the Minutemen breaking the law that no one would ever hear about.

The Minutemen were patrolling on state trust land that they had entered by passing through private property. The owner of the private property, Mrs. King, came out to the highway to inform us that we were not allowed access to her land, so all we could do was wait on the side of the highway and listen to the Minutemen's radios. We waited outside a few hours, until a large truck pulled off of the highway. Out jumped a big white guy wearing full camouflage and army boots strapped tightly around his ankles. On cue, the 'ding' of the video cameras being turned on by legal observers broke the silence.

"Hey Ray," yelled the big man with the goatee as he jumped out of the truck with a cigarette in his hand.

"What's up Jim, it's nice to see you," I responded. "Long time no see." It was none other than Jim Wade, the Minuteman with whom I spent hours in the middle of the desert last July who found himself one of the stars of my documentary. Most everyone seemed shocked that I was having a friendly conversation with a vigilante who looked like he just got back from driving around the streets of Baghdad looking for roadside bombs to dismantle. Legal observers gathered around and began to take pictures of us as we exchanged pleasantries and tried to get caught up.

"That Simcox is fucking nuts," explained Wade. "He's off his rocker. Did you hear he married some 24 year-old and is milking her for her money? We are out here trying to save lives, but his guys don't care about the poor migrants." I could sense that Jim was getting ready to go off on one of his rants about really caring about the migrants and being humanitarian, but I just let him go on. "I can't tell you how many lives I've saved out here. These coyotes are ruthless, they just don't care. They rape the women, make them carry drugs. This is slavery here." Wade continued, "I have sympathy for these people, if I was in their shoes I'd be doing the same thing."

I'd heard similar arguments countless times and have since heard them many more times. There was a time when I actually wanted to believe it. Jim gave the typical Minutemen rant. He's an environmentalist trying to save the desert and wishes the Sierra Club was seeing the path of destruction left by migrants. He wants a guest worker program, but only after the borders are secured. Which is a brilliant strategy used by the far-right. You can say you want a certain policy to the media, but only after another policy is implemented, when in fact the latter is impossible to ever achieve. They might as well say they want a guest worker program, but only after all of the water on the earth is gone. Regardless, I could sense some of the younger volunteers really being in awe. Here was a real, live vigilante dressed in head-to-toe camo. He was ready for war and they were actually getting to listen to what made him tick. The same curiosity seems to grip the American public, and if you only listen to the sound bites played on television or written in newspapers, people are likely to see the Minutemen as rational, compassionate beings.

I have yet to exactly time it, but there is a point where the Minutemen relax a little bit and run out of their canned human rights sound bites. The last time I interviewed Jim, it took about 25 minutes to get to that point, but this day it would take a few more hours. He invited legal observers to ride along with him and his rogue group of Minutemen, known as 'The Minuteman of One." The Minuteman of One was started by Fred Puckett. You can usually find old Fred wearing a dirty pair of overalls and a baseball cap. His moustache resembles Yosemite Sam, the cartoon character who tries to shoot Bugs Bunny, and his demeanor is pretty similar as well. An undercover reporter caught him on tape saying that the Minuteman of One "do it like they did 40 years ago in Vietnam" – that is, "go out two at a time and take them down hard."

Why Fred decided to split from the Minutemen and form his own group is a subject of debate, and I'll only tell you what he told me. He complained about the leadership being too controlling and strict, actually referring to Minutemen's National Director of Vetting as a "bitch." While I am not sure what the Director of Vetting actually does, I can attest that Connie is not the nicest person in the world. Of course, Fred's biggest concern was that the Minutemen were not hands-on enough and that they didn't even provide water to migrants because they were afraid of being sued. Fred wants to drive around the desert and check for lay-up spots, not simply sit in his car for eight hours staring at the desert. He actually wants to be out there "saving lives." What Fred wants to do is mimic the Border Patrol. The only difference is that he lacks a badge, hasn't received a psychological evaluation, and does not receive a paycheck.

There is no love lost on the other side toward Fred and his group. It is even rumored that Fred made a vague threat to the Minutemen and hoped that none of their people got caught in his crossfire, because his people carry long-arms. Indeed they do. Jim invited legal observers to drive with Fred and himself to a popular lay-up spot so that he could show them all the trash migrants leave behind. The only ones to volunteer for the special mission that involved riding in the back of Jim's pickup were the young college students, who quickly jumped in.

As the truck drove away up the highway, Professor Amster came up to me and asked, "Do you think they'll be okay?"

"I hope so," were the only words I could think to say. "Besides, if anything goes wrong, they'll just call us on their radio." I am not sure if it was he or I who was more relieved, that is until we realized that none of the people who had jumped into the truck were carrying a radio. After trying to reach each of them by cell phone, we sat nervously for over four hours, awaiting their return. The minutes passed by much more slowly after the sun went down, and the desert sky was filled with stars. The beauty of being back in the desert was overshadowed by my nervousness. I felt so stupid having let people leave without making sure they had a working radio.

Professor Amster would occasionally make a nervous joke, but I assured him that everything would be alright and that I knew where Jim lived. This didn't do much to ease his stress, and I learned later just how nervous I should have been as well. While Jim and the crew were rambling down the dirt-paved Coleman Road, they came upon a group of migrants who were getting into a large white van. When Jim placed his pick-up in front of the van, everyone inside of the van jumped out and ran back into the desert. Jim had arrived at a pick up spot where migrants who had been walking for days in the desert were to meet with coyotes who would give them a ride into Phoenix and then secure transportation to whatever city they were headed to. While many deaths occur due to lack of water in the desert, many people also die in vehicle accidents, especially when thirty people are thrown into a van and the tires are blown out by the Border Patrol.

None of the vigilantes chose to pursue the migrants into the desert, probably because the legal observers had already turned their cameras on. Instead, the vigilantes went through the van and rummaged through the migrants' personal belongings. Border Patrol agents eventually arrived and a few minutes later the stillness and darkness of the desert was destroyed by one of the Border Patrol's helicopters flying low and shining spotlights in search of the migrants. I am sure the vigilantes were reminded of their days in Vietnam. The night ended with a group of migrants being led out of the desert by Border Patrol agents.

The next day, my fellow legal observer realized he had lost his wallet the night before. After searching everywhere, we assumed the wallet fell out of Jim's truck when he was driving with him and Jim boxed in the van that was beginning to load a group of migrants. After spending a few days trying to decide whether or not to drive into the splinter group's headquarters, we finally drove in.

In retrospect, perhaps driving into the parking lot of the Veterans of Foreign War (VFW) Hall in Three Points, Arizona, was not the best idea. The Minuteman of One and his splinter group of vigilantes used the desert area surrounding the VFW Hall as their headquarters and camping grounds. Large Marine and U.S. flags flew overhead, and camouflaged tents and large pickup trucks occupied the ground. A genuine patriot's playground.

As soon as we got out of the car we were quickly greeted.

"I am going to kill those ACLU fuckers!" shouted the 60-plus year-old man as he reached into the back of his pickup truck to pull out his AR-15. He wrapped his right hand underneath the handle of his assault rifle and used his left hand to point the barrel of the rifle in our direction.

"I think I am going to stand behind Mr. Puckett," I shouted as I stepped behind the dirty-looking, overall-wearing man who dubbed himself the 'Minuteman of One'.

"Calm down, just calm down," Fred Puckett told the old man. As I stood behind Fred, whom I had earlier mistakenly called Kirby, I saw Jim place his body in front of the AR-15 and encourage the old man to put the rifle back in the truck. We eventually left the compound without recovering the wallet, but thankfully we were still in one piece. I would have been quite pleased if that had turned out to be the most nerve-wracking day of the month.

Close to death

Just a few days later we were sitting outside of the Minutemen's headquarters waiting to follow them out for their night patrol. Three of us were just across the small highway that runs north-south next to the corral that sits about 26 miles from the U.S.-Mexico border. From the street, we could see the Minutemen's night patrol huddled in a circle, as if waiting to break for the line of scrimmage. The day shift was in the circle as well, and the group probably numbered around 40. As we were leaning against our cars looking into the compound, the movement of the dry bushes to our south caught my attention. It was probably about one hundred yards down the highway on our side of the desert. There did not appear to be any wind, so I told the other two observers that I was going to drive down just to make sure it was not a group of migrants.

I drove down the road and got out of my car where I had thought I had seen the brush moving. What I found was a shell of a man. His skin was so dark I could not tell what his ethnicity was, and I had no clue if he spoke Spanish or some other language.

"Q'vole compa," I called out to him. As he stumbled out from behind the bush, I took in his bald head, bloody nose, and filthy clothes and watched as he limped toward me, dragging his right leg behind him.

"¿Quiere agua, quiere comida?" I asked.

"Estoy perdido," he responded. He described how he got separated from his group and told me that when I glimpsed him, he was getting ready to approach the ranch across the street to see if they could give him some food and water. I advised him that going to knock on the Minutemen's door would probably not be in his best interest. He was so dehydrated and hungry that I had to explain it to him about four times before he actually seemed to comprehend me. I was trying desperately to explain this to him as fast as possible, because I knew that at any moment, the Minutemen caravan might leave the ranch and come right in our direction. When I had driven over, they had yet to gather into formation with each car lined up behind the other, but I knew they were already running behind schedule.

I looked nervously over my shoulder every few seconds, fearful of what would happen if the entire caravan of armed vigilantes came our way. The desperate man begged me for a ride and confessed that the bottle of yellow liquid he was carrying with him was his own urine, which he had been drinking for the last day and a half after spending four days walking in the desert. He told me his name was Angel, and he was crossing the border to be reunited with his family in Chicago. Angel was having a tough time getting by in his native Acapulco, a popular tourist destination for the wealthy around the world. He spoke in broken sentences while looking into my car and asking for a ride. I learned that he had been separated from his group of about 30 people two nights before, when they were approached by what he thought were private citizens with high-powered assault rifles. He was not sure what had happened to the rest of the group and was unaware of what direction he was walking in.

Angel again asked for a ride. I explained to him the law as I learned it in the classroom. If I was caught with him in my car, I could get five years in jail, be fined thousands of dollars, be forever branded a felon, and the Border Patrol would confiscate my car. I told Angel that we would have to turn around and drive right by the Minutemen, and they would notice an unfamiliar face in the car, especially a face as sunburned and bloody as his. Angel responded by saying he would lay down in the backseat and nobody would see him. He emphatically stated that he could not wait any longer. His one request besides a ride was for a Coca-Cola. While nearly dying from dehydration in the middle of the desert, he was craving for the cold, carbonated liquid to pass through his dry throat.

What I did next would make me a potential felon but leave my conscience clean. It was still daylight, and given the amount of Border Patrol I had seen around during the day, I thought it was best to wait for the cover of darkness. I instructed Angel to climb back underneath the barbed wire fence and wait under a bush and when the sun went down a car would honk its horn and he could come back out of the desert for a ride to Tucson. As he was turning around his right hand gripped an imaginary coke can, and he raised his arm to his mouth, again requesting a Coke. I told him I was not sure if we had a Coke, but that someone would be by in a minute to leave food and water for his stay until night time. I walked back to my car and before opening the door, I looked back in Angel's direction. I saw him wobbling from side to side, unable to place his full weight on the soles of either foot because of the enormous blisters beneath his bloody socks. Though he was moving as fast as he could it appeared to me that an obese 90 year-old in a walker could have moved more quickly to get to the other side of the barbed wire fence. I again looked at the highway and hoped that neither the Border Patrol nor Minutemen would come around the corner before Angel reached his cover.

I did a u-turn, and in under a minute I was back to where my two fellow legal observers were waiting. As I got out of the car, the Minutemen caravan was getting ready to leave. We tried to act as routine as possible and started filming while smiling and waving at each vehicle as it exited the compound and began to move down the highway. I tried my hardest to remain calm but am sure that the image from the camera I was carrying shows a bouncy picture that would give anyone watching it a headache.

We watched as license plates from Washington, Idaho, Alabama, New York, Iowa, and Arkansas drove out of sight. Thankfully, none of them stopped in the area where I had just been. I told my fellow legal observers what had happened and asked if they could drive down the road when things looked calm and leave food and water on the other side of the barbed wire fence. I looked in an ice chest that was in the trunk and smiled when I saw a six-pack of Coke. During the legal observer trainings it was made clear that assisting migrants in this fashion was explicitly prohibited. Giving food and water was certainly allowed, but rides were not. However, there were only three of us on this shift and I knew that I could trust the other two to keep this secret. After spending nearly 72 hours together in a highly intense and stressed-filled weekend, I knew where my colleagues' hearts were, and I was confident that I could trust these two individuals with my life.

I sped down the highway in a rush to get to an area where I could get cell phone reception. As I drove north on Highway 86, I did not pass a single Border Patrol agent and cursed myself for not just putting Angel in my backseat as he had requested. Within 20 minutes I arrived at the gas station in Three Points and pulled my car off to the side of the road, impatiently waiting for my Blackberry phone to get reception. I dialed the phone number of a friend whom I will call Marilyn. Marilyn answered but explained that she was far away and would not be able to make it to me until late at night. I thanked Marilyn, but told her I thought we had to move just after sundown because if we waited until much later, very few cars would be on the road and a lone vehicle on the highway would be even more suspicious.

I then placed another call to someone we'll call Vicki. As I was waiting for Vicki to pick up the phone so I could explain what was happening, Fred Puckett pulled up behind me. Before he got out of his truck, I hung up the phone and was quite happy that he did not walk up behind me as I was explaining our plan. Parking next to the one public toilet in the town probably was not the best idea, but I hope the reader can understand that I had to make that stop before making phone calls. Fred politely said hello and as soon as he was in and out of the bathroom I again called Vicki. Vicki is the kind of woman you see at the grocery store, smile at, and never remember. Her smile and quiet voice puts you at such ease that you feel that you have known her for years. She's Anglo, in her early 40s, and is one of the least likely people you would expect to risk her comfortable lifestyle to help out someone she has never even met. Perhaps the only person who looks less likely to transport someone unlawfully is Marilyn, only because Marilyn is probably 30 years older, and her hair is completely white.

I told Vicki what had happened, and she only asked how soon she needed to be out in the desert. I asked her if she wanted another one of our friends to ride with her and she thought it would be best to have two people in the car as opposed to what appeared to be her driving by herself.

We made plans to meet up in a couple of hours, and I then called James to see if he was available. James was up for the task and agreed to meet up with Vicki and me in a couple of hours. I headed back south on Highway 86 and heard over the radio from my other legal observers that everything went well, and they had caught up with the Minutemen and were set up behind them. I suggested we meet back in front of the Minutemen compound to strategize for the rest of the afternoon and then turned the music up and cruised down the highway at a steady 65 miles per hour.

My fellow legal observers had already arrived when I pulled up outside of the compound. I got out of my car to give them the update; after talking for a few minutes, I looked south and saw Angel standing on the side of the highway. "What the fuck is he doing?" I screamed, tossing my keys to one of the legal observers and motioning him into the driver's seat. I jumped into the passenger seat so that I could get out quickly to talk to Angel once we reached him. "Let me know if you see anything," I called back to the other legal observer who was staying outside the Minutemen's compound.

We drove down the highway and before my car came to a complete halt I asked Angel, "What's up?"

"I can't wait any longer, just whoever comes next it does not matter. I just can't wait any longer. I don't care if it's Border Patrol or the racists, I can't wait," explained Angel. Even though Angel had gotten the food, water, and Coke, he was afraid that he was just going to be left in the desert and that nobody was ever going to come back. I explained to him that I had called some friends and that they were going to come just after dark to pick him up. He again repeated that he could not wait any longer, and just then I heard the rumbling of a diesel engine.

Living a block from the U.S.-Mexico border meant that I became quite familiar with what a Border Patrol truck sounded like, and I did not need to turn around to know what was coming down the highway. At that moment I got a call from the legal observer waiting outside the compound, warning me that a Border Patrol truck was coming our way. I hoped the truck would just drive past, but as the truck drew closer I could hear it slowing down, and I turned to see it veering off of the pavement and heading right in our direction.

Angel and I were standing face to face, I with my back facing to the north and Angel looking straight at me. "Just kick back against the side of the car and don't say anything about us planning a ride, just say we gave you food and water, you got it," I told Angel. "Just kick back and relax, try to be cool." He agreed to not say anything and leaned his backside on the side of my car, carefully placing the dry branch he was using as a walking stick in front of him.

The passenger side door was swung open and I placed my left forearm on the top of the open door, allowing my body weight to shift to my left leg so I would look as comfortable and relaxed as possible as I turned to greet the Border Patrol agent. My throat had quickly become dry and I took a deep breath and swallowed before smiling and asking the Border Patrol agent, "How's it going?"

"It's going well," responded the young agent with a military style haircut and chiseled face. He had rolled his window down but remained in his truck and left the diesel engine rumbling. If he had turned off his truck, he probably would have heard the thumping of my heart. "Did you call in some illegals?" the agent asked.

"Nahh," I responded as I grinned sheepishly. "That's not our role out here, we're legal observers, we're out here to make sure the Minutemen don't beat on anybody. If I see them beating on anyone then I'll make sure to call you." I had spent countless hours training people on how to use their body language to defuse a possibly violent situation with the Minutemen and was hoping that my stance and tone was giving the impression that I was completely relaxed and not the least bit nervous or intimidated.

I am sure Angel did not have a clue what I was saying, but out of the corner of my dark sunglasses I could see him nodding his head in agreement. "Well, someone called in some illegals on the side of the road, but

I do not see any," said the Border Patrol agent as he glanced at Angel and then looked back at me and smiled. "Have a great day," he said before rolling his window back up and driving back on the highway heading south.

I looked inside the car at my fellow legal observer, who was leaning over the steering wheel with his jaw wide open. It took a minute to believe what had actually just happened, and I was happy that once we were able to speak again, I had earned Angel's trust. "So, just go back and wait and someone will honk and then I come out?" he asked.

"That's right, we'll see you in a few hours," I responded as I watched him again waddle back toward the barbed wire fence. We drove back down the highway and plotted on how to go about getting Angel to safety. The more we talked about what to do, the more I thought about what could go wrong and the potential fallout from our attempting to help Angel. Getting caught would mean that the legal observing program would be cancelled permanently and the Minutemen would know that there was no one to monitor their actions. The ACLU would surely receive an unbelievable amount of bad publicity for having one of its employees engage in illegal activities. This would mean disgrace for all those who stood up for me and gave me the opportunity to assume a leadership position within the organization. I would just be another young male of color who lacked the control to follow the rules of a civilized society.

Then of course there was jail, which would mean not being able to return to law school and not having the ability to continue my work. No more traveling, speaking at universities, eating at nice restaurants, staying at posh hotels, or any of the other benefits that come with being a somewhat known and respected human rights activist. Every time I looked at the sky, the sun appeared to be in the same place, and it felt as if time was standing still so that it could enjoy watching my mind and my conscience quarrel with each other. I began to verbalize my anxieties, and my fellow legal observers continuously reassured me that everything was going to be fine. They even went as far as to offer to leave me at home while they drove the lead car to show Vicki and James where Angel was. If they got caught, they were willing to say that they were acting without my knowledge.

Within my gut I had that same piercing feeling that I had as a child when my brothers would run into Mexico to see how far they could touch before coming back. Back then I knew the Border Patrol would catch them, and that is why I ran back home. This time I did not want to run away and break my arm.

I was ready to cross the line. We met Vicki and James just after sunset and the plan was for them to follow us to where Angel was waiting. When we pulled off to the side of the road, they would know to honk their horn and get out to wait for Angel. With no lights on the side of the highway and the sun long retreated, it was difficult to ascertain the exact location where we had left Angel earlier in the day. Riding down the highway was quite easy, as we were not the ones who would be transporting Angel to Tucson. It was Vicki and James who were at risk, yet their demeanor was as relaxed as if they were driving to pick up a relative to take them to a holiday dinner. The road was clear of Border Patrol agents, and the Minutemen had set up post well south of the compound. All was going as planned and I hoped I would not have to make any phone calls to search for legal representation for Vicki or James. If they were pulled over, they were going to say that they just found Angel on the side of the road and were not going to mention anything about us.

We pulled over and saw Vicki and James pull behind us and kill their lights. We drove on down the highway and spent the rest of the night sitting behind the Minutemen. As for Vicki, James, and Angel, they all made it back to Tucson safely, and eventually all three ended up safely with their families. There were still roughly 27 days left in the month of April, and that day would not be the last time I called James.

A strange sense of liberation comes with knowing that you can break the law. I am not talking about any physical rush brought on by adrenaline, but a mental sense of calm and peace. I had seen too many people suffering in the middle of the desert, all of whom had simply accepted no as an answer after the first time they asked for a ride. Angel was different – he was by far the closest to death of anyone I had ever seen, and this combined with his asking for a ride even after I said no really made me think about what the right course of action was. For too long I had hidden behind the law. I was too attached to my privileges to engage in the morally right action. Is giving someone a ride so that he does not die and can go on to support himself and his family really breaking the law? Or is the government breaking the law by refusing to allow people to enter and enacting policies that result in over four thousand bodies being discovered on the border? There were many free hours in the desert to ponder the answers to such questions.

The desert

Most days, the Minutemen would simply set up in an area that we lacked access to. Since Mrs. King had denied us access onto her land, we were unable to reach the state trust land where the Minutemen often set up. We drove into the city in order to find detailed maps that might show an entrance from a side road and thought that we had found a path. While my small Honda was not much for four-wheel driving through the desert, the husband of a cousin of mine who lives in Three Points offered to take a few of us out in his full-size Chevy truck.

We set out midday to search for the path that might get us onto the state trust land. Driving off of the highway and turning down dirt roads gave us an opportunity to appreciate the beauty and solitude of the desert. I grabbed onto the roll bar in order to keep from hitting my head on the ceiling and enjoyed the view of the small desert trees and bushes that rested in front of the Baboquivri Mountains. The Baboquivri Mountains separate Pima County from the Tohono O'odham Indian Reservation, and we crossed over reservation land looking for an alternative entrance.

The floor of the desert is covered with small rocks and dry, yellow grass placed in between the cacti, palo verde, and ocotillo trees. In each direction, there is a backdrop of small mountains and the open blue sky that my eyes so desperately miss when I am not in the Southwest. The desert sun is intense, but not like being in Phoenix. In the desert, you don't have the sun reflecting off the concrete; instead the foliage and desert floor absorbs it. It is still a deadly warmth in the summer months, but with an adequate amount of water in your system it feels like the sun is attempting to give life, not take it. The clouds are so close you feel you could have a conversation with them or the mountains that are a distance away but not blocked by large buildings. The quietness of the desert is occasionally broken by the violent sound of a Border Patrol helicopter flying overhead or the quick movement of a small rodent or bird.

The desert is the perfect location to think about the meaning of life and wonder why the majority of my time is spent between buildings walking on pavement. While my eyes have been fortunate to see the finest works of art in the Louvre, Musée d'Orsay, the Tate Modern, and the Anthropology Museum in Mexico City, I have yet to see a human creation that can rival the sense of beauty and calmness that emanates from the desert. I imagine, however, that when it is over 120 degrees and you are out of food and water, the desert is anything but beautiful.

Finding locked fences on the alternative paths, we headed back to the Minutemen's outpost and met up with the group of legal observers who were keeping eyes on the Minutemen. I had already received a call from legal observers that members of the media were waiting for an interview. After we had been sitting down for only a few minutes, a cameraman and reporter pulled up at our location. There were no markings on their vehicle, so I assumed it was an out-of-town crew using a rental car. With a rushed look on her face, the reporter walked briskly toward me and stuck her hand out to shake mine. "Hi, it's nice to meet you, we've been waiting to talk with you," she said.

"Sorry for keeping y'all waiting, who are you with?" I asked.

"We are with Fox News," she replied.

"Fox National?" I asked. She responded in the affirmative.

"Well, thanks so much for the opportunity," I said, "but I do not give interviews to Fox."

The reporter then went on the same rant that I had heard a few times before from the *Hannity and Colmes* crew, the *O'Reilly Factor*, and Lou Dobbs' staff after turning down requests for interviews from them. It seemed as if all the far-right wingers' lackeys went through the same training on how to get someone to appear on their shows. Fortunately, their appeals to educate their audience and get my ideas across to the "other side" were not a priority for me, so I persisted in denying her request.

Then she instructed her cameraman to start filming. "You predicted that the Minutemen were going to be violent, have you seen any violence out here?" she asked while sticking the microphone in my face. I looked at my cousin's husband and nodded my head – the universal sign to all Chicanos that it is time to leave. We started walking toward the truck and the cameraman and reporter followed us step-by-step while the reporter continued to pepper me with questions. I finally made it back into the truck while the cameraman placed the lens of his camera next to the window, paparazzi style.

"¡Qué pendejos!," said my cousin's husband as he started his truck and we drove off. As we drove down the Minutemen's line, he got his first glimpse of what the Minutemen looked like. He looked in amazement as we were only 20 minutes from his double-wide trailer and he was seeing gun-toting white people from out of state camped out searching for people that looked like him, his wife, and his young children. "I can't believe this is happening right here," he said.

He sported a shaved head and baggy pants and his clothes reminded me of the outfits I would don as a teenager before heading out to cruise the streets and listen to old school music and hip hop coming from the 12-inch speakers in the trunk.

"¿*Vas a ir a la marcha?*" he asked.

"I am not sure, I think I'll just stay out here," I responded to his question about whether or not I was going to be attending the march. April 10 was being promoted heavily in the Spanish-language media as a national day of action.

A historic immigrants' march in Phoenix

Street demonstrations were planned all across the country, and in Arizona there were marches planned in Douglas, Tucson, and Phoenix. In every radio, print, and television interview in Spanish, I was encouraging people to attend and was hoping that the turnout could surpass the 20,000 that took to the streets of Phoenix on March 24. While I desperately wanted to attend, I knew that everyone else did as well, and that would mean that there would be no legal observers out watching the Minutemen.

Hearing reports that the Minutemen were going to be heading to the marches to counter-protest put me a little more at ease, and I drove up to Phoenix early on the morning of April 10. The march was beginning at the Veterans Memorial Coliseum and I began to encounter traffic 15 blocks away from the venue. I had driven to the Coliseum on many occasions, but had never had an experience like this. For as long as I can remember, the coliseum has hosted the annual State Fair, and as a child I remember hustling out in front of the entrance on Thursdays. Thursday was wristband day, where for $20 you could buy a yellow wrist band that would give you free access to all rides, as opposed to having to buy tickets for each ride. My friends and I would wait outside of the exit and ask people who were leaving if they would give us their wristbands, or offer to buy them for $5. We would then sell the wristbands to those entering the park for anywhere from $10-$15 and pocket the profits. Inside, the coliseum held more special memories. It was on the coliseum's basketball court where I remember walking with tears in my eyes to shake hands with then-Phoenix Suns legend Kevin Johnson, who handed me a trophy for my team's second place finish in the Boys and Girls Club State Championship.

In the bumper-to-bumper traffic, I saw more than a few pickup trucks filled with Latinos dressed in white shirts with jubilant smiles, honking their horns. Today was not a day to cut someone else's lawn, lay tile on someone else's roof, or clean someone else's house. This day was about unity, love, and resistance. I finally found parking and made my way to the area where people were gathering. I passed families pushing their young children in strollers, couples holding hands, and people carrying signs opposing H.R. 4437. Perhaps because there were so many people in a small area, my cell phone was unable to make calls out, and after what seemed like the hundredth attempt, I finally got through to my mother and we were able to meet up.

Occasionally we read or hear a string of words that touch that inner chord and lead us to want to take action. On this day, the chords of over 200,000 people were reached, and it made a beautiful sound. Of course there were a small handful of counter-protestors there, and one of them I recognized was my buddy Timothy the Nazi. Timothy was standing alone at the intersection of 19th Avenue and Van Buren. I stood behind him, but was sure he did not recognize me; in fact I am sure he did not recognize anyone. He stood as still as a guard in front of the Queen's palace, with a stoic look emblazoned on his white face. There were so many people at this intersection that I began to feel claustrophobic after waiting for over fifteen minutes for the march to begin. In the time I was standing by Timothy, I did not hear a single person make a negative comment toward him or attempt to engage him in dialogue. While he stood still with his anti-immigrant sign draped over his shoulders, thousands of families marched east, first toward downtown Phoenix, and then west toward the Arizona State Capitol, and there was nothing that a neo-Nazi or anyone else could do to stop the masses. It was impossible for me to make it to the front of the march, so I simply strolled along somewhere in the middle. I was enjoying walking alongside people I had never met and was again happy to not see anyone I recognized. Jokes were told, and occasional chants were yelled, including the words, "*¡Sí se pudo!*"

I was getting text messages to make my way to the front of the line and finally figured out that I could cut through a side-street and wait for the beginning of the procession. I was surprised that the first line of marchers was well surrounded by a security detail that was pacing the speed of the march and ensuring that the path before the marchers was clear. After finally getting through the security detail, I took the traditional arm-in-arm position of the front row of marchers alongside congressmen, reverends, state legislators, and community leaders.

It did not take me long to realize that I would have felt more comfortable staying in the back. The lead marchers were not telling as many jokes as the people in the back, and their stern faces seemed staged for the cameras. Additionally, the attempts of the many bilingually challenged in the front to chant the Spanish slogans were hurting my ears. Finally, we arrived at the State Capitol and made our way to the stage. The small grass area in front of the stage was quickly filled, and it was interesting to see the masses simply keep marching and heading back to their cars as opposed to listening to the slew of speeches that were planned. I guess they figured the people had already spoken.

When I returned to the desert, I could not help but laugh at what now appeared to me to be the absolutely miniscule amount of volunteers the Minutemen had, or for that matter had ever had. Of all the anti-immigrant demonstrations, rallies, and patrols I witnessed, I probably only saw about 3,000 people. Nonetheless, the amount of damage that a handful of armed hate-mongers can do should certainly not be underestimated. There were still more than twenty days left in April.

Patrolling on State Trust Land

One effort to limit the Minutemen's patrols backfired. It was apparent from the maps we purchased that virtually all of the Minutemen's activities were occurring on state trust land and not private property. Under Arizona State law, one cannot enter state trust land without a special permit to hike, camp, hunt, or fish; simple permission from the leaseholder is not sufficient. I informed ACLU of Arizona Executive Director Alessandra Soler-Meetze of our discovery and sent her a draft of a letter to the Arizona State Land Commissioner asking him to remove the Minutemen from state trust land. Alessandra balked at the idea and was afraid that it would appear that the ACLU of Arizona was attempting to circumvent the Minutemen's First Amendment right to protest.

I made the argument to Alessandra that we were not telling the Minutemen that they could not march through city streets or have a rally in front of the State Capitol; rather, we were encouraging the State Land Commissioner to enforce the Arizona Constitution and prevent a hate group from unlawfully using state trust land to hunt for human beings. Nonetheless, Alessandra refused to allow the letter to be sent. I contacted members of the media and requested that they look further into the state trust land issue. About a week later, an employee of the Arizona State Land Department appeared at the front gates of King's Anvil Ranch. I recognized the emblem on the side of the truck and stood with my mouth open as he drove toward the Minutemen. All of us who were sitting in front of the ranch looked at each other and wondered if it was really about to happen. We had spent the past week talking about how wrong it was that the Minutemen were using state trust land and feeling upset that the ACLU of Arizona was not putting pressure on the State Land Department to take action. After a few minutes, we heard the following transmissions on the Minutemen's radio.

"This is Pineapple for Too Tough. Over."

"This is Too Tough, go ahead Pineapple, over," responded Simcox.

"Yeah, Too Tough, there is some guy here...uh, says he is from the state or something...says that we do not have permission to be out here, that we need to leave, over," responded Pineapple.

"What?" screamed Simcox into the radio.

"He says he is from the state, over."

"I'll be there in a minute," said an agitated Simcox. Silence was all that came from the radios, and I took out my newly-purchased cell phone and walked around excitedly looking for a spot where I could get more than one bar of reception. I began making calls to the newspaper reporters to tell them what had just happened. It was about 30 minutes later that we saw the dust being kicked up and a truck driving in our direction. We waited in front of the gate, and the Arizona State Land Department employee pulled off to the side and got out of his truck to grab a bottle of water out of the back of his camper. He appeared to be a little shaken up and I assumed he had just had his first intense encounter with some pissed off anti-government folks.

"Pretty tough crowd in there, huh?" I asked. He looked at me, puzzled, and I pointed to the radio and told him we had heard how upset the Minutemen were when they learned they did not have the proper permits to be on state trust land. I said, "I guess they just do not understand that even though the leaseholder gave them permission to be on the state trust land, they still need to apply for a permit and be engaging in a recreational activity. Plus, they are conducting a group activity and have not paid the proper group fee, and I seriously doubt they have the insurance as required for a group permit." The agent seemed to perk up; it was probably the first time in his life that anyone outside of his department had a working knowledge of the laws that he enforces on a daily basis.

"Right, this is state trust land and you need a permit to be out there. This ain't about politics—it is about enforcing the law as written," he replied.

"The law is the law," I responded. "I guess now they'll have to file the proper paperwork and wait in line like everyone else." The irony was just too much for me to resist. Just then we heard chatter on the Minutemen's radio.

"So what are we going to do, Too Tough?" asked a voice that sounded like Pineapple's.

A quick response came from Too Tough. "We are going to do the same thing that we do to all other idiots; ignore 'em."

"Oh, did you hear that, Simcox just said that they were not going to listen to you and they are going to stay there. So what happens now, do you call the Sheriff's Department to come out and enforce the law?" I asked the State Land employee.

"Well, normally folks just listen and do as told, but if they don't, then yes, you are correct, I am supposed to call the Sheriff's Department," he answered. I was not sure if it was he or I that was enjoying the conversation more about the intricacies of Arizona State Trust Land law more. After spending hours in the library a few years ago researching the law, reading over Barnett's contract, and trying to come up with arguments against renewing Barnett's lease, I was finally able to have a conversation with someone about laws that no one else really cared about.

"Well, I have the Sheriff's number here if you want to give him a call," I responded. "You could probably use the support, these are some really whacko, anti-government folks, and I wouldn't want them to take out their hate on you." Unfortunately, the employee did not want to raise more problems than he had already created, and given that it was getting late in the afternoon, he was probably just concerned with making it back to Tucson at a reasonable hour. I told him I would give him a call if the Minutemen were back on state trust land tomorrow and he politely gave me his card.

The next day the Minutemen were back on state trust land, so I called the agent but only got his voice mail. It was one of those intensely hot days were you roll up your sleeves and place your lawn chair in the shade underneath one of the small desert trees. The sun moves quickly, and it seemed that about every time I was getting comfortable, I would have to move the chair to a different spot to remain in the shade. At around 1 p.m., my phone rang, and it was my favorite reporter from *The Arizona Republic* newspaper. She informed me that the Arizona State Land Department was claiming it had made a mistake. Just then a Border Patrol truck whizzed by at what must have been over 80 miles per hour, and I had to ask the reporter to repeat the last part of what she had just said. The reporter had spoken with the State Land Department and the officials were now stating that they did not mean to send out one of their employees the day before. The leaseholders were claiming that they contracted with the Minutemen to pick up trash and fix fences on the state trust land, and they were therefore employees of King's Anvil Ranch.

The smiles and laughter of the day before were replaced with a sense of disappointment and frustration. Out of all the days we had been watching the Minutemen, we had never seen them come out with a single trash bag in the back of their pickups nor did they ever talk about repairing any fences. The phone rang again and this time it was a new reporter from the *Arizona Daily Star*, Brady McCombs. I had tipped off McCombs a few days earlier after getting his name from a columnist at the Daily Star whom I trusted. Unfortunately, the reporter with whom I had worked the year before was no longer with The Arizona Daily Star, and in retrospect, I probably should only have called the reporter whom I trusted.

McCombs had also heard that the State Land Department was claiming it was a mistake, and he asked how I felt. Still extremely upset, I went ahead and answered him truthfully. Of course, I should have realized that my comments would appear in the newspaper the next morning under an unsympathetic headline. "ACLU Unable to Oust Patrolling Minutemen," read the bold letters in the *Arizona Daily Star*. In the article, King—the leaseholder—called us misguided youngsters from out of town and was angry that the ACLU did not care about her constitutional right to property. The article was buried in the inside of the Tucson-based newspaper, and I was hoping that nobody would see it. My hopes did not last that long and I soon got a call from ACLU of Arizona Executive Director Alessandra Soler-Meetze.

Alessandra was upset that the article mentioned that the ACLU contacted the State Land Department the week before and asked if I had sent the letter. I told her I had not and that the reporter should not have said that we contacted the State Land Department the week before. Although I believed that we should have contacted them and mobilized a large amount of people to call them as well, I had not done so. Nonetheless, Alessandra was upset that I had told reporters that they might want to look into the issue and demanded that I give no more interviews, telling me instead to send all requests to her. It was the second time I was censured by the ACLU, but this time I had already grown tired of giving interviews, so it really was not much of an issue. The month was almost over, and I could not wait to get out of Arizona and back to the comforts of working under Will Harrell and the ACLU of Texas. The Minutemen were enjoying their momentary victory, and all smiled widely and waved as they drove by us after their morning shift.

Simcox was especially boisterous, as he rolled down his window and shouted, "Nice try, Ray. You're going to have to try a lot harder than that when messing with me—a lot harder." I simply smiled and wished him a nice day.

An unexpected guest

We drove back to the small, unfurnished house we were renting in Three Points to use the bathroom and recharge the batteries for the night shift. I was on the phone with James, who was driving down from Tucson, when we heard a knock at the door.

We were always careful when driving home and never went to the house if we even had the slightest suspicion that we were being followed. Of course, by this time in the month, we assumed that everyone knew where we were, as the house was used as our meeting location, and it was not uncommon to see 40 people around the house wearing legal observer t-shirts. In this small community of about 100 houses in the middle of the desert, it was certain that the new kids on the block were being talked about. I told James I would call him back and then asked Ryan if we were expecting anybody other than James for the night shift. He said no. We both looked at each other and Ryan walked to open the door. I stood back near the bedroom, after a few seconds Ryan turned back at me with a grin on his face and said, "You are not going to believe this."

I walked toward the door and outside I saw someone with disheveled hair, skin as dark as mine, and sleep still in his watery eyes, carrying a two-gallon jug filled with water. His wrinkled shirt, jeans covered with souvenirs from the desert and constant glances to the floor all suggested that he was a nervous migrant who had been walking in the desert for days. From his short, skinny frame, and mild voice I would have guessed he was from one of the southern states of Mexico, and I was leaning toward assuming Guerrero or Oaxaca. Still something just did not seem right. His water jug was already filled so he could not just be seeking water. All of the migrants I had talked to in the past said they only take the risky step of knocking on someone's door if they think they cannot go on because they are out of water. Additionally, he had knocked on the door only a few minutes after we had arrived, as if he was waiting for us to walk in the house.

"*¿Cómo le puedo ayudar?*" I asked him.

"I'm lost and I am hungry," he responded in Spanish while looking more at the pavement in front of the door than in my eyes.

"What's your name?" I asked as we continued our dialogue in Spanish.

"My name is Eusebio, I've been walking for four days and have not eaten for two days. I got lost from my group…."

Before he could finish his sentence, I cut him off. "How did you get the water?"

"The person at the house over there gave me the water," said Eusebio as he pointed west along the road on which we drove in. "It was kind of them to give me water, but she said that she had no food and told me to leave or she would call the Border Patrol."

"How many other houses have you knocked on?" I quickly asked.

"Just about all of them, but no one is home, you are only the second house that has answered." Given that it was around 4 p.m., it made sense that not a lot of folks would be at their houses, but I still was not sure if he was really a migrant or someone working for the government trying to figure out what we were really up to. I knew that the government had sent undercover agents to spy on Rev. John Fife and those involved in the Sanctuary Movement when they were assisting those fleeing from violence in Central America.

I had read stories and heard from people around Douglas that the Border Patrol uses undercover agents to pose as migrants in order to infiltrate smuggling rings. I had thought in the past few weeks that we were perhaps giving a little too much information about our actions over the radios. Knowing that members of the humanitarian group No More Deaths were being prosecuted for transporting migrants they had found in the desert to the hospital, my mind was still not at ease.

"How can we help you?" I asked Eusebio.

"I was hoping for some food and a ride," he replied. Just about every migrant I encountered in the desert first asked for a ride so I was not surprised by his request; however, I needed to talk with him a little bit more to dispel my uncertainty.

"We can give you food, but sorry, it is against the law to give you a ride," I told Eusebio. "Come on in and have a seat." Eusebio entered the house and took a seat on one of our luxurious lawn chairs that we carry with us from the desert into the living room. Ryan prepared some food for

Eusebio, and I took a seat next to him and continued to pepper him with questions.

"So where are you from?"

"I am from Oaxaca."

"What city in Oaxaca?"

"The capital, Oaxaca City."

"Were you born in Oaxaca City?"

"No, I was born in a small village in the mountains not far from Oaxaca City."

"What's the name of the small village?" He responded with an indigenous name that I could not pronounce and had never heard of. I was really wishing that I had made a trip to Oaxaca before and could ask him more questions about his native land, but unfortunately I was stuck. "What kind of work do you do?"

"I am a bricklayer. I was not earning a lot in Oaxaca, and my wife is expecting a baby. I told her I would come to the United States and save up enough money so that we can have a proper house to raise our child in," explained Eusebio. I tried quickly to think of more questions that would give me a better sense of whether or not Eusebio was being straightforward with me. Everything that popped into my head were questions that any good undercover agent would have an answer to: how much had he paid, where was he going, how did he get separated from his group, who is the mayor of Oaxaca City, what day is the big festival, who is the governor of Oaxaca. I was turning into a goddamn Mexican Federal or Municipal Agent trying to discern whether the person in front of them was really from a small village in southern Mexico or actually from Honduras or Guatemala.

Just then Ryan served Eusebio the plate of food he had prepared. Eusebio began eating as if someone was about to take the plate away from him and he would never get food again for the rest of his life. There was no thank you, or kind words that an undercover agent might have given in order to gain sympathy from the liberal do-gooders. Eusebio simply ate like a man who had not had a meal in days and was lost in a vast desert thousands of miles from everything and everyone he knew.

I walked into my room, closed the door, laid on my inflatable bed, and cried.

About 15 minutes later the front door burst wide open. My jaw dropped, and I thought I was about to be busted.

"What's up guys?" asked James.

Ryan and I laughed hysterically, "You scared the shit out of me man, didn't anybody teach you to knock!"

James looked around the room and his eyes fixated on Eusebio. "¿Qué tal?" he asked Eusebio. Eusebio responded that he was doing fine and then Scott addressed us. "Legal observers my ass!" James, who earlier in the month had assisted with another family reunification as previously mentioned, had no problem getting along with our new friend.

Eusebio came out of the shower with his hair slicked down, clean clothes, and sporting a large smile. Needless to say, James did not join us that night on patrol, and I heard that he and Eusebio had a nice, quiet dinner in Tucson.

"That was great"

The endings were not always joyous. A few days later we were again playing "move your chairs into the shade" on a sun-filled day. A discussion between Ryan and me was quickly halted when we heard over the Minutemen's radio that a migrant was seen south of station 10. We were by now accustomed to leaving our chairs under the bush and driving down the Minutemen's line only to later hear that the apparent sighting was actually a cow, rancher, or Border Patrol agent. I ran around the front of the car into the driver's seat while Ryan sat in the passenger side, turned the video camera to the on position and made sure the still camera was within his reach. He cupped the video camera in the palm of his hand as the dust storm my tires created engulfed stations one through nine. We arrived at Station 10 to find a migrant sitting in a lawn chair in the shade of a four-door, black F-350 with Colorado license plates. The Minutemen to whom this truck belonged were a white couple who appeared to be in their early 60s. The two had been with the Minutemen all month and were some of the few Minutemen to never give us a dirty look or say anything foul to us. The man and the woman were both still standing in the bed of their truck, each sporting small sidearms on the side of their hips. I stopped the car on the edge of the small dirt road and walked toward the man sitting in the shade of the truck. I got down on one knee to be at eye level with him, told him who we were and what we were doing, and then asked the standard questions.

"*¿Quieres agua, quieres comida?*" He answered that he wanted water but declined the offer for food. He gave his name as Miguel and said he was from the central state of Michoacán. A Minuteman from a different post arrived and jumped out of his jeep, and Ryan turned the camera in his direction. The burly man's face was covered with the long hairs of his salt-and-pepper beard, and his sunglasses covered just about the rest of the skin on his face. His suspenders ran over his disproportionably large belly, which was attempting to escape his skintight black shirt.

"Are you filming me?" he screamed at Ryan. The Minuteman was obviously perturbed, but I remained focused on Miguel, trying to make sure he was comfortable. I was also anxious to gain Miguel's trust and find out whether he was assaulted or directed to stop by the Minutemen. I remained on my knee talking with Miguel while the Minuteman laid into Ryan.

"I know my rights. Turn that camera off. You can't film me without my permission," stated the Minuteman.

"Actually, we are in a public area and I have the right to be filming," Ryan responded.

"No you don't, I know my rights, now turn that goddamn camera off," the Minuteman yelled.

"Well sir, I don't mean to make you upset, but I am going to keep this camera on."

"The hell you are not!"

I began translating the conversation for Miguel as by this time he was obviously interested in what was going on. I motioned for Ryan to turn the camera off and he did, much to the delight of the gun-toting Minuteman, who was probably not sure what his next show of bravado was going to be. A few other Minutemen arrived to enjoy their booty and take some prized pictures, which they would certainly show off back home. I could just imagine what they would be saying. "Look, here's the illegal we caught, that's one more job we saved for an American." I asked Miguel whether he had gotten lost from his group, but he explained that he had not.

"I do not have any money for a coyote, so I just decided to start walking through the desert on my own," stated Miguel. "Everybody said I needed a coyote, but I thought that with the love for my family in my heart I would be able to make it without one. I have three kids back home who I love and I will do anything to make their life better. I do not want them to suffer how I suffered." Miguel's eyes teared up, and he threw his head over the back of the chair and looked toward the large blue sky. "Dear God, what am I going to do? I do not have a peso, not a single peso. I had to sleep in the plaza in Altar because I ran out of money."

I told him about the migrant center in Altar, and then he asked what was going to happen to him when the Border Patrol came. I told him he would be taken in the Border Patrol's truck or van, fingerprinted and photographed and placed with other migrants in a holding cell. When there were enough migrants there they would load up the large bus with limo tinted windows and drive them back to the border. His look of confusion turned into a look of fear. He left three young children and his wife back home waiting for the financial support he promised. There was no way he could return to Michoacán after being gone for less than two weeks. Not only did he lack money for a coyote, but he lacked enough money for a meal after the Border Patrol dropped him back off across the border. I tried to conjure up some words to give him hope, and he responded by saying that if God wanted him to succeed then he would succeed. And if God did not want him to succeed, then it just was not meant to be.

When the Border Patrol arrived, I gave Miguel more food and water to put into his bag, and I heard a Minuteman yell something about aiding and abetting. The Border Patrol agent arrived and went through the routine. Miguel was ordered to stand up and walk to the truck. He grabbed his backpack and slung it around his left arm. He turned to the Minutemen in the bed of the truck and said, *"Gracias,"* and then looked at everyone else and repeated his thanks without the slightest hint of animosity or difference in gratitude for us or the Minutemen. As Miguel ducked his head and walked into the back of the truck, the Minutemen began to applaud. They yelled "thank you" to the Border Patrol agent, and he smiled back at them before turning on his diesel engine and driving away.

The month was still not over. On the last day of patrols for the month of April, I was hoping to enjoy a calm, peaceful send-off. The Minutemen had planned for their final patrol to end at 4 p.m., and I was constantly looking at the sun, hoping it would move quickly across the sky. The Minutemen's numbers were exceptionally low and we counted only nineteen people on patrol. Amongst the patrollers were four new G.I. Joes. While most all Minutemen carried firearms, there were only a select few that earned the title of "G.I. Joe Minutemen." There was no need to debate amongst ourselves whether or not these four were deserving of special attention. Dressed in matching military-style khaki pants and army green long-sleeved shirts, the four appeared to be in their late twenties or early thirties. All wore dark sunglasses and stood over six feet tall. With their survivalist demeanor and guns strapped to their thighs, it was certain that they did not come simply to sit in lawn chairs. It was probably safe to assume they were either ex-military or still in the armed forces. It was probably also safe to assume that they were not organized neo-Nazis from the National Alliance. At least the African-American G.I. Joe was probably not. I sat in the passenger seat of my car, and the only sound I could hear was the cracking of the peanut shells in my mouth. I was dreaming of the city and could not wait for 4 p.m. to say a final goodbye to the Minutemen and drive to Tucson to get Indian food. I was thinking of what I wanted to scoop up with my garlic naan and had it down to saag aloo and palak paneer.

My thoughts of food were put on hold when over the radio we heard a deep voice whispering about sightings of migrants south of station nine. "Isn't that where the G.I. Joes set up?" I asked Ryan.

"I'm afraid so, buddy," responded Ryan as he closed the driver's-side door and went to start the car.

As soon as station one saw us they gave the familiar warning that I was tired of hearing, "Here comes the ACLU!" I had survived three long months of only listening to the two-way radio and resisting all impulses to hold down the button and respond. We spotted the G.I. Joes standing between a row of thorn-filled bushes with binoculars in hand. It was probably impossible for the migrants to even notice that they were being closely observed. We decided to drive down a smaller road heading south to warn the migrants of what they were about to run into.

As soon as we got out of the car, we could see two bodies walking toward the Minutemen at station ten. About 50 yards south of station ten was a man wearing a blue baseball cap, a long-sleeved white t-shirt, and carrying a backpack. Next to him was a heavier set woman with a black jacket covering her arms and her frizzy, bleached blonde hair pushed back in a ponytail.

As the couple approached the Minutemen the man with the backpack spoke first, *"Hola."*

"*Buenos días,*" added the woman before the man could finish saying hello.

"We are lost," added the man as they continued to move toward the Minutemen.

"Please, help us," said the woman.

I hustled over to where the Minutemen were at, and as I was walking up I heard an armed Minuteman standing on top of the camper of his camouflaged pickup truck speaking to his fellow Minuteman. "Just ask 'em to sit down and take a break. We'll get 'em taken care of."

"Uh huh," responded the man with the backpack, who obviously understood what the Minuteman said. He translated for his partner. I looked to the south and there appeared to be more people walking out of the desert.

In the distance appeared four figures, the darkness of their skin seeming to match their dark clothing. One of the figures was noticeably smaller than the other three, standing only as high as the knees of the shortest person in the distance.

"*Mira un niño, no bueno,*" said the Minuteman standing next to the migrants in very bad Spanish.

"We were going to Arizona, but we got lost."

"*Muy cansado el niño,*" responds the Minuteman.

"*Sí,*" was the unanimous response. Everyone could tell that the young child was tired.

I began to speak to the migrants. "We are with human rights, against the vigilantes, have you heard of the vigilantes?" The migrants all responded in the affirmative. "Well, these are them," I stated, pointing to the Minutemen.

"Take us to where you are going," pleaded the woman, with a sense of desperation in her voice.

I told the migrants not to worry, that we had our video cameras and the vigilantes would not do anything to them. "So they won't take us," asked the woman. I told her that when we are around they do not take people, but that unfortunately we are not around all the time so we cannot really be sure what they do when we are not there. "Is it still far to the highway? To Arizona?"

"Well, we are in Arizona, but the big highway is still far away," I answered. The piercing sound of the approaching baby's crying fills the silence that had followed my response.

"They have telephones," said one of the men who had recently joined the group from what appeared to be out of nowhere.

"Tell them to let us borrow one, so we can call," said the woman, with a note of excitement.

"Well, the problem is that they already called the Border Patrol," I stated as the woman sighed a breath of fear. "I think in 15 minutes the Border Patrol will be here. You have the right to keep walking, but I think…."

"No," responded the short, chubby man with a moustache who had just walked up. As we were speaking, the mother of the baby, a short woman wearing a black beanie just above her hair that was wrapped in a bun above her neck, crouched to the ground and her young child walked behind her and grabbed onto her neck while continuing to wail. A tall, skinny migrant who appeared to be in his late teens softly caressed the baby's head as the mother stood upright.

With the baby safely on her back, the woman bent to the ground to pick up a piece of cloth and wrapped it once around her waist, covering the buttocks and legs of the young baby. She pulled the long ends of the cloth over her shoulders, and the cloth made a cross just above her breasts as she reached behind her back to tie a knot with the remaining ends of the cloth.

The group became excited when I told them that we were already in Arizona. "So how far is the highway?" the man with the backpack asked. We were surrounded by small highways, and I was not sure which one he was talking about.

"Are you trying to walk to Tucson or to Phoenix?" I asked.

"*A Tucson,*" answers one of the men, pronouncing the letter c. They were trying to figure out how much farther they had to keep walking, and I was not looking forward to giving the answer, as I too often remember the looks on the faces of migrants when they hear that they are still days away from reaching their destination.

"It's about a day and a half more of walking," I stated, as the entire group sighed in unison. When they asked the distance to Phoenix, I guessed that it would be about three more days of walking. Some looked immediately to the ground, and the woman standing directly in front of me rolled her eyes to the sky and gasped for air before stating, *"Ay, muchacho."*

A soft rumble drew our attention to the empty sky to the east. "That's the Border Patrol's helicopter, it will be here in a few minutes," I told the group.

"Why did you call them?" asked one of the migrants to the Minuteman. The Minuteman who claimed to speak Spanish and had been somewhat conversing with the migrants until then all of the sudden acted as if he did not know what he was asked.

So I helped translate. "He asked why you called the Border Patrol."

The chatty Minuteman did not have a quick response and all he could come up with was, "that's our job."

Simultaneously, the same migrant who asked the first question asked another question, but this time in English, "Are you going to call my mom?" The chubby man with the white shirt began to laugh at his own question and the Minuteman did not respond.

Since there appeared to be at least one member of the group who was interested in confronting the white guys with the guns standing in front of them, I decided to ask a few more questions. The noise of the helicopter was getting louder, and I knew it would only be a few minutes before the Border Patrol arrived.

"So how come you wanted to come to the United States?" I asked the group.

"To work," answered three of the migrants, one after another.

"Necessity," answered two others. "To move ahead."

The young man got to his feet and stated, "If there was work there then we would not come here."

"I sympathize with these guys," stated the Minuteman. "I've worked with them before."

"Then why is he turning us in," responded one of the women.

"As you can see, I speak a little bit of Spanish," said the Minuteman, looking at me instead of the migrants. "And I didn't get it from sitting on my butt; I worked with Hispanics all my life, *toda mi vida*."

"We don't want to do anything bad. We just want to arrive, work, and move ahead. Move our family in Chiapas ahead," said the chubby man, gesturing toward the small baby. The woman with the pink polo shirt raised her right hand to wipe a tear off the cheek of the mother carrying her baby and smiled into her eyes as if to say, "Don't worry, everything will be okay." She then used her other hand to wipe a tear falling from her own cheek. By now it was almost impossible to hear the person standing next to you as the Border Patrol helicopter was hovering directly in front of us, nearly blowing the hat off of my head.

Ryan handed out food, juice, and water to the group, and I tried to tell them not to worry – that the Border Patrol will treat them well.

"That's not true," responded the woman with the frizzy hair. "When we get to the station, they throw everything we have in the trash. The water, they just dump it on the floor." The woman made a kicking motion to show how the Border Patrol kicks sleeping migrants to wake them up. She winced in pain and said, *"Ay, no."* The chubby man asked the woman to show me her leg. She was initially embarrassed, but she handed her water and food to her friends and pulled her left pant leg above her knee.

The red lines ran up, down, and sideways from the top of her sock to her kneecap, leaving one to wonder what it must feel like to have your jeans rubbing against the cuts with every step that you take. I kneeled down to take a closer look, but she shied away when I asked to take a photo. I explained that people have to see what it is like to cross in the desert, and eventually she agreed. As I was cleaning her wounds, everyone turned to the east to see another dark-skinned young man with a backpack walking out of the desert. The helicopter finally left and the desert was once again silent as the migrants ate their food and waited for the arrival of the Border Patrol. "Are the others still out there?" I hear one of the migrants ask the young man who had just come out of the desert.

"Yes," responded the exhausted young man slowly and quietly, his eyes remaining fixed on the vast desert he had just walked out of. His hair was a mess and a small patch on the back stood straight up, showing how he must have laid on his back on the desert floor the night before.

A truck door slammed and someone yelled in Spanish, "How many are there?" The baby began to cry again as one of the migrants counted the bodies around him and responded that there were eight.

"With the baby?" asked the Border Patrol agent.

"Nine with the baby," answered back the migrant.

"We walked a lot…we walked up, and we walked down… one day we are going to cross," said the teenager, pushing his long bangs behind his ears and cupping his hands behind his head as he leaned back against the telephone pole.

"One day, but not today," said the woman with the frizzy hair as she laughed and choked on her food.

"Maybe one day you won't have to walk through the desert to work," I stated.

"That would be better," said the woman.

The young man uncrossed his hands, and his smile disappeared as he crouched back down to the dirt and said, "Three nights and two days."

"Three days and two nights in the trash can, for nothing," chimed in a short, chubby woman with a baseball cap and a backpack.

The Border Patrol agent had left and the baby continued to cry.

I asked the man with the white, long-sleeved shirt and backpack if this was his first time in the United States. He responded that he had been here before and had worked in construction in Delaware. "Before it was one night to cross. Now it is three nights…three days…and one more, four nights." With more agents and technology put on the border each year, migrants are forced to cross in even more remote areas, making the journey continually longer and deadlier. No longer can the journey be made in one night, and as it becomes more difficult to cross the border, more people are deciding not to return home. While migration was traditionally circular, in that people would work in the United States and then return home only to cross again at a later date, people are now forced to stay in the United States and look for a way to bring the rest of the family to join them. Hence an increase in women and children crossing the border.

The Minuteman called my name and asked me how much water the migrants were carrying. I ignored him and remained focused on my conversation. Finally, he decided to address one of the migrants, asking in Spanish if they had more water and whether it was enough for two days. "Yes," responded the man I was talking to. "We have six liters."

The Border Patrol agent returned and told the migrants to get in the truck. He ordered two of the women and the baby to get in the cab with him and told the others to sit in the open cab in the back.

"Hey guys, thank you," stated the Border Patrol agent to the two Minutemen.

"Thank you," they responded.

"Good deal. We'll go ahead and take it from here," said the Border Patrol agent.

The Minuteman asked if the Border Patrol were the ones that called in the chopper, and the agent responded in the affirmative.

While the Minuteman and Border Patrol agent were talking, the short chubby woman with the backpack slowly moved toward the back of the truck. Unable to bend her knee, she dragged her left foot behind her and was having obvious difficulty jumping into the back of the raised truck. The man with the long-sleeved, white shirt jumped out of the bed of the truck and assisted the woman in clearing the tailgate, which was a few inches higher than her head.

"You guys get anything, give us a call, we are in the area," said the agent to the Minuteman. "That was great."

Reviewing the videotape of this incident further etched the screams of the young baby into my mind. I rewound those last words of the Border Patrol agent and listened to them multiple times. "That was great." How far have we come as a nation, as a civilization, to consider such an event "great"?

Chapter Ten

Walking through the Desert

It was an extremely tough way to end the month. The Border Patrol drove off taking the eight people and the baby, and we quickly moved our location farther away from the Minutemen. The roaring of the chopper was long gone, and in a matter of minutes the desert returned to its peaceful existence. I needed to be alone, so I walked north of the dirt road down a slightly worn path that the migrants probably would have used to keep walking. I soon found myself surrounded by the blooming ocotillo trees and thin green bushes. The only external sounds were the occasional rustling of the wind through the desert foliage, but it was the cries of the young baby that filled my mind. Over and over again, the wailing of the young child repeated. The baby might not remember being carried across the desert, but for the rest of her life her options would be limited regardless of the fact that she had no control over where she was taken as an infant. If they made it to a community in the United States, the child could graduate first in her class, become president of the National Honor Society, an all-state track star, prom queen, and then graduate summa cum laude from the most prestigious college in the nation and would still be unable to get a job because she did not have a social security card. Perhaps she will some day dream of being a doctor, lawyer, politician, social worker, or school teacher, but will be unable to contribute to society because she lacks a certain number. I am completely skipping over the difficulty of having to get a driver's license, board an airplane, pay for college without federal financial aid, and the many other obstacles faced by the thousands of individuals who were brought across the line at a young age, many of whom have no recollection of their "native" country. Or consider the trepidation you would feel as a ten year-old child if you came home from school to an empty house and later learned that your parents had been deported during a workplace raid during the day. These and other injustices are an unfortunate reality in the era that we live, in and it is somehow acceptable for the government to kidnap someone from the community they live in. I've heard stories about mothers who were still breastfeeding their young babies being deported and not being allowed to even see their child before being treated like a criminal and removed from the country.

To assist young people who lack documentation many have championed the DREAM Act. While the DREAM Act has been put forth in different forms, the idea is federal legislation that would allow young people who were law abiding and are pursuing higher education or the military a chance to legalize their status. A common slogan used by activists is that children should not have to suffer for the sins of their parents. While I fully support a pathway for anyone to legalize their status, I find rhetoric such as the proceeding "sins of their parents" quite troublesome. Youth should not be forced to demonize their parents by referring to their being brought to this country as something negative. The parents of undocumented youth simply wanted what every parents wants, a better future for their children. DREAM Act students should be proud that their parents sacrificed leaving the land and country they were so familiar with in order to give them a better life. Instead of quick slogans that seek to veil dream act students with pure innocence, the focus on the bigger picture should not be lost. Indeed, the granting of "Deferred Action" to some undocumented people between the ages of 15-30 should not stop people from fighting for the rights of all undocumented people, regardless of their age when they entered the country, whether or not they have a squeaky clean past, and how old they are today. The Deferred Action program offered by the Obama administration does not contain a path to residency or Citizenship; it does not confer any rights to those currently undocumented. Instead, it gives work authorization to those who qualify and is a promise from the government that the people granted deferred action will not be deported while the program is in existence. While we can celebrate a promise to not temporarily deport someone, we must also demand a process through which all can legally remain in the country.

We must not forget the comment the young man made minutes after being stopped by the Minutemen, "*Un día vamos a cruzar.*" Translated those five simple words means, "One day, we are going to cross." He spoke the words with a sense of hope, displaying the resilience of the human spirit. Here he was, a young man from Chiapas with nothing but a backpack on his shoulders and the clothes on his body just having been defeated by the biggest, baddest, most militaristic government in the world—a government that spends billions of dollars on underground sensors, camera towers, fencing, helicopters, humvees, night vision technology, thousands of well-armed agents, all with the aim of keeping him from crossing the border. He had just walked through a desert that has taken thousands of lives and came upon a group of gun-toting crazies, yet his sense of hope was not crushed. It was almost as if he was saying, "Go ahead and try to keep me out, put up some more fences, hire more agents; I'll still find a way to get across. You may have a temporary victory today, *pero un día vamos a cruzar.*"

The fallout of the Minutemen

Years have passed, and I no longer train people to follow the Minutemen. Thankfully, my good friends the Minutemen self-imploded. The small group of rag-tag, right-wing whackos became too popular for their own good. Donations poured in from across the country, and it was not long before infighting over the money tore the organization apart. As briefly mentioned in Chapter Eight, numerous Minuteman leaders and volunteers began questioning the whereabouts of hundreds of thousands of dollars in donations to the Minutemen. The challenge to the organization's leadership over financial accountability became public, and the organization fell apart. I found it interesting to read an article in *The Washington Times* by Jerry Seper, essentially detailing the downfall of the Minutemen. A few years back, I wrote a report while working for the ACLU that showed how Seper's reporting in *The Washington Times* inflated the number of participants in the Minutemen Project and gave the impression they were a much larger group than what they actually were. Seper's 2010 article mentioned how Simcox allegedly threatened to kill his wife, their three children, and any police who came to protect them. It quoted former Minuteman Bob Wright, who you may remember as old "Chrome Dome" who was running the patrols in New Mexico, as saying that Simcox should be "pitied for [the] personality disorder that has brought him to such shame." Always giving Simcox more than an opportunity to say whatever was on his mind, Seper reported that Simcox blamed the success of the Minuteman Project for his "falling short in all my relationships, most notably my duty to my wife and family." He said his primary duty now is to "get my whole person behind my nexus of love, my feelings, my thoughts, my actions - my God and my family come first." Although Simcox was still somewhat popular on the speaking circuit and politicians sought his endorsement, that pretty much came to an end when the domestic violence charges came to light. While for a few years Simcox remained outside of the media spotlight, in 2013 he was arrested and charged with two counts of molestation of a child, two counts of sexual conduct with a minor, and one count of attempted molestation of a child. According to the Phoenix Police Department, he was arrested because there was probable cause to believe he had sexual conduct with girls who were under the age of ten.

The other co-founder of the Minuteman Project, Jim Gilchrist, also ran unsuccessfully for political office. He is less crazy than Simcox and has yet to have any major meltdowns, but the infighting reached him as well when supporters attempted to oust him as President of the Minutemen and the fight eventually went into the courts. After being victorious in court, but losing civil defamation lawsuits, a recent report alleged that he now spends his time attempting to sell his endorsement to political candidates. As published in *Politico.com*, three Republican campaigns that sought Gilchrist's donation that refused to hire a consulting firm closely linked to Gilchrist, lost out on his endorsement. In one campaign, Gilchrist went on to endorse the rival candidate. The article quoted a radio host who interviewed Gilchrist about endorsing the candidate with a less stringent record on immigration as saying, "Jim Gilchrist and his Minuteman organization is a sham front group that is clearly selling endorsements to whoever will buy them."

Some of the other Minutemen members mentioned in this book have not hidden from public view after an embarrassing scandal or attempted to simply earn a few dollars from their new fame. Laine Lawless, mentioned in Chapter Six when she claimed I inserted a "white power" chant into the documentary I co-wrote and co-produced, now spends her time trying to defend the senseless killings orchestrated by her vigilante friend Shawna Forde. Tired of following the protocol of the Minutemen, or if you believe the Minutemen, she was kicked out of the group for erratic behavior, Forde decided to form a different border vigilante group, the Minutemen American Defense (MAD). Forde told a reporter that MAD was not a group who sat in lawn chairs, rather they were a vital militarized outfit that runs recon missions in the desert. On May 30, 2009, Forde orchestrated an attempted robbery of a house she believed belonged to a drug dealer. Her plan was to rob the house and use the proceeds for her vigilante group. Forde, Jason Bush, and Albert Gaxiola posed as immigration agents and stormed the house, but found neither drugs nor money. Instead, they ended up shooting and killing nine year-old Brisenia Flores and her father Raul Flores. Brisenia's mother was also shot, but survived only because she pretended to be dead. After trials in Pima County Superior Court, which included heart-wrenching testimony from Brisenia's mother, Forde, Bush, and Gaxiola were all convicted for murdering Brisenia and her father, amongst other charges. On February 22, 2011, Forde was sentenced to death, as was Bush a few months later. Gaxiola ended up receiving life without the possibility of parole.

While Forde and Bush await executions from the State, another vigilante decided to take his own life, but not before he savagely killed a few others. Jason Todd Ready, who was the individual mentioned in Chapter Six when Laine Lawless claimed I inserted a white power chant after his speech, went on to form his own vigilante group called U.S. Border Guard. Dressed in full camouflage and carrying high powered assault rifles, Ready's group certainly presented the image of a bunch of loons out looking for trouble. Ready had previously tried his hand at local politics and was mentored by SB 1070 co-author Russell Pearce. After unsuccessfully running for a seat in the Arizona House of Representatives in 2004 and for a City Council seat in the City of Mesa, a suburb of Phoenix, in 2006, Ready shed his mainstream politics disguise and self-identified as a Neo-Nazi. On May 2, 2012, Ready shot and killed four people in a domestic dispute, before taking his own life. Among the victims were Ready's girlfriend, her daughter, her daughter's boyfriend, and a fifteen-month-old toddler. Ready had previously referred to the toddler as being "half-ugly" because of her half Latina heritage. At the home Ready was living in, agents found military-issued grenades, police and Nazi uniforms, white supremacist propaganda, and assault-style rifles.

Neither Forde's or Ready's murders were surprising to me. What is surprising is that more violent acts have not been attributed to any of the vigilante groups. I know these crazies have perpetrated other acts of violence, but they have simply not been caught by law enforcement. As long as the government encourages these groups to patrol the border, by responding to their calls for assistance and refusing to arrest them for unlawful imprisonment, impersonating law enforcement officers, and other crimes, the vigilante groups will persist. While their numbers are dwindling given what happened to Forde and Ready, the vigilante issue nonetheless remains a reality for those trying to cross the U.S.-Mexico border. Instead of it being the media-hungry Minutemen, there are now only fringe groups of Neo-Nazis that patrol alongside the federal government.

After the leadership fell apart, the volunteers who did not start their own vigilante killing squads essentially morphed into the Tea Party. In 2010, a group of us protested a Tea Party meeting along the border, and it was essentially a reunion, watching the same people attend the Tea Party meeting that attended the Minutemen Project. It doesn't make sense to me how people who are supposed to be about less taxes and less government advocate for billions more to be spent on the border, but there were the same people heading into the meeting.

While I am grateful the majority of the Minutemen are no longer patrolling the border, I do have to give them credit for increasing the anti-immigrant sentiment in Arizona, and throughout the nation. Essentially, the Minutemen mainstreamed hate. By taking the bold action of taking guns to the border, the Minutemen further polarized the immigration debate and moved it much farther to the right. Their radical, drastic action created a space that made it politically acceptable for politicians to put forth anti-immigrant proposals. Despite initially being very small in numbers, the Minutemen were successful in creating the image that the "crisis" was so bad that private citizens needed to go to the border to stop the "invading, criminal Mexicans." Nothing is farther from the truth, but political theater is not based on facts, but perception.

Arizona's assault on immigrants

Thus, the modern Arizona was born. Politicians realizing that the anti-immigrant sentiment was the new ticket to national fame quickly rode the Minuteman wave. When the Minutemen left the desert, it did not take long for elected officials in Arizona to take over the assault on immigrants under the auspices of attrition through enforcement. The idea of "attrition through enforcement" was developed by anti-immigrant Mark Krikorian. The idea is essentially that undocumented immigrants will "self-deport" if their day-to-day life is made more difficult by government officials and the private industry at all levels. Essentially, what the anti-immigrant crowd wants is a police state where you are snitched on by your local school teacher, librarian, employer, or neighbor, if you cannot affirmatively prove your immigration status.

The slow development of the attrition through enforcement strategy in Arizona can be seen as beginning in 2006. However, the origins of this can be pushed back ten years, to 1996, when then Motor Vehicle Division Director Russell Pearce proposed and successfully achieved denying driver licenses to those unable to prove legal status. In addition to the previously mentioned Barnett Bill that took away punitive damages for undocumented immigrants, another ballot initiative was approved by 78 percent of those who voted in 2006. This initiative denied bail for immigrants charged with serious felonies. Soon after, the Arizona State Legislature passed into law A.R.S. 13-2319, the state's anti-smuggling statute. It would not be long before former Maricopa County Attorney Andrew Thomas —who unsuccessfully ran for State Attorney and was eventually disbarred— began charging those who were crossing the desert with conspiring to smuggle themselves into the country and thereby charging immigrants —not just the coyotes— with a "serious" felony. This meant that even if they wanted to fight their case, they would need to remain in jail as opposed to being let out on bail.

The assault continued with Proposition 300, which denied the benefits of in-state tuition, a lower price than those from out of state have to pay, to undocumented youth, no matter how long they had been living in Arizona. In 2007, the Arizona State Legislature passed the Legal Arizona Worker's Act, which was upheld by the U.S. Supreme Court despite a vigorous challenge. While there have been relatively few prosecutions under the new law that was supposed to punish employers for hiring undocumented workers, the idea of "attrition through enforcement" was solidified in the preamble of S.B. 1070. The *Support Our Law Enforcement and Safe Neighborhoods Act*, more commonly referred to as SB 1070, was signed into law by Arizona Governor Jan Brewer on April 23, 2010. At the time of its passing, it was referred to as the broadest and strictest anti-immigrant piece of legislation in modern history. While there are various facets of the legislation, the piece that got most of the attention was the requirement that law enforcement officers attempt to determine an individual's immigration status during a "lawful stop, detention or arrest" when there is reasonable suspicion that the individual is an "illegal" immigrant. Civil rights organizations mobilized quickly to file lawsuits against S.B. 1070, but it was the intervention of the federal government that got most of the attention. The United States Department of Justice filed suit to prevent Arizona from enforcing some aspects of the law. Their argument is legally known as "pre-emption" which pretty much means, "Hey, Arizona, it's our job to arrest and deport undocumented immigrants, not yours." And oh has the federal government been busy doing just that.

The role of the Federal Government

While the attention is focused on S.B. 1070 and similar pieces of attrition through enforcement legislation across the country that followed, the fact that the Obama Administration has been deporting more people than previous administrations remains a side-note. A 2011 article from the *Los Angeles Times* reported that the Obama administration deported a record number of undocumented immigrants for the third straight year, with the latest year having a whopping 396,906 deportations. While recent pundits claim the Obama administration has been misrepresenting the number of deportations by including people who were sent back across the border without a formal deportation, the fact remains that other dramatic changes have occurred under President Obama's watch. As if it is not enough to simply rip someone from their family and deport them, the federal government has also dramatically increased prosecutions against undocumented immigrants. Yes, instead of deportation being enough punishment a record number of people are also being put behind bars for "illegal entry" or "illegal re-entry" into the country. According to the Transactional Records Access Clearinghouse at Syracuse University, "illegal re-entry" is the number one crime that federal prosecutors now charge. The report further stated that between 2002 and 2008, prosecutions for first-time illegal entry in district courts that line the border increased 330 percent. Prosecutions against immigrants are so vigorous that data from the U.S. Sentencing Commission showed that Latinos made up 50.3 percent of those sent to federal prison despite being only 16 percent of the U.S. population during the first nine months of fiscal year 2011.

If anyone doubts the numbers, they need only come to the federal courthouse in Tucson any weekday at 1:30 p.m. to watch Operation Streamline. Brought straight from the desert, some having walked more than a week and being near death, 70 immigrants a day are brought into the special proceedings courtroom on the second floor of the federal building. Attorneys are allowed three hours in the morning to meet with five to six clients, explain to them the U.S. criminal system, identify any possible defenses, and ultimately inform them of the option to plead guilty to illegally entering the country at 1:30 p.m. I previously represented people in Operation Streamline, and some of my clients have been from small villages where Spanish is rarely spoken and have only a few years of education. While those who speak indigenous languages in Mexico are supposed to have their cases dismissed, there have been occasions where hearings have been put off for weeks so that an interpreter can be found to explain to the person who was simply seeking work why they will be put in federal prison for up to 180 days.

While my clients are shackled at their feet and handcuffed, I make my best effort to explain to them that they are caught-up in a political battle where the federal government is trying to show the public that they are being tough on immigrants. I listen to their reasons for crossing the border, sick family members, hungry children, a desire to work for a few months to save enough money to build a house for their family; sometimes we cry together, and in the end the decision is almost always to plead guilty. Despite the fact that there are ways to "win" the case, the person would have to stay in a federal detention center, likely run by the private prison company Corrections Corporation of America, longer than it would take to even get a trial. The government makes the plea offer in a strategic manner, so they get the benefit of another conviction while the immigrant gets less prison time than they would if they fought the case. There are others who have no legal defenses and are sentenced to six months in prison, all for trying to get to this country to reunite with their families or find work.

Governments have for years made efforts to keep people from exercising their freedom of movement, and undoubtedly they will search for more creative ways to fortify borders and make life more difficult for those living inside the country. The United States has contracted with private corporations such as Boeing, and the border is turning into a playground and new profit maker for the defense industry. The Wackenhut Corporation contracts with the government to transport migrants caught in the desert to detention centers, and I imagine it will not be long until the Border Patrol is replaced or augmented by private soldiers.

Putting morality into the immigration discussion

From following crazies in the desert to sitting in a courtroom and explaining to immigrants that the federal government is sending them to prison for being poor and from the other side of the border, I've seen a lot of hate and dehumanization in the past decade. Arizona has gone from punishing immigrants for attempting to earn a livelihood and has now even gone as far as attempting to ban the history of all Latinos, not just those without documents. Shortly after signing S.B. 1070, Governor Jan Brewer signed H.B. 2281, which bans classes in public schools that advocate ethnic solidarity, promote overthrow of the U.S. government, or cater to specific ethnic groups. This was a specific attack on the successful Mexican-American Studies (MAS) program in the Tucson Unified School District (TUSD), and it is the only program that has been targeted by Arizona Attorney General Tom Horne and his successor, John Huppenthal. Caving into pressure from the state government, the TUSD school board voted against appealing a decision from an administrative law judge that found the MAS program in violation of the Arizona law. I was present at the meeting, as were hundreds of others in opposition to the destruction of the MAS program, and not a single person spoke against appealing. Speaker after speaker pointed out the independent study that found the MAS program did not promote the overthrow of the government and instead increased students' overall scores and chances of pursuing college. Students of the program spoke in favor of appealing the negative decision as did policy makers and parents. Despite the overwhelming support for appealing the decision, the school board voted to not appeal, effectively ending the MAS classes and leading to the books used in those courses being boxed-up and taken out of the classrooms. This banning of the books has received international attention, and students have not sat by idly as their education and history is attacked. What board members failed to realize is that drastic moves such as taking away books and banning courses will simply radicalize youth more and encourage them to take bolder steps against those in authority.

    Bolder steps against the oppressors in positions of power are exactly what we need, and we need it now. People in positions of power will not stop the oppression toward our communities until they feel the pushback from the grassroots. Arizona has been slowly turning up the heat, with each new anti-immigrant or anti-Latino act increasing the temperature. Until the grassroots creates a level of chaos that matches the level of insanity put forth by those in positions of power, the anti-immigrant actions and sentiments will only slowly get worse. Attempts to reach the "hearts and minds" of those in the middle have not worked. We don't need better talking points to reach those in the middle; we need bold actions with the "radical" demand that all people have the right to live, love, and learn wherever they please.

The people on the right are not afraid of being bold in their demands. Be it cries for a "stronger" border, greater interior enforcement, or banning of books, the idea is still the same. Let's use the power of the nation-state and local governments to make life more difficult for other human beings so they will either not come into our country or they will leave. Not only does this concept violate the "Golden Rule," it is just simply disgusting to think that people spend their time and our resources on figuring out more ways to make the lives of other human beings worse. Why not spend all of that time and energy instead on looking for ways to create jobs or re-structure economies so people would not be forced to leave their countries of origin? How about figuring out how to build more bridges instead of more fences? Why do we not figure out how to create ways to build community and lessen the xenophobia and racism as opposed to kicking people out?

In short, let's put morality into the immigration discussion.

On the moral scorecard, how is the United States doing right now? Well, over 4,000 people have died trying to cross the U.S.-Mexico border in the past 14 years since the implementation of the operations shifted migrants into remote, inhospitable areas. Border residents with dark skin are consistently treated as criminals and racially profiled despite many having roots in the area that pre-date the United States of America's acquisition of the lands. Young people are denied opportunities to contribute to society because they lack a social security card, and mothers and fathers have been extracted from their families for simply going to work. Each workplace raid separates families and negatively impacts the lives of thousands of people, while a more heavily militarized border has kept migrants from returning home to visit a sick loved one or attend their parent's or child's funeral. Meanwhile, the entire country benefits from the sweat and labor of the undocumented immigrants we demonize, and more people can afford to purchase homes, eat out at restaurants, and vacation. If every U.S. citizen spent a day considering how undocumented migrants have contributed to the quality of life enjoyed in this country, then perhaps immigration would not be seen as charity but as a benefit. Imagine having to make a list of every single thing in your daily life that has been put in your hands after having been touched by an undocumented worker. There is a good chance that the sheets, pillow cases, and your clothes that say "Made in the U.S.A" were in fact "Made in the U.S.A. (by undocumented migrants)." The fruit you have for breakfast. The hamburger that you had for lunch was probably slaughtered by an undocumented migrant, loaded by one, unloaded by another, and cooked by another. Let's not forget who fed the cow and harvested the grain that fed the cow and who washed the dish it was served on. Make the list for an entire week and see all of the possibilities you come up with. Then, after making the list, go the next week without the use of any of those goods, products, or services.

Migration is one of the greatest moral challenges facing humanity in the 21st century, and it is time we looked at it as such. Is human mobility a human right? According to international law, everyone has the right to leave the country they are in, but there is no corresponding right to enter any other nation-state. Are you supposed to live on a boat in the middle of the ocean to exercise your right? Put more concretely, do people have a human right to go where they please on the earth to search for work that will improve their quality of life and the lives of their loved ones? Before you answer the question, let me share with you a hypothetical example I like to use adapted from John Rawls. If you are a religious person, let's imagine that you are having a conversation with your Supreme Being. For the sake of simplicity, let's say that God calls you up to heaven to ask you a question. God asks you whether or not you think human mobility is a human right, but before you can answer He gives you the following information. After answering the question, you will be sent back to earth as a completely different person. But, you will not know your gender, sexual orientation, country of origin, citizenship, education level, or color of your skin. All you know is that you will be one of the 6.6 billion people on Earth, so the chance of you returning as a U.S. citizen is extremely slim. With Asia having 60 percent of the population, odds are you might end up there, and keep in mind that with more than 170 million people in Latin America than in the United States of America, it is more likely that you would end up a citizen of a Latin American country. Your mind wonders as you do the math and think of the myriad of possibilities of who you will soon become. Perhaps when you are sent back to earth you will find yourself a Honduran migrant who spent 30 days riding on top of a freight train through Mexico, having been assaulted by gang members, seeing friends' legs cut-off attempting to board trains and having been robbed by Mexican government officials. Maybe you'd be peeking through the U.S.-Mexico border looking at one of the 21,370 Border Patrol agents while being monitored by the National Guard on camera and staring at the vast desert that has taken thousands of lives. Or, maybe you would find yourself a migrant who has just left the coast of Africa on a flimsy raft trying to reach Europe.

Now you can answer the question.

There are some people who will declare that human mobility should be a human right, but it is just not practical. They will point to the same numbers above, and show that logistically, it is just impossible for all the people of the world to migrate, they just would not fit. Let's keep in mind that a 2005 report from the United Nations estimated that only 191 million people, roughly 3 percent of the world's population, migrated internationally. And contrary to what might be public opinion, they did not all leave Mexico for the United States. In fact, more international migrants can be found in Europe (64 million) and Asia (53 million) than the 44 million in North America. While the United States of America is home to the largest amount of immigrants compared to any other nation-state, the fact is that according to the United Nations, four out of five international migrants are found in nations other than the United States. I know it must be hard for many U.S. citizens to believe, but not every single person in the world wants to come to the United States.

Additionally, if there was free migration, how many people would choose to go home and return after a certain period of time as opposed to being forced to stay for fear of the difficulty of re-entering? While militarization might not deter people from crossing in the first place, there are studies that show that it has decreased circular migration and more migrants are turning into immigrants and permanently settling in the United States. Free movement back and forth might actually be a "benefit" to the xenophobes who want only to exploit the labor of migrants but not want them to become life-long members of the society.

Have you ever wondered to yourself why the island of Puerto Rico is still populated? Why do not all of the people who were born in Puerto Rico head to the United States to live permanently? As a "commonwealth" of the United States, Puerto Ricans do not require a work visa to live or work anywhere in the United States. Given the opportunity to move freely back and forth between the island and the main land United States, many Puerto Ricans leave their homeland for a short time, but eventually return despite the vast economic disparities and lack of job opportunities in Puerto Rico. Granted there are many factors to take into consideration, including the U.S. subsidies to corporations in Puerto Rico and the difference in the minimum wage between Puerto Rico and other Latin American countries, but it is worthwhile to study how others can enjoy the same freedom of movement that Puerto Ricans possess.

This is also a good time to mention that freedom of movement will not solve all the problems of the world. In fact, I've never talked to a migrant who has wanted to leave the world they grew-up in behind to move to an entirely different country and culture. In a perfect world, people would only need to exercise their human right to visit the Grand Canyon or enjoy a day in San Francisco or a night-out in New York City. The real need is an economic system where people are not exploited and forced to leave their homes. While such a solution is beyond the feeble mind of this ignorant brother from the border, what I do know is that the immediate suffering and deaths occurring in my community can be stopped tomorrow by recognizing an individual's human right to cross political boundaries to find work.

I am confident that there will be a day when a child can walk to a library and check-out a book about migration in the late 20th and early 21st centuries. The child will be astounded to learn that thousands of people died attempting to "unlawfully" enter nation-states. During this time period, human mobility will be so universally recognized as a human right that children will find it difficult to believe that there was actually a point in history where people could not travel freely around the globe. The child will read about how the disempowered and disenfranchised of the world organized across borders to demand recognition of what they knew in their hearts. Perhaps this child will be your great-granddaughter, and realizing that you were alive during this time period, they will take the book to you and ask, "What did you do when so many people were suffering and dying?"

History is unfortunately all-too-full of examples of human beings objectifying and abusing other human beings. Fortunately, history is also full of examples of human beings standing up against injustices and struggling for a better and more just world. Now is the time to write this history. We know the problem, and we must not be timid in demanding the solution. You might not be a rich person, famous, or think of yourself as powerful, but you do have your body. You control your actions and can decide whether or not to let the laws of nation-states keep you from doing what you believe is morally the right thing to do. You can choose whether or not to cross not only physical borders, but mental ones as well.

This is an issue of freedom and liberty. These two concepts are freely used in the United States of America. Supposedly we fight to defend freedom and liberty as if they are statues in a museum to be protected. But what about the rights and privileges associated with those terms? Human beings, like all other animals, should not be restrained by prisons, cages, or borders. And what about your freedom? Should you be restrained from assisting someone in improving his or her life if you so choose? Currently, the U.S. Government can fine and imprison you if you decided to assist your fellow human being in unlawfully crossing the border in furtherance of their remaining in the United States, or if you harbor someone already in the United States. It is quite disappointing to have a law on the books that criminalizes those who attempt to help their fellow human beings improve their lives. One would think that in a truly civilized society, such actions would be rewarded with the assistance of the state, not with its punishment.

In his book, *What Are Human Rights?*, Maurice Cranston notes that the Greek word *eleutheria* and the Latin word *libertas* both have their origins in the idea of being unimpeded in the exercise of movement. He writes, "There are some grounds for thinking of the right to freedom of movement as the first and most fundamental of man's liberties." Cranston is not the only writer to make such statements. Arguments in favor of human mobility as a human right can be found in the works of Immanuel Kant, Alan Dowty, Roger Nett, Joseph Carens, Jonathon Moses, Veit Bader, Rainer Bauböck, Kevin Johnson, Teresa Hayter, Ann Dummett, Maria Jimenez, Luis Cabrera, Antoine Pécoud and Paul de Guchteneire, Peter C. Meilaender, Stephen Castles and Alastair Davidson, Mark Tushnet, John Gray, Mehmet Ugur, Robert E. Goodin, and *The Wall Street Journal*. While the logic of *The Wall Street Journal* may fall more in line with the thinking of Adam Smith, it is worth noting that free movement cannot be dismissed as the sole idea of communist or socialist crackpots or liberal philosophers and academics.

My goal is not to give the impression that the idea of human mobility as a human right has legitimacy only because capitalists or academics are advocating it. I had the privilege to be able to work with two friends to conduct focus groups with undocumented migrants who were either living in the United States or about to cross the border. Of course, the fact that some were Mexican citizens being interviewed in Mexico means they were not at the time undocumented. In fact, most people described as undocumented actually have some sort of documents, even if not the ones needed to enter the United States of America. Nonetheless, this shows that even the politically correct term of "undocumented" is a misnomer. My apologies for digressing. We were trying to figure out the legal consciousness of undocumented migrants. That is, why do they choose to break the U.S. immigration laws but not break other laws such as robbing from someone or stealing a car? If one feels that it is morally acceptable to break U.S. immigration laws, but not other laws, then why is that so? Many of the answers led me to the conclusion that undocumented migrants should not be seen simply as economic refugees, but in fact are making a political statement. Every footstep in the desert can be seen as an act of civil disobedience.

The underlying themes found during the discussions with migrants were that border controls were unjust, and there exists a serious lack of inequality of treatment as seen through racism and discrimination based on economic status. Crossing the border in search of work can be seen as a political statement about equality. I am a human being, all human beings are equal and I am going to exercise my right to free movement. To further illustrate the points let me share with you some of the quotes from migrants.

> Right now in the United States, there isn't a law that is capable of stopping us. They treat us how they want. The United States has enough power to treat us in whatever way they think

we deserve; but no, we're human too. —*Dany, migrant from Honduras*

Simply to know that over there [Mexico] one enters without anything. Without asking for passports, they can enter there [Mexico]. But when one comes over, one cannot. That makes you grow furious because you have to show them your papers, and they ask you to be in school or working [to get a visa], they ask you for a lot of things to come here. And they only cross over whenever they want. —*Jose, migrant from Mexico*

Also, not only is there racism in the United States, but also in our country and in Mexico. There's racism everywhere. Just because we're Latinos they think that we're low, I don't know, but God made us all equal as humans. But we don't think the same way they do. They think that we're a plague. —*Fernando, migrant from Honduras*

They say that there are two [paths for migration], one with thorns, rocks, animals and another, that is much freer with pavement that you can cross in a car. You seek out that route and can't find it due to the economy and you have to go the other way despite the risk of getting thorns stuck in you or eaten by an animal. You have to suffer through it. That's the way for the poor people. The way for deputies, governors and presidents is the other way. To get a visa you need to have a high economic status, that's it. —*Dany, migrant from Honduras*

The migrants we interviewed were clear in expressing their understanding of their oppression. They can plainly see the inequality of treatment through the fact that U.S. citizens can freely travel to their countries but they cannot do the same in the reverse direction. The people we spoke with were clear in seeing this inequality in existing because of racism and lower social economic class. So that is the identification of the injustice and the analysis of its source, and what about the solution? Those I met are very specific in providing a framework for a long-term struggle.

> I think that we should be able to enter freely into any country because we're equal as human beings. We are all worth the same. —*Guadalupe, migrant from Mexico*

> Here we should have something [discussing European Union] similar so that the United States, México and parts of South America have fewer problems. Those that give to others can help shape perspectives on equality that can help develop countries that are in debt. Just like Europe. In Europe, if I'm from Spain, I can go to Ireland or Germany and I can work for the European economy. —*Ricardo, migrant from Mexico*

> I think that we should have [the] liberty of going wherever we want, as long as it's for work, because we all come for the same thing. Because we come to cooperate. So then I tell you that what they're doing to us is committing an injustice against us because we're illegal. —*Alejandro, migrant from Mexico*

> Yes well this, I think that the right to immigrate that every human being has it, even if he doesn't have papers. Because when they arrived from Europe they arrived, they arrived here without a visa paper to take away the ancestor's land. I don't feel illegal in America because I am a native of America. I think that whites who live over there are more illegal. —*Roberto, migrant from Mexico*

Fernando puts it in the more traditional terminology when he says, "[o]pen the borders." Saul explains the pain one must endure to exercise human rights.

> ...and I tell you, who has been damaged has been us the poor who are trying, who even lose their lives sometimes, to go and earn a dollar, because I tell you, I have left my home, and I have left my two children, and I don't know if I will see them again, I don't know if I will ever see my family again, and can you believe, like a human because we're all human, tell me. You leave the United States, you leave by plane for here in Mexico, but you know that if God permits, if nothing happens to the airplane, you will return, because you have your job, to your place of origin, and everyone [is] calm, but us, we sleep on the street, we sleep in the hills, we risk our lives, you think that we want [to ride] this stupid train, is it an easy thing? No. Look, my feet are beaten, because of what, because I have slipped, because the wheel has almost grabbed my feet, all beaten up, because the train doesn't come easily, it doesn't come easily, it comes and you with the thought and with saying well I have to pass, to give my children a better life, like I said a while ago, if I didn't have toys, I want my children to have some, if we, my mom and dad, we lived the entire time by charity... I don't ask God to give me riches, but also not for me to be in this poverty that I'm in...it hurts, it hurts as a parent, it hurts, if you're the father of the family. I don't know if you're a father already...no, not yet, the day that you are, you will realize that your children, you don't like it when anyone despises your children, I prefer it that they hit me...but don't do anything to my children, not even a bad look, like I'm saying, and all of that makes one risk your life to enter here.

Despite the strong testimony from migrants, there appears to be an understanding that the privileged of the world will never be able to fully empathize with what undocumented migrants must endure. As Dany stated, "[t]he only way would be for them to live in the prisons we feel and sit where we sit." Furthermore, Dany stated:

> But they should put themselves in our shoes, walk on mines, ride a raft, walk in the heat, go without water and then after all that suffering, see what they think about immigration. It would be a good way for them to feel what one feels and has to go through.

Migrants were passionate in sharing their stories of struggling to cross borders and equally passionate in explaining their political and philosophical thoughts. These were not the testimonies of some more economic refugees in need of charity; these are visionary leaders in need of more followers.

A long struggle

It has been an unbelievable privilege and pleasure to be able to write this book. I know I have not been able to do justice to the interactions I have had with so many amazing people, but I hope that you have enjoyed my humble attempt to shed a little bit of light on what will someday be seen as one of the grossest human rights violations in the history of the United States. Most importantly, I hope you feel compelled to become a follower. There is not a need for anyone to speak for anyone else or to empower anybody. Instead, now is the time to take action and follow in the footsteps of those who have already led the way. Be as militant and radical as you can be, non-violently of course. The past few years have seen students chain themselves together inside the Tucson Unified School District's meeting room in opposition to banning MAS classes and DREAM Act students engaging in civil disobedience and being arrested without fear of being deported. Such actions are long overdue, and to stop the escalation of violence directed toward our communities, further actions are desperately needed. I believe a strong argument can be made that Obama's deferred action program came about because DREAM Act students were engaging in civil disobedience throughout the country. We must not let the granting of deferred action to some undocumented young people detract us from the bigger picture. It's time to stop saying no and start saying yes. Yes, people have a right to support themselves and their families, a right to cross borders to find work, to live, to love, to learn about their history, to remain unchained and outside the walls of a prison, to pursue a higher education, and a right to live a happy life free of fear of an overreaching government.

The struggle will be long and extremely difficult, but we have the migrants' experience as an example of how to move forward. Regardless of how many more miles of fencing are added or how many more thousands of agents are sent to the border, people we will find a way to cross. We will face more tanks in the desert, vigilantes, unmanned aerial vehicles, sensors, cameras, and anti-immigrant legislation. There will be times when it feels as if we are on our fourth day walking through the desert. Out of water, and with nothing but desert in front of us, we will want to quit because the path looks too difficult. But with the love in our hearts, that is the same love that migrants have for their loved ones back home, we will persist.

Un día vamos a cruzar.

About the Author

Born in the small bordertown of Douglas, Arizona, Ray Ybarra Maldonado is a Stanford-educated attorney who took a two-year leave from his studies to directly intervene in the vigilante movement that was starting in Arizona. While working for the American Civil Liberties Union, Ybarra Maldonado was instrumental in starting a major civil rights lawsuit against one of the vigilantes, and trained hundreds of volunteers and spent months following the Minutemen as they patrolled the U.S.-Mexico border. He co-wrote and co-produced the award winning documentary, *Rights on the Line: Vigilantes at the Border*, and he has been quoted frequently in the national and international media on the topic of immigrants' rights and the vigilantes.

Ybarra Maldonado is a noted public speaker who has given presentations at Harvard, the University of California at Berkeley, the Universidad Nacional Autónoma de Mexico, and dozens of other universities, colleges, and community groups across North America. Ybarra Maldonado has testified in front of local and state government entities and his work has been profiled in the Intelligence Report, *Stanford Lawyer*, and in a documentary that premiered at the 2006 Sundance Film Festival, entitled *Crossing Arizona*.

As a trial attorney, in the anti-immigrant state of Arizona, he has attained not guilty verdicts on felony charges for immigrants in both state and federal court. He has also won cases at the 9th Circuit Court of Appeals on behalf of migrants, and currently remains in the trenches fighting to stop deportations in the Florence, Eloy, and Phoenix immigration courts and representing immigrants charged with state and federal crimes.

Ybarra Maldonado attended Cochise Community College in Douglas, Arizona on a baseball scholarship and graduated Summa Cum Laude from Arizona State University with a degree in Religious Studies. He previously volunteered at migrants centers in Agua Prieta, Sonora, and Tapachula, Chiapas where he assisted with cleaning, preparing food, and conducting human rights discussions.

Ybarra Maldonado is currently a non-residential fellow at the Stanford Center for Internet and Society and he lives with his wife and child, Ray Emerson, in Phoenix, Arizona. Prior to marrying his wife, Dr. Angeles Maldonado, he was "Ray Ybarra", and legally has changed his name to "Ray Ybarra Maldonado." Ray and his family are avid fans of the Arizona State Sun Devils, Stanford Cardinal, and all things Arizona (minus the anti-immigrant politics).

Made in the USA
Las Vegas, NV
22 July 2021